DOING CHURCH

a practical guide,
by those who do it…

Other Resources by William D. Watley

- 10 Steps to Financial Freedom
- African Presence in the Bible
- African American Pulpit
- Are You the One?
- Breaking Financial Barriers
- Bring the Full Tithe
- Exalting the Names of Jesus
- From Mess to Miracles
- God Wants You To Grow
- Less Than Tipping (book)
- Less Than Tipping (guide)
- Poems by a Son, Prayers of a Father
- Preaching in Two Voices
- Preparing Joshua
- Roots of Resistance
- Sermons from the Black Pulpit
- Sermons on Special Days
- You Have To Face It To Fix It

CDs / DVDS

DVD Set
William Watley at The Potter's House

DVD Series - *"Vision for Recovery"*
Don't Underestimate Yourself
Ingredients for Recovery
More than Meets the Eye

Individual DVDs
From Being Taken to a TakeOver
Men Are Builders Conference

CD Series "Vision For Recovery"
Facing People When We Have Been Damaged
When It Won't Go Away
Broke But Not Broken
Obedience Will Not Leave You Empty Handed

Individual CDs
From Being Taken to a TakeOver
The Foolishness of the Cross

CD Sets
10 Steps to Financial Freedom
William Watley at the Potter's House

DOING CHURCH

a practical guide,
by those who do it…

VOLUME II

Edited by
William D. Watley, Ph.D.

New Seasons Press
Newark, New Jersey, USA

All scripture quotations are taken from the New Revised Standard Version (NRSV), New International Version (NIV), or the King James Version (KJV) of the Bible unless otherwise noted.

For copies contact:

Rev. Dr. William D. Watley, Senior Pastor
St. James A.M.E. Church
588 Dr. Martin Luther King, Jr. Blvd.
Newark, New Jersey 07102
(973) 622-1344, Ext. 111 (office)
(973) 622-6912 (fax)
www.williamwatley.org

New Seasons Press, 2010
Printed in the USA
ISBN 978-0-9972409-8-6

Dedication

Saints Still Walk Among Us

Dr. Elliot Mason
1922-2010

Spiritual Father and Mentor

Servant of God, well done.
Rest from thy love employ
The battles fought, the victory won
Enter thy Master's joy

Acknowledgements

I am grateful to my friend of long standing and editor of more publications than she cares to remember, Mrs. Carolyn Scavella. She has helped birth, as well as shape this publication in a variety of ways. Over the past twenty-six years you have served as sounding board, first reader and primary redactor for every publication I have written. I am extremely grateful for the blessing you continue to be to me personally, to my family and to the Lord's cause. You are an outstanding example of classy Christian womanhood and loyalty. This, along with many other reasons, provides the rationale for my dedicating this work to you. My prayer is that the Lord will pour back into your life everything and more for all that you give to so many of us who are privileged to know you, to love you and respect you.

I am also grateful to Rev. Marcia Sapp Salter who did so much of the preliminary and non-glamorous grunt work that turned this dream into a deliverable. I am grateful for your love for the Lord, your enthusiasm, commitment and creativity as you execute your responsibilities, as well as your teachable spirit. I am also grateful for the keen eye and anointed gifts of the Executive Minister of St. James A.M.E. Church, Dr. Raquel St. Clair, who also did some of the proofreading for this work. My gratitude also extends to my daughter beloved, Mrs. Jennifer Watley-Maxell and Felicia Kennedy, for their invaluable contributions to the editing process.

The people of St. James A.M.E. Church in Newark, New Jersey have grown, struggled and suffered with me in my efforts to *do church* among them…and sometimes on them. I am truly blessed to have had the privilege of serving as pastor to such a supportive flock of Christ.

Last, and certainly not least, I am grateful for my spouse and companion of over 40 years, Mrs. Muriel Annette Lewis Watley.

You have never wavered in your support and understanding down through the years, as I have sought to make full proof of the ministry entrusted by God into my care. Thank you for looking after our family when I was not around, and for praying for me in season and out of season. Thank you for your particular contribution to this work in terms of your proof reading and helpful questions and suggestions.

To God be the glory! Great things God has done and continues to do in all of our lives as we attempt to *do church* in a way that honors our Lord Christ.

Contents

FOREWORD

Ministry in the 21st century has been a new and challenging experience. Fundamentalists and liberals alike have to retool themselves to meet contemporary challenges. The old scripts are being abolished and the new ones scrutinized as leaders grapple over what stays and what is to be excluded from the crock pot of post-modern leadership.

As much as we attempt to maintain our image of intellectual absolutisms, the reality is, uncertainty is one of the tools God uses to create a thirst for knowledge. It is there, at the humility of plaguing questions, that seeking, knocking and asking begins. To be sure we have new challenges, some of which even the Bible doesn't directly address, yet its truths help to fence in our debate within the scope of orthodoxy.

The idea of collective reasoning isn't new. You will remember that the early church used it to keep them from deviating too far from their brand and mission. The first experience they had with Jerusalem that brought about Pentecost must have been amazing! Imagine the enthusiasm in which the disciples left Jerusalem filled with fire and armed with the demonstration of the Holy Spirit. These men, who had been trained at the feet of Jesus Himself and filled with His Holy Spirit, must have been confident that they were ready for the challenge of their day.

However, it wasn't long before they found themselves bombarded with questions about inclusion, interpretations and protocol: Who would be required to be circumcised and who wouldn't? How did they prepare for a church whose diversity threatened the traditional ideas of sanctity and holiness? What role would women play in this new and exciting organic church whose growth was paramount with its rampant division? How could they garner the strength of its people when so much compartmentalization threatened to divide the baby born on the cross?

Quickly these sagacious men learned that the fire of Pentecost alone wouldn't be enough to hold the church together. Neither the oratorical skills of Peter, nor the intellectualism of the newly converted Apostle Paul were equipped to circumvent the constant bombarding of distracting ideas. Yes, there were reports of great miracles and yes, there were great movements growing out of desert lands and city streets alike, but there was also dissension and egotism that corroded the underbelly of the movement.

Jerusalem Again

It was under the staggering weight of these and many other responsibilities that a cry was made to gather again in Jerusalem. This time it wasn't to wait on a great demonstration of the Spirit, nor was it to hear the burning sermons of those touted to be gifted with swelling words, and inspirational monologues. No, this time they came to Jerusalem with the best of the best. Like Olympic champions gathering to win the cup, these men came to pursue the prize of a deeper understanding for the future and to benefit from their collective debate. Like the Passover bread shared by the twelve, each one had a part of the whole. Jesus had well demonstrated to them that each of them held within himself a part of the mystery of the memorial body of Christ!

So they gathered again. From camel backs to worn sandals, every mode of transportation was employed to bring together pieces to a place of wholeness. The outcome would determine whether Holy Days would be observed, or whether meats offered to idols would now be consumed. They wanted to know how to proceed with the organizational infrastructure of the church in a way that didn't virally contaminate or corrupt the living organism of the church for which Christ died.

I shudder to think what might have happened had they not loved the church more than they romanced their perspectives. They sought common ground for the sake of the coming generation. Their return to Jerusalem would inevitably create debate. It would assuredly cause discourse. But at the end of the day, they hoped to anchor ideas from which they could extrapolate a new creed and lift the old rugged cross no longer weighted by the uncertainty that drove them there.

The sun was hot, the room crowded, and dust filled the air as they sat, like Native American chiefs around the evening fire, to openly debate each other for the sake of theological posterity. Sometimes the debate might have been like frolicking children, but more often than not, the debate would likely stir the fire of incivility. And only their shared love for Christ, his cross, and the church would keep it from erupting into an argument akin to a bar room brawl! The reward they sought from this crossfire of ideas was a clarion call to new and heightened direction. It was from this premise that the New Testament and its burgeoning church would survive its embryonic stages and emerge out of the embers of debate with the blueprint for leadership and living! They succeeded and the church moved forward, trimmed of the fat meat of archaic ideals and toned by reasoning on issues not addressed by any teaching to which they had previously been exposed. Today, we are the benefactors of that debate.

Fast forward to our days and times. This is a needy time in which we live. Many leaders in the church have lost their way. Some have imitated what they couldn't create. It is a day where the vision, purpose and goals of the church seem unclear. What is clear, however, is that someone has to act now. My friend and brother Dr. William Watley has been commissioned by the Master Himself to gather a collective pool of reasoning for our times and leave these thoughts in a book for the coming generation. He, himself, is no lightweight thinker. So many react when he blows the trumpet in Zion and reaches for the collaboration of the unified perspectives of highly respected clergy!

I met Dr. Watley personally several years ago and knew almost immediately that we would be friends. Perhaps because I was in part mesmerized, no actually I was stunned, by the profundity of his rationale and his often uncanny ability to be planted on principles sacred to the church while still able to transition to a message cut to the continuity of contemporary relevance. His ability to intellectualize without becoming entombed in the shrine of humanistic self-aggrandizement, opened up the way for a crossbreed of inspirational and yet intellectual comrades from various circles of thought to engage in this work, since he, himself, is not a limited man.

Who better than a man steeped in church leadership for over forty years and yet trained by the scholarly, without acquiescing his convictions for his credentials, to determine who would be the select group of thinkers that would be gathered together in this work called, **DOING CHURCH**?

I welcome every reader to eavesdrop on the ideas and concepts shared in every turned page, like hungry minds gathered at the windowpane of an upper room, filled with the aroma of a well-prepared smorgasbord. Listen with your heart while you read with your eyes the collective reasoning of this hand-selected team of thinkers, to grace every page in this book with a rich and substantive discussion. But greater still, is its ability to move the discussion to conclusion. For I am sure you realize, as I do, that discussion without conclusion is engaging but ultimately fails to be gratifying. What this book and its varied authors provide is a template far beyond the parading of ideas into the goal of an absolute conclusion. It is written to the intent that it might cure the ills of this critical moment.

Dr. Martin Luther King Jr. spoke of the fierce urgency of now. This is a new "now" with a new "fierce urgency." That is why my heart leaps in joy as I watch Dr. Watley's rapid and yet regal response in this critical work to the fierce urgency of our "now" moment! His thoughts are like a drum major with his baton held high. He sets the pace and rhythm to which we march. His book blows the whistle to which each reader will march into the mausoleum of truths, the museums of theological warriors, and the mosaic cross-pollination of ideas from which the church will increase its impact without reducing the blood of Christ to the cherry red Kool-Aid of mediocrity! Without this father of the faith's commitment, our impact globally will weaken to water and never evolve to the rich wine of a process worthy of the church itself. We will, through his teachings, think globally and not be limited to an asphyxiatingly narrow manipulation of thought that keeps us channeling a universal God into a city councilman whose vision is for a small region. God's leaders need a message that transcends the community and goes on to transform a generation!

I am therefore proud to lift my pen to push forward Dr. Watley's march into leaving both a legacy and pointing to an absolutely irrevocable destiny to which the Holy writ says is the inheritance of the remaining leaders who would usher its followers into the place where hearts and minds touch and agree. For it is there where asking anything, is possible from that union. I only ask that you, with an open mind, prepare to shift into high gear as you have been invited to join the voyage to the bottom of absolute truth and thereby know with all certainty that we preach the doctrine of the apostles with the flare of our contemporary generations no less artfully than our spiritual ancestors did. But our focus must be tailored, and custom designed to an abiding understanding of our times.

Bishop T. D. Jakes,
Senior Pastor, The Potter's House of Dallas, Inc.

Preface

When the Day of Pentecost had come, they were all together in one place. And suddenly from heaven there came a sound like the rush of a violent wind, and it filled the entire house where they were sitting. Divided tongues, as of fire, appeared among them, and a tongue rested on each of them. All of them were filled with the Holy Spirit and began to speak in other languages, as the Spirit gave them ability.

Now there were devout Jews from nation under heaven living in Jerusalem. And at this sound the crowd gathered and was bewildered, because each one heard them speaking in the native language of each. Amazed and astonished, they asked, "Are not all these who are speaking Galileans? And how is it that we hear, each of us, in our own native language? Parthians, Medes, Elamites, and residents of Mesopotamia, Judea and Cappadocia, Pontus and Asia, Phrygia and Pamphylia, Egypt and the parts of Libya belonging to Cyrene, and visitors from Rome, both Jews and proselytes, Cretans and Arabs---in our own native languages, we hear them speaking about God's deeds of power. All were amazed and perplexed, saying to one another, "What does this mean?" But others sneered and said, "They are filled with new wine."

But Peter, standing with the eleven, raised his voice and addressed them, "Men of Judea and all who live in Jerusalem, let this be known to you, and listen to what I say. Indeed we are not drunk, as you suppose, for it is only nine o'clock in the morning. No, this is what was spoken through the prophet Joel...

Now when they heard this, they were cut to the heart and said to Peter and to the other apostles. "Brothers, what should we do?" Peter said to them, "Repent, and be baptized every one of you in the name of Jesus Christ so that your sins may be forgiven; and you will receive the gift of the Holy Spirit. For the promise is for you, for your children, and for all who are far away, everyone whom the Lord our God calls to him." And he testified with many other arguments and exhorted them, saying, "Save yourselves from this corrupt generation." So those who welcomed his message were baptized, and that day about three thousand persons were added. They devoted themselves to the apostles' teaching and fellowship, to the breaking of bread and the prayers[1].

So reads the account of the Day of Pentecost according to the New Revised Standard Version of the scriptures. The Day of Pentecost has traditionally been called the birthday of the church. Of course the events of Acts 2 is not the first time that the community of faith or baptized believers in Christ is referenced in the scriptures. As early as Matthew 16: 17-18 in response to Simon Peter's confession of faith that the Lord Jesus Christ is the Son of the living God, the Master replies, "Blessed are you, Simon son of Jonah! For flesh and blood has not revealed this to you, but my Father in heaven. And I tell you, you are Peter, and on this rock I will build my church, and the gates of Hades will not prevail against it." However, even though the Lord had referenced the church and expressed an international vision for the work of the church before the momentous events of Acts 2, the Day of Pentecost is still considered the birthday of the church in a number of traditions because of the outpouring, infilling and empowering presence of the Holy Spirit. On that day the Holy Spirit saturated the 120 worshippers who were gathered in the upper room. The coming of the Holy Spirit to the whole church, and not simply to a few scattered individuals who were in the mix, meant that the church became the corporate evangelical voice and gospel body of Christ in the world.

Since the first three thousand souls were joined with the 120 worshippers on that day, the record of growth and the sphere of influence of the church over the past 2000 years are beyond measure. The number of Christians runs into the billions while the number of congregations and communities of believers can easily reach the hundreds of millions. The organized church denominational structures and para-church fellowships is mind boggling, and the educational, medical, economic, and outreach institutions that minister to the poor, the victimized and the voiceless is staggering. When one looks at the stellar record of the church over the past 2000 years one can truly proclaim, "Look at what the Lord has wrought through the efforts of those

---

[1] Acts 2:1-16; 37-42

who represent and proclaim him as Lord and Savior to the world." The church has indeed come a long way since the Day of Pentecost.

Any casual reading of history, as well as ordinary observation of the current times, also recognizes that the church has had anything but a stellar record over the past two millennia. When one looks at some of the dastardly and shameful things we as followers of the Lord have done in his name; and, as we have represented his cause, we can often be accused of crucifying the Savior again and again and again. Too often we have twisted and perverted the Gospel to suit our own ends. We have all too often portrayed ourselves as more petty than powerful; as the envious rather than the excellent, and as the compromised rather than the committed. There have been times when the church has been the church that strengthened the arms of oppressors rather than the voices of the oppressed.

In our own times we have seen the image of the church, and the body of Christ damaged and fractured time and again because of misunderstanding, bickering, turf wars, doctrinal fights and scandals. We as the followers of Christ have managed to fight over everything from the traditional church dividing issues of baptism, Eucharist and ministry to newer issues such as music and liturgy, sexuality and alternate lifestyles, prosperity and a plethora of justice issues. When one looks at the litany of abuses done at the hands of the church in past and present times, one is also tempted to raise one's hands in horror and proclaim, "Church of the living Christ, your sins are legion!"

Why does the church have such a contradictory and checkered history as well as a turbulent present? Reasons include human sin, pettiness, greed, error and doctrinal disagreement. The spiritual warfare that evil wages against the church to prevent the spread of the kingdom of God, in a domain that evil has mistakenly claimed for itself, is also a theological factor. When one looks at the impediments to the church becoming the bride and body of Christ, without spot or blemish; when we consider the church's greatest blessing and bane - we humans who administer, serve, and represent it, the reality is that even after glorious achievements and a two thousand year history of existence, many times we still don't know how to do church very well.

We know how to sing about church. We know how to pray for the church. We know how to preach about the church. We know how to express our faith and belief in the church. We know how to defend and fight for the church. We know how to write about the church in both poetry and prose. We know how to study, research and analyze the church. We know how to quote the Bible regarding the church. We know how to organize and structure churches. We know how to do everything but live out the implications of the gospel as the church. Even after all this time and experience in being the church, we still don't know how to *do church*, live the church and even be the church very well.

From the oldest among us to the youngest, from the most seasoned to the least experienced, from the most sincere to the most selfish, from the most giving to the most exploitive, from the most degreed to the least formally educated, whether we are clergy or lay, male or female, rich or poor, no matter what our ethnicity, we as members of the body of Christ called church, still have trouble doing church. We still make a number of plain old ordinary human and even stupid mistakes administratively, in spiritual formation and development, in formulating, expressing, and implementing vision, and in our normal dealings with each other as human beings.

To put the matter succinctly and plainly, we as church people, whether leaders or followers; whether we are in the pulpit, the pew, the classroom, or the administrative office as support staff, or denominational officials, we do some really dumb and stupid things. Too often in our attempts to stand up and represent the Lord, we stumble over our own feet and end up on the ground looking up, scratching our heads and licking our wounds, as we ponder how we got ourselves into some situations. We question, how did something that started out so well and felt so good and so right, end up in such a mess?

Hopefully, this book will help address some of the common, ordinary issues and challenges we as the people of God face in our efforts to do church. We have drawn together some of the best minds and practitioners of our time who have established themselves as imperfectly proficient in doing church. While none of our contributors is perfect, each has impeccable credentials, credibility, and a proven track record in the areas in which they have written. I am sure that you as a reader will appreciate both their personal and transparent writing style and their authoritative and academic contributions.

Although each of these writers is African American by ethnicity and although they write from the perspective of the cultural milieu of the African American religious ethos, the quality of their ministry, the poignancy of their insights, the serious and studious nature of their articles, and the integrity of their walk and witness, bring a message and has valuable insights for the kingdom of God as a whole and for the church universal. I shall forever be grateful to each of the contributors whose offerings have made this publication the living reality that it is, and the blessing to the kingdom it promises to be.

William D. Watley, Ph.D.
Spring, 2010

DOING CHURCH
administratively

"So You Want to Build a Church or Buy a Building?"

Floyd H. Flake

"Now, my son, the Lord be with you, and may you have success and build the house of the Lord your God, as he said you would."
I Chronicles 22:11 NIV

Introduction

The building of a church is one of the most difficult challenges that a Pastor or congregation will face. Therefore, the planning phase is essential to determining how the building will be utilized presently and in the future. This is important in assuring that the facility will accommodate anticipated growth. The process requires that every possible projected function can be housed in the facility.

The building should not be built merely based on the existing facility's capacity, but with a view for additional program and ministry space. The needs assessment should focus on an analysis that allows for a facility that is big enough to meet the forecasted needs, but not so big that it has excess space that will not be utilized. The church is a capital asset that oftentimes sits vacant more than it is occupied. Therefore careful thought must be given to assure that the ministry functions take full advantage of all of the space. The key to a successful building program is embodied in planning that is appropriate for an outcome that lends itself to a sustainable building that is adaptable for as many needs as possible, within the constraints of the budget.

Since the building is primarily for religious, rather than sectarian usage, consideration should be given to making certain that its aesthetics are conceived with a view of God's expectations. The input of pastors, members, architects and others are important, but ultimately a religious facility should be an expression to God.

Pre-construction Requirements

Most municipalities have strict requirements for building a religious facility; therefore, the appropriate professionals are necessary to determine whether the project will require variances. Furthermore, certain zoning restrictions only allow for buildings that meet the categories that are germane to the particular community where the facility is being constructed. These issues will require professionals who are aware of the locality requirements and have the capacity to assure that they are met prior to the completion of planning. The cost of not resolving these necessary site issues in advance can be exorbitant. The best way to get these issues resolved is to check with the building department and if necessary hire a consultant who is versed in these matters to be the expediter for the project.

In some localities, the city council or community boards may have to approve the project, even if it is a church. Therefore, it is wise to contact the local officials during the planning phase. It is better to have them as partners in the project than trying to include them after a problem evolves. Furthermore, they can often refer you to sources that can help expedite the project, particularly if you have limited knowledge in the area of construction and building.

Planning
The first question in the planning phase centers on whether there is a legitimate necessity for buying or building a new church facility. That is the trigger to the conversation about which option best suits the future needs of the congregation.

The most important question for the congregation is "Do we want to build a new church or buy an existing building?" The rationale for building from the ground up is that there is a greater chance that at the end of the process the church will have a building that will meet most of its needs. In buying an existing building, many of the fixtures are already in place and the readjustment cost is high. We once lost over $150 thousand on a rehabilitation project because when it was finished, many of the systems within the building broke down. It would have been cheaper to demolish the building and build a brand new structure. Once we looked behind the walls, we found areas that had to be completely restored, so our initial investment turned out to merely be a down payment on what ended up as a $500 thousand rehabilitation project.

The focus of the project must incorporate the facility's capability for meeting the total needs of the ministry. If the purchase of a building that accommodates all of the program and worship needs fits within the budget category of the congregation, it might be a good choice. Generally older buildings that have been abandoned by congregations have many needs that are unknown until you begin to operate within it. In most cases your maintenance issues in a new build are fewer than those found in an older facility.

I have noticed in many instances where pastors have decided to start a new ministry, they have elected schools, stores, strip malls, or warehouses which generally cost less money and more often than not, do not require exorbitant amounts of capital for maintenance. The Rev. Charles Macklin, pastor of The Sanctuary at Kingdom Square has done a phenomenal job with a strip mall in Capitol Heights, MD. Not only were they able to make a portion of the mall a sanctuary, they lease to IHOP, Bally

Fitness, and several other businesses. In Memphis, TN, the Rev. Stacey Spencer, pastor of New Direction Christian Church, purchased a significant portion of a mall and converted part of it into a sanctuary; subsequently adding a school. They also have a restaurant; where each Wednesday, they have community functions and sell lunches.

Much of the success in the planning phase will be determined by the vision of the people to see beyond the historical limitations of what a church should look like. The Reverends Macklin and Spencer's ministries are effective because their facilities allow them to generate income to help pay for their worship centers. The operative model for building of ministry should be considered in the context of its multi-purpose capabilities.

The role of the planning committee must encompass the totality of ministry needs and the means of meeting those needs within or by expansion of the structure. Therefore the planning committee must consider designs that create the best opportunities for some degree of multi-use of various parts of the building. Investing in a church requires a vast amount of capital dollars for a facility that is often empty. Thus, it is imperative that the plan allows for additional uses outside of the times of worship. A capital investment of the magnitude that building a church demands requires that every effort is made to utilize every aspect of the building in as many ways as is possible.

It is impossible to be aware of all of the needs of the congregation in the future, especially if there is significant growth. Therefore, it is necessary to plan well, using the best assumptions that are available in relationship to your projected growth in congregants, programs and ministries. One of the most important factors governing the planning phase is getting a majority of people to come to an agreement on what the outcome should be. That means the pastor or committee chair has to take the responsibility of determining when to bring this phase to closure. Remember that the objective is to get majority support and be aware that no matter what the conclusion is there will be some members who will be unhappy with the outcome. The overriding factor should not be the color of tiles on walls or even material choice, but whether or not the ultimate agreed upon plan will meet the predetermined objectives.

Design

The building design is generally in the mind of a pastor or leadership group; however, the key person is the architect. Therefore, it is essential that the architect has a heart for the people and the project. Ultimately, the design should become a positive statement of the sentiments of those who will occupy it. The architect should approach the project with an attitude that this building is God's house. The architect can help expedite the process or cause major postponements as you move forward.

To the best of your ability, check the background and record of the architect to determine if he or she has a history of delivering on time and with the quality expected by the hiring entity. A good architect will work with the contractor and the planning committee in material choices that have great long-term value. This is essential to the ultimate maintenance of the building. Furthermore, an architect with a good reputation in the city can generally move agencies that have responsibility for decisions that impact the building process to respond in an expeditious manner.

The worst things that one can encounter in a building project are delays that are caused by the inability of timely responses. They impact negotiations with the bank, payments to the contractors, and build up the emotional tensions of the congregation that is awaiting the day of entry into their new building.

One of my favorite architects was Harry Simmons, who designed the Senior Center, The Cathedral and the School. He understood well how to move the project, but also how to make sure that the vision for the end product would make the statement that expressed the feelings of those who were part of the process of bringing it to the fore. When an individual builds a new home, they expect it to be a reflection of who they are; therefore, the building of a church ought to be synonymous with how the congregation feels about God.

Once the planning committee has decided what type of building they wish to have, then the process moves to choosing the materials that bring out an expression to both the internal and external aesthetics. The role of the architect is to project the character of the building in a manner that invites the community to come in. It should answer the question, "What statement would we like this church's presence to make to the community of which it is a part?" As a rule, architects have their own ideas about what the building should look like, but ultimately it is the decision of the owner that should prevail.

The next question is, "Who will select the materials for the building?" This is important to the degree that attractive facades are very expensive; however working with the architect you can often find facades that meet your standards, but are not quite as costly. An example might be, choosing an expensive block as opposed to brick as the outside façade. Brick is generally more expensive than block, but block is larger and less expensive to lay, thus reducing the cost of labor. The savings on the labor side allows for more money to be spent on the internal aesthetics of the building.

Internal facades should be chosen based upon some analysis of anticipated wear and tear; some portions of the building where the public assembles may have a higher grade than other areas where there will be much less traffic. The pricing of tile does not necessarily mean that it will have a longer life cycle; so the most important thing is its practicality, durability and attractiveness.

The sizing of rooms should be determined by the anticipated usage. Choir rooms may be larger than those used for Sunday school classes. Dividers can be used to create more multi-purpose space, so that the same room can serve dual functions. Special attention should be given to nurseries to make certain they meet the standards in size and decorum that have been set by governmental agencies. Furthermore, in the areas where there are small children, there are specifics in relationship to toilets, cabinets and other furnishings that must be addressed.

Since office space is such a vital necessity, much consideration must be given to its design. I am convinced that you rarely have enough office space in a growing church, especially where there is an anticipation of creating new ministries. However, to the degree that it is possible, the projection must be made in advance, otherwise you will eventually cut into program space.

The biggest challenge is determining the appropriate sizing for each office, depending upon its function and its need. In the more contemporary offices, like Bloomberg, LLP, there are very few offices with walls. With today's modern technology, many people operate in a large space together, with areas defined by opaque dividers. The key is designing for the utilization of more technology with less dependence on space set aside for individual workers.

I discovered when we were about to build The Cathedral that one of the greatest concerns of the members was adequate restroom facilities. Be aware of the fact that women generally need more space. (You really cannot build enough.) If the building has more than one floor, then restroom facilities should exist on each floor. Of particular concern is the availability of sufficient restrooms for women and men with changing stations for babies.

The Sanctuary

The area for worship must be carefully planned so that an atmosphere is created to encompass as many worship functions as possible. For instance, we knew in advance that our choirs were large, so the choir stands were designed to accommodate up to 200 persons. We were also aware of the vast size of the dance ministry, so the aisles were designed wide enough to accommodate them. And, because we wanted to emphasize music without placing a limitation on the number of instruments, the staging area for the band was built sufficiently large. However, we discovered that the band area got rather small as we augmented the instrumentation to better accommodate the size and height of the building. As some point, we will restructure the band and choir areas because our music ministry has grown well beyond our projections and expectations. As I stated earlier in the planning phase, you can only make your best assumptions, but it does not mean that you will not ultimately find the necessity of making changes, especially if the congregation grows.

Modern sanctuaries require significant amounts of technology; plasma screens, audio-visual equipment, speakers, and recording apparatus. The capability for making DVDs and CDs for immediate sale following worship and other events is critical. The greatest value is the ability to have worshippers share the gospel with others who may not have a personal church experience. It also has the potential to generate significant revenue that creates another stream of income beyond total dependence on tithes and offerings. The equipment pricing will initially seem exorbitant; however, prices have gone down significantly, and the return on the investment will more than justify the cost over time.

In order for these functions to operate well, they must be incorporated into a lighting format that enlivens the setting. These are tools for use in discipling and extending the ministry of the congregation. There is also a necessity for creating on-line access for worship to be relayed via the Internet. Pews must be comfortable enough so that people will enjoy worship.

The ancillary uses of the building must also be considered in the design phase. Will the building require space for community activities? Where will the Sunday school and other educational programs be housed? Is there a necessity for a kitchen; and how should it be sized in relationship to the rest of the building? Is there a need for a chapel?

The architect and structural engineers will need to work with the local government in relationship to zoning issues, parking requirements and other outdoor spaces. Lastly, consideration should be given to the possibility of expansion. In most urban cities, it is almost impossible because of the density of the population. So, the buildings must be built with the consideration of vertical growth.

The planning phase also includes land analysis to determine what the zoning regulations are in the area where you choose to build. In some instances, you will face height restrictions, setback requirements and/or limitations on size. For example, in Nassau County, New York, they generally deny requests for a church building with more than a 1,200 seat capacity. Near where I live, a church had begun its excavation five years ago, and the county shut them down because they were building a 3000 seat facility. Recently I noticed that they had started the project again, but now they have determined that they must build a much smaller facility.

The rules are different everywhere; that is the reason I stated earlier that you should confront the zoning issues very early in the planning stage. When incidents like this occur, you are not able to recoup the funds that have been expended, so those are dollars lost. It is better to hire an attorney who understands zoning to help in assuring that your goals will be met without unnecessary delays.

The structural engineer is critical to the success of the project because they must analyze water tables and the amount of stress the building can handle. There are some variables that you will not be able to control, even with the best analysis.

When we built The Cathedral, we hit the height of the underground water table at 13 feet. However, when the excavation was completed and we were ready to lay the foundation, the water table tested at 21 feet. We were fortunate to negotiate with the Building Department to allow us to raise the building; however it meant that if we kept the same design we would be over the legal height limit. Eventually we determined that the original plans for a 14 foot ceiling in the basement would be reduced to a 9 foot ceiling, and with the

City's approval, we were able to continue the project. However, the original foundation and the sidewall that we had begun constructing stood for over a year before the City came to its final decision on the matter.

In most building projects there will be some unforeseen occurrences that might mitigate against the timetable; however, if you work diligently with all of the parties and are willing to make adjustments, it is possible to succeed in the end.

Budget

The budget is the most important aspect of a building project because it determines how much building you can afford. An analysis of the current revenue streams, tithing members and attendance are the critical components of designing an appropriate budget. Three major questions should be answered in the budget process. How much money can we raise? How much can we borrow? And, how much can the facility earn?

The rule of thumb is that a safe debt percentage is 30% of your annual income. We have found that a capital campaign can be useful in generating additional revenue before the project has started and even more so, after the project is completed. Generally the Capital Campaign should start a year or two before the beginning of construction so that funds are flowing in for the soft costs that are associated with the building. The campaign continues throughout the building process, hopefully picking up steam along the way.

Once the project is completed and the congregation has seen the new building, their confidence and commitment rises to a level wherein they are more motivated to give. The capital campaign should continue because it energizes older congregants and serves as a mechanism for new members to have a programmed means of giving. That is a significant requirement because the outlays, expenses, and financial requirements of the church have generally grown; that is certainly the case if there was a necessity to get a mortgage to finance the building. This new expense can become a burden if the giving is not continuously rising to meet all of the new obligations.

I have discovered that a capital campaign is most effective when one of the professional capital campaign groups lead it, rather than the church trying to save money by not employing such an entity. They are professionals who have the knowledge from many other churches that is essential in not making unnecessary mistakes or losing focus on the ultimate goal. If the program is operated correctly, they will generate much more revenue than the dollars you pay them to oversee the process. The more money you raise, the less money you have to borrow, and the shorter time frame you have to establish for the repayment of the loan. This reduces the interest cost and puts the church in a better position financially to meet its future goals. With attractive ministries that support membership growth and the attraction of the new building, offerings will generally rise; however because the growth is gradual, it may take several years before your budget becomes balanced.

Borrowing

There are a number of churches that have been blessed to raise enough money to build a church, school or multi-purpose facility without any debt. However, the majority must secure financing through a bank or other form of lending institution. Therefore, audited financial statements become a necessity for bank evaluation. The bank will look at how you manage your current operations and capital to determine if you have the internal capacity to repay the loan. If your statements are shoddy or incorrect; it sends a red flag to the lender and makes it difficult to get financing.

In most instances your building becomes security for the debt, which means that if you do not pay according to the schedule; your property can be seized. There is normally a requirement for a reserve amount of cash that is placed in a separate escrow account, which is not to be used in the daily operations of the church until the loan is repaid.

Every loan is processed by the bank based on loan to value (LTV); which determines whether the property value can justify the loan amount that is requested. The differential between loan and value becomes the church's responsibility. The bank will generally maintain some oversight over the church's finances until they feel secure that all obligations will be met in a timely fashion.

If the project is expected to earn income, the projections should indicate how much in income is anticipated, and the cycle in which the income will come. This is an area where you must be extremely careful so that you do not incur taxable income, which will have deleterious impact on a church that is registered in the state as a non-profit organization. The bank will evaluate everything that is a part of the design and construction including the quality of material, the artistic value of its finishes, and the space that is made available for both worship and other ministerial purposes.

Some years ago we built the Allen Christian School, which many churches are doing if they are located in communities where educational opportunities are limited. We discovered that the bank where we had been doing business for years would provide a building loan for the school. I talked to about 10 banks before finally meeting the president of Carver Bank, who then brought City Bank of Newark and Freedom Bank of Brooklyn to the table to jointly accommodate our needs. Unlike a home where the mortgage is sold to an agency like Fannie Mae or Freddie Mac, church loans are generally held in the bank's portfolio. Therefore, they seek to either spread the risk among several banks or not take the risk at all. When they consider churches and church supported schools, they generally try not to make the loan.

From my experience the key is not giving up, but continuing to pursue the goal that provides an opportunity to create a better environment for you congregation and community. In most cases, if you are diligent in the pursuit of the loan and can justify it, you will be able to find an institution that is willing to take the risk. However, your financial statements must be top notch. Your ultimate goal in financing should be to burn your mortgage within seven to ten years. That is generally possible if your mortgage is no more than 30% of your annual budget. Any excess funds that you garner should be placed against your principal to reduce interest costs, or in a reserved fund so that you can have the assurance of security in case some unforeseen event should occur.

Professional Team

Mario Hodge, who is a building consultant, informs me that budgets are impacted or protected by the team of professionals who will lead your project. Therefore it is necessary to shop around both for quality and price. The selection of the professional must be judicious to the degree that you know their track record, whether they have legal liabilities outstanding, and if they have a history of finishing the projects to the satisfaction of the client. Many churches have been severely hurt by choosing a person who has been helpful to the church, so they are convinced that there is no reason to check their background. Building a church should be dealt with like any other responsibility where you expect a quality result. The members of the professional team must be committed to building a project that glorifies God and not themselves.

Oftentimes architects and professionals will use your project to make a statement about themselves and drive your costs well beyond your budget. If their reputation has not been established already, then they are probably not the best choice for your project. Rev. Elaine and I took our architect to look at churches in Florida and Maryland and Georgia because we could not find comparables in the New York area. We needed to know, as you need to know, the latest technology and models that are working well in newer churches that are similar to what you expect to build. If the team is good, it will protect you from costly overruns, liabilities, risk exposures, as well as financing penalties.

You must take responsibility for having input in all areas of your development and learning those things that you don't know. During my early years, starting with the Senior Center, I learned to read blueprints and to package my own loans. I felt that I needed to be included in the discussions in a knowledgeable way. Subsequently, it has benefited me significantly to have this knowledge as I have used these skill sets to continue the growth of Allen's developments. The best way to learn how to oversee your project is hiring a project manager and letting them guide you as you learn the process for building your own projects.

Make sure that your professional team is able to communicate with one another. That has been made easy by conference calls and e-mails so there is no excuse for a project not moving along in a timely fashion. If any of the professionals are not performing, they should face financial penalties until they respond positively.

Furnishings

Furnishings should be compatible with the décor of the building. Its main purpose is to provide a comfortable aesthetic for the congregants and the persons who are working in the facility on a daily basis. The choices should be made on furniture purchases from designs which will not be discontinued, because inevitably with growth, there will be a need to expand. Most of all, cheap furniture does not have a long life cycle, and is therefore a waste of money.

There are many parishioners who think that the church should be furnished with their used furniture. In their spirits they mean well; however, the ultimate goal is to have an attractive offering unto God and to the people that you are inviting into the kingdom.

Timeline

When the decision is made to enter into a building program, the assumption of growth must be included in the building analysis.

The new facility must be appealing in order to serve as an attraction for new members. One of the reasons that cities build major athletic stadiums is in an attempt to appeal to the fans. The church's offering of Jesus Christ as Lord and Savior is much greater than a sports offering, therefore its facility must be at least equally appealing to persons who are looking for a place of worship. The timeline is generally determined based on the ability to bring all of the components together to work cohesively toward closure. Although you cannot judge all of the potential pitfalls that can slow down the process on the front end, it is still important to set a terminal date so that people will work diligently toward it. Their hopes are raised when they have some idea of when they will enter their new home. The excitement of it causes them to generally give more toward the building project as they watch the daily escalation that will soon culminate in a dream that comes to reality. There is a point where if there have been a number of postponements and the process has slowed down, the pastor, leaders and planning group must position themselves to encourage people to believe that progress is being made. If the psychological moment passes where people begin to question what is happening to their money, there is an uphill battle to try and regain their confidence. So, everything possible must be done to assure that the timetable is adhered to as much as possible. Once people lose faith in the project, it is extremely difficult to convince them that the grand opening will surely come if they are patient enough to wait. To avert any negativity, there are three things that a timetable must have:

1. A realistic time frame for beginning and completing the project.
2. Financial commitments that give reasonable assurance that there are enough resources to finish on time
3. A commitment to prayer, faith, and fasting on the part of the people.

The Issue of Pastoral Authority and Control

Richard Franklin Norris

The African Methodist Episcopal Church was born in the midst of a time when the critical need for pastoral care and leadership were at the height of need and necessity for a people striving to become free and stable. The quest for economic stability and personhood in a society that was too often hostile, oppressive and filled with stress and deprivation created a climate ripe for the presence of religion and mutual aid. The church offered a vehicle for pooling of resources and mentoring for those without skills and the capacity to access the necessities to sustain the individual, to say nothing of the family. The church under the leadership of a caring shepherd offered a haven of hope and opportunity for self-help. Beyond the elements of faith and religion were the elements of mutual aid, fellowship and family. The church was a place that offered self esteem and respect for individual personhood. Central to this community of hope was the watchful care of dedicated pastoral leadership.

Such a community of faith was critical to the stability and advancement for a people faced with challenges beyond any that can be fully understood in society as we now know and experience it. It was the church and the creative leadership of pastors who were endowed with trust, respect, power and authority that fostered hope for a people otherwise adrift in a sea of challenge. They were spiritual leaders and at the same time symbols of hope for an improved quality of life, economic deliverance and educational enlightenment. Coupled with both symbolic and actual power and authority, the pastor was central to the destiny of a pilgrim people with few, if any, other options,

The need for discipline and guidance was central for the navigation through the maze of life for a people oppressed, deprived and systematically excluded from access to opportunity and a reasonable dignity and quality of life. The pastor was often the source of encouragement hope and possibility for a community with limited skills and less opportunity. Resident in the pastor was the perceived wisdom, power and key access to both spiritual and secular upward mobility. Coupled with these ascribed attributes was the capacity to control much of life as it was experienced in the early days of the African Methodist Episcopal Church. That capacity to control reached into every facet of the life of a people searching for respect and grasping for the bare necessities of life, food, clothing and shelter. This power and control often meant the difference between access and exclusion from life altering opportunities.

It is for these reasons, among many others, that the pastor became the reservoir and repository for power and authority. No other leader in the Black community had the access to people power and influence, as did the preacher. While there is a consistent thread that runs through the realities of what was and what is, there has been a major paradigm shift in the way that these realities shaped the influence and impact of the Black preacher and the congregations that serve and lead.

While the reality of power and influence have always been there, the use and power in the hands of many preachers has evolved into a tendency for over use and abuse of the resident power of the pastor. Historically there was an understanding of the power of restraint and control in the use of power and authority. The current trend seems to be the greater exercise of unbridled use and power and control. It is no secret that we have always been a clergy-led church but the measured use of power and control has historically been characterized by restraint. The shift in the controlled use of power has in many obscured the appropriate use of authority and the measured use of power.

Hans Finzel in his book entitled, *The Top Ten Mistakes Leaders Make,* identifies what he believes to be the elements of failure that haunt would-be leaders. The use of a military model that has the leader barking out orders to an uninspired following often results in abuse when unbridled exercise of power is inflicted on followers.

The model of servant leadership has been eroded to the point that shepherd leadership, has been replaced by the model of a driver, often lacking compassion and restraint. This is a shift from the very fabric of what has made the church the true body of believers and the empowering capacity to belong and participate in the body of Christ. This shift impacts the quality of ministry. The issues of power and authority are at the core of what makes the church effective or relegates it to existence in an abyss of irrelevance and ineffectiveness. It is a threat to every phase of the life of the Christian Church as we have come to know it. The paradigm change has lead to eroded confidence in the leadership in many churches. It is an era driven by prosperity religion where the prosperity rarely extends beyond the circle of leadership.

Power is often addictive. It often extends and inflates its influence and control moving from progressive to oppressive and often abusive control. Because the pastor is both respected and trusted, there is a deep-seated potential for exploitive exercise of authority and power. Often the abusive leader looses the capacity to discern the shift of leadership style that diminishes their effectiveness and undercuts their influence that defined their arrival on the stage of leadership. It is too often so subtle that it creeps in unnoticed becoming a part of the accepted mode of operation. It evolves into a style that infects the mental process to the point where it becomes difficult to separate that which is ethical from what is oppressive and authoritarian. It thus thrusts the church from its rightful place as a haven of peace and refuge for those starving for the security of a community of faith.

Jesus said that those who would be greatest among us must be the servants. J. Oswald Sanders is right on when he identifies the model of servant leadership. In his book, "Servant Leadership" he offers this prospective: "In stating that primacy in leadership comes by way of primacy in servanthood, Jesus did not have in mind mere acts of service, for those can be performed from very dubious motives. He meant the spirit of servanthood, which He expressed when he proclaimed; "I am among you as He that serves."

Isaiah 42:1-5, a messianic passage, reveals what the spirit of servanthood means and outlines in his prophetic fore view the features that would qualify the coming Messiah as the ideal Servant of the Lord. Israel had been chosen by God to be His servant through whom He would reveal Himself to the world. But the nation failed, Jesus succeeded gloriously, and the principles of his life must be the pattern for ours."

Sanders heralds a litany of principles that help define servanthood. He lists: Dependence on God in that even Jesus emptied Himself in conforming to God's will (Philippians 2:7). Approval: chosen of God and delighting to conform to His will. Modesty: True servants allow their faithfulness to acclaim their works and not their own flamboyant arrogant self-advertisement. Empathy: Kind, understand in the leadership of the weak and afflicted. Optimistic: Inspiring leadership cannot emerge from a spirit of pessimism. Anointing: Isaiah 61:1-2 declares that "The spirit of the Lord God is upon me; because the Lord hath anointed me to preach good tidings unto the meek; he hath sent me to bind up the brokenhearted, to proclaim liberty to the captives, and the opening of the prison to them that are bound; to proclaim the acceptable year of the Lord, and the day of vengeance of our God; to comfort all that mourn."

If the "mainline" church is to exercise the resurgence of life, giving renewed personhood in its ministry; there must be a recapturing of the spirit and ministry of servanthood. It is an established fact that churches that serve while offering inspiring worship opportunities will grow while those detoured to the narrow constraints of self preservation and self enhancement will continue to stagnate, afflicted by self inflicted wounds. The new age of the church is an age of new wine that must be housed in new wineskins. New technology demands that the church of the twenty-first century embrace the new while preserving the fundamentals of the faith that bring life and hope in a difficult world. The leadership of the church must cling to the principles of Christ that allows for the work of the Spirit of God to provide the strength and guidance that leads in the path of righteousness for His name sake.

It has been said that, "Power corrupts but absolute power corrupts absolutely." There is a glaring resistance to the spirit of inclusion that shares power and authority in the church. When leadership is not inclusive and shared, the church is weakened and the failed development of disciples leaves the membership weak and unable to participate in the making of other disciples. It erodes the development of the capacity to develop a priesthood of all believers that empowers the church to become the true body of Christ. Shared leadership as defined in terms of true discipleship strengthens the body, leaving little room for the festering of discontent and rebellion. True disciples tend to hunger for the living God who inspires, empowers and makes fruitful productive servants. Blessed are those who have more disciples than members.

The Discipline of the African Methodist Episcopal Church makes clear in its mission statement the focus of the church's ministry identifying it as a servant-oriented institution. That mission is to: "Minister to the social, spiritual and physical development of all people." The objective of the church is the empowering of its membership in the area of "(1) Christian discipleship (2) Christian leadership, (3) current teaching methods and materials, (4) the history and significance of the A.M.E. Church, (5) God's biblical principles and (6) social development of which all should be applied to daily living."

There is no place in the mission statement of the church that encourages a concentration of power and authority in the hands of a single person, but in the hands of true disciples of the living God. The powerless tend to become the hotbed of discontent and disruption in the local church as well as in the denomination. We are challenged to be the liberating, empowering followers of Christ who is the true head of the church. When the membership of the church is informed and empowered, the life of the church becomes vibrant and filled with an engaged body of believers contributing to the growth of the church. An uninformed powerless membership will be stagnant and lethargic, bereft of motivation and a will not be all that God intends for them to be. They are relegated to a place beneath their full potential and possibility. What a waste of human resources. Yet too many leaders filled with their own perceived greatness, miss the wealth of ability resident in the hands of informed inspired disciples.

If a leader is to be great, that greatness is not self-bestowed. The measure of one's worth is ascribed by others and not one's self. Jesus did a spot check when he asked his disciples "Who do men say that I am." If we want to know the true measure of who we are we must measure the impact of our perception as seen in the eyes of others. If the church is to be the true body of Christ it must have a true picture of what the Lord requires. He requires that we "Do justice, love mercy and walk humbly with God." It means that we do the right thing, be fair and just in all of our ministration. We must be merciful. Not demanding an eye for an eye and a tooth for a tooth. Temper justice with mercy. Thirdly we must embrace humility. It has been said that when people are full of themselves, it is then that they are most empty.

One should strive never to use all of the power they have. I have become more keenly aware, since becoming a bishop in the church, of the awesome power resident in the office entrusted to me. Like one driving a high-powered automobile, it becomes clear that there is much more power under the hood than a prudent person should ever dare to use. In like manner, pastors have far more power than is wise to use. If one becomes consumed by the quest for power and authority of their own making, they create an atmosphere charged with fear, distrust and anarchy. Effective use of power and authority demands that use of it creates a respect for it like one must have for electricity. When respected and handled in accord with established principles there is an almost limitless capacity for productive use. In like manner, proper respect for the use of power and authority can open the doors of opportunity and achievement. When a lack of respect is shown, a formula for destruction can be the result.

The issue of authority and control in the hands of the pastor has the potential to either make a church greater or to diminish its ministry depending on how that authority and control are applied. Power in the hands of a small, self-centered leader may result in tyranny and oppression. The misuse of power has reduced many congregations to a shadow of what they once were. It is amazing how a church, in the hands of one pastor who rules with a selfish autocratic style, results in the decline of that congregation. The succeeding assigned pastor of that same church soars on the wings of an empowered membership that share not only the power but the vision and aspirations of that pastor, who is large enough to see the possibility of a shared leadership.

Ruling with an iron hand often results in a stiff-necked response, riding on the wings of resistance, resentment and rebellion. Ours is an age of diminished loyalty to the denominational brand. When people have a wide range of choices and where there is not a welcoming environment; people vote with their feet and embrace a choice that is welcoming and to their liking. In the absence of a sense of opportunity for inclusion and empowerment, there are many who will not be herded into a place where their brain must be disconnected if they are to belong. A real leader seeks to exercise the growth and development of the potential of the membership of the place where they serve. This is in no way intended to advocate weakness in the leadership of the pastor, but it is to advocate making room in the tent for all who would seek to enter and serve.

Having pastored six congregations, some more challenging than others, I found that a common thread connected all of those ministries. That common thread was the desire of most of the members to see and help their churches do well. When met with a respect for the creativity and abilities of the people, they embraced the vision of the leadership, some quickly and others more slowly. There will never be unanimous agreement on every issue but when the thoughts of the people are respected and considered there tends to be better cooperation and support. I have always listened to the people though it was not always the appointed time for the vision they shared. Respecting their contributions was important not only for them and their feelings, but for the good of the body as a whole.

Now there are times when the leader must stand his ground, based on what is best for the church. Not every idea of the pastor is perfect but there are times when the pastor must be the shepherd of the flock. Pressing one's own vision, needs to be done with room and respect for other ideas whose time may come at a later season. Don't kill the vision but remember the words of the prophet who advised that the vision is for an appointed time and though it may tarry, wait for it. Sometimes it is the vision of the leader that will have to be put on hold. Remember that the pendulum swings both ways. There may be times that your vision must tarry. The strong-arm approach may be so destructive that, while well intended, many spirits may be so damaged that recovery may not be possible.

It is clear that the A.M.E. Discipline places certain power and authority in the hands of the pastor, but the life of the church is more important than the ego of the leader. I had a pastor whose membership was all but completely gone say that he did not have a problem because all of the opposition was gone. He missed the big picture. Almost all of the members were gone never to return. The exercise of power and control had resulted in a church that was so much weaker and its ministry had proved beneficial to every church in town but not their own. How tragic was the result of that power and control. A more inclusive ministry may have produced a better result.

Many of the problems result from budget issues that too often create civil war in the local church. Money is usually only a problem when there is not enough of it. The proper allocation of resources makes a difference in the spirit of the church. Too many pastors make the mistake of improper allocation of resources. There is a misguided thought that every church is a self-sufficient full time pastorate. The truth is that many of the congregations that make up our Zion are not churches that can sustain a full time pastor receiving a full-time living wage. If an attempt is made to make a part time appointment support a full time compensation level, that ministry is destined for failure. At the same time a full time pastorate paying full time compensation while receiving part time service is also prone to trouble.

In conclusion, the proper use of power, authority and control will spell the difference between success and failure in the ministry of a pastor. The inability to be flexible and inclusive can result in limiting the quality of ministry in a local church. Following the principles set forth in scripture and the guidelines in the Discipline can make a difference in the life of the pastor and the churches that they serve.

Order in the Church

Sir Walter Mack

One of the elements of ministry that is a necessity for "Doing Church" in the twenty-first century is to give honor and reverence to the place of "order" in the church. It is important that order is put in proper context because in many churches either order is lifted up over any other function of ministry, or order is treated as something optional, obsolete, and not necessary for "Doing Church".

Order is derived from the Latin word *ordo-inis*, which means methodical in its structure, or in its verb form it means, "to arrange" which is derived from the word *ordinare*. Theologically, God has a methodical arrangement for the church, and the effectiveness of the church is often measured by how the church extends, exercises, and interprets the order that God established for the church in its inception. Alexander Pope once declared, "order is heaven's first law." If this perception holds any merit of truth, then it becomes obvious that order should be one of the primary laws, if not the very foundation for any ministry that is serious about "Doing Church".

While I believe that having order in the church is vital for the function of ministry, my opinion about this matter derives from a very personal experience during my tenure of ministry. Upon graduating from the Duke Divinity School at the age of 26, I was called to pastor a rural church in North Carolina. Although this church had experienced progressive ministry in its 106-year history, upon my immediate arrival, I detected a church that was severely out of order. The lack of order in this church manifested itself during my first church meeting when contention and conflict erupted to the point that reprehensible anger and clear profane language were expressed, even during the benedictory prayer of that meeting. The divergence centered around a deacon who had tremendous influence in the church. Not only did he have influence, this deacon also had an indeterminate amount of responsibilities; he served as trustee, treasurer, Sunday school superintendent, and not to mention that he was a relative to many of the members in the church. As a result, this deacon would often defy order by implementing his plan for the church- instead of acknowledging the church's plan. Consequently, confusion and strife manifested among many of the members, and indeed, much of it deviated from his ability to control ministry direction. His interpretation of order was "whoever has the money, determines the order." This self-determinate factor alone gave him precedence when it came to order because he was the overseer of all the church funds.

Over a period, of time this kind of operation became arduous for me as the pastor, and also unbearable for many of the other officers and members of the church. In fact, this predicament only worsened as there was sure evidence of integrity violation with misappropriate handling of money, an abuse of authority and position, and even more, a shameless display of stubbornness marked with an intentionally disrespectful spirit and attitude. Soon after, when the officers, the congregation, and I confronted this "church leader" about the truth and transparency of his actions, his ambivalent conduct became hostile and elevated. This belligerent display of defamed behavior produced an intense level of negative emotions throughout the ministry.

Irrefutably, this one member convinced five others into driving a wedge between the membership. This out-of-order group caused premature dismissal of meetings due to unruly conduct, interruption of church worship services because of ungodly behavior, and finally a resorted movement to have under-cover sheriff deputies in attendance at Sunday morning services because of the possible threat of gun violence. These insidious and begrudging acts not only affected the body of Christ, but also in fact caused bifurcation and division between family members and life-long friends. The church was despairingly out of order, however, to add impact to injury, the church ended up in court with a judge making a recommendation to this group of six, that if they did not want to abide by the desires of the majority, they needed to consider leaving, and they did. When this splintered group left the church, the church began to blossom and grow exponentially. The spirit of the church shifted from a feeling of malignancy to a feeling of ministry. Worship services were filled with power and evangelism took a new thrust. The finances went into overflow because trust and accountability were in place, not to mention the unsaved desired to be saved.

When order was taught, explained and demonstrated, the church was able to witness God bring light out of darkness, clarity out of confusion, peace out of perplexity, and order out of chaos. This accomplishment did not happen by osmosis, but there were many intentional actions that took place so that "order" could prevail. Through preaching and teaching about "order", the church began to look at matters differently, and understood that much of what was manifested upon my arrival, was a direct result of things that were out of order prior to my arrival. As a new pastor, I perceived it to be monumental that if we were going to "do church" we were going to "do church" with order. Therefore, in the transition from "disorder" to "order" emphasis had to be placed on the church understanding divine laws and principles which collaborate with being a church that possessed order. When the church began to operate in the realm of walking in order, they witnessed a new way of "doing church" that truly gave God honor and glory for the things that God had done. This transformation occurred because they understood a new revelation about order and the proven benefits that followed.

Therefore, this chapter will focus on how we "do church" and how we do it with order. What is the intent of order? What causes the lack of order? Who does failure of order affect? What are the benefits of order? How do we establish order, and what are some of the practical ways to implement order in the church?

A Place of Violation and Establishment of Order

[1] And the entire congregation lifted up their voice, and cried; and the people wept that night. [2] And all the children of Israel murmured against Moses and against Aaron: and the whole congregation said unto them, Would God that we had died in the land of Egypt! Or would God we had died in this wilderness! [3] And wherefore hath the LORD brought us unto this land, to fall by the sword, that our wives and our children should be a prey? Was it not better for us to return into Egypt? [4] And they said one to another, Let us make a captain, and let us return into Egypt.
[5] Then Moses and Aaron fell on their faces before all the assembly of the congregation of the children of Israel. [6] And Joshua the son of Nun, and Caleb the son of Jephunneh, which were of them that searched the land, rent their clothes: [7] And they spake unto all the company of the children of Israel, saying, The land, which we passed through to search it, is an exceeding good land. [8] If the LORD delight in us, then he will bring us into this land, and give it to us; a land which floweth with milk and honey. [9] Only rebel not ye against the LORD, neither fear ye the people of the land; for they are bread for us: their defence[a] is departed from them, and the LORD is with us: fear them not. [10] But all the congregation bade stone them with stones. And the glory of the LORD appeared in the tabernacle of the congregation before all the children of Israel.

[11] And the LORD said unto Moses, How long will this people provoke me? And how long will it be ere they believe me, for all

the signs which I have shewed among them? [12] I will smite them with the pestilence, and disinherit them, and will make of thee a greater nation and mightier than they.

If there is any passage of scripture that exemplifies the establishment of order and the violation of order all in the same moment, it is the experience that is written in Numbers 14:1-13. In this passage Moses has already received the report from Joshua and Caleb about the land that was flowing with milk and honey- a place called Canaan. Israel had everything they needed to possess the land, with the exception of confidence to do it.

Their confidence was diluted by what they saw, and not what they knew. What they knew was that in Numbers 13:2, God released Moses to obtain the land, to take it and possess it. Moses followed the plan by sending one leader from each tribe on this mission to see the future possession and return with a report. Among the spies were two men, one by the name of Joshua who represented the tribe of Ephraim, and Caleb who was a descendent from the tribe of Judah. The assignment was to investigate the land to find out the defensive ability of the Canaanites, while also finding a place for agricultural advancement. When the Israelites arrived at the land, they indeed saw land flowing with milk and honey; cities that were large and fortified, and inhabitants that appeared as giants. After forty days, the spies went back to Moses carrying with them grapes from the Valley of Eschol, which served as a symbol that the land had great harvest and prosperity. This was their land to possess; however, it was the other things they saw that took them off of their destined course of possessing what God had already promised. They also saw the occupants of the land, the descendants of Anak as giants, and themselves as grasshoppers (Numbers 13:30-33). They therefore rejected the opinion of Joshua and Caleb to overtake the land, but rather retreated in their desire to go back to Egypt and insulate themselves in slavery.

This reality surfaces in Numbers 14, where we find the Israelites organizing a hostile church conference. The top agenda item of the day involved rejecting the plan that Moses, Aaron, Joshua and Caleb were suggesting. This rejection is apparent because verse 1-3 declares… *And all the congregation lifted up their voice, and cried; and the people wept that night.* [2] *And all the children of Israel murmured against Moses and against Aaron: and the whole congregation said unto them, Would God that we had died in the land of Egypt! Or would God we had died in this wilderness!* [3] *And wherefore hath the LORD brought us unto this land, to fall by the sword, that our wives and our children should be a prey? Was it not better for us to return into Egypt?*

It was the congregations desire to go back to captivity rather than follow the vision, follow the plan God had given them, and possess the land God had promised. William Faulkner declared, "The past is dead and buried. In fact, it isn't even the past". (Walter Earl Fluker, *Ethical Leadership-The Quest for Character, Civility, and Community*, Fortress Press, Minneapolis, p. 61). They chose to defy the order, and "do church" the way they wanted to "do church." They wanted to stay in the past. Defying order is not the same as confronting an issue. Confronting an issue may be done to get clarity, to be more informed about details, to make certain that the task is in our ability, and can be done with a very cooperative spirit. One should never diminish healthy confrontation. As a matter of fact, invite it sometimes. However, healthy confrontation is not the same as a defiance of order. Let us consider a few elements that led to this obvious revolt and abandonment of God's order to possess what was theirs to have.

The Violation of Order Always Begins With A Murmur

This spirit of the congregational "murmuring" against the direction that Moses was taking is very real and operative in ministries today. The murmuring that Israel offered up was synonymous to a lament, and it stemmed not only from the fear of facing the giants in Canaan, but Israel was murmuring because while they had come out of Egypt, it is apparent that

Egypt had not come out of them. In other words, they had on band-aids from Egypt, but the wounds had never healed. There is a popular thought in identity dialogue that declares, "Hurting people often hurt people". Israel was hurting because their options were limited; they felt that their snatching and quick deliverance out of Egypt was not rewarded by a place they had to labor to obtain. In other words, if we are going to have to fight giants, we may as well labor like slaves in Egypt.

Egypt a place of stripping identity, is now their desired place for identity. They now desire to become what they once despised. To add impact to injury, the only vision that they had of themselves was to see themselves dead. *Would God that we had died in the land of Egypt! Or would God we had died in this wilderness!* How could they see a way to possess a land that was flowing with milk and honey, when the only view they had of themselves were their bodies in caskets? Erich Fromm calls this necrophilia or being lovers of death. According to Fromm, "necrophiles 'are fascinated with all that is not alive, all that is dead; corpses, decay, feces, dirt…and they come to life primarily when they can talk about death. They tend to dwell in the past, not in the future, and are enamored by force and violence, which supplants sexuality and spiritual relations with visions of power and conquest" (Walter Earl Fluker, *Ethical Leadership-The Quest for Character, Civility, and Community,* Fortress Press, Minneapolis, p. 74,). Israel was not just depressed, but they were tombstone depressed, and now their depression is surfacing through their murmuring.

This action is most likely to happen in churches especially when there are members who practice what psychologists call "displaced emotions"- when someone's experiential hurt and pain is transferred on to someone else. The resurfacing of an emotional injury often provokes this action. In other words, anger from the low self image and the institutionalized oppression that had been an intricate part of Israel's enslavement in Egypt, is now being transferred on to Moses, Aaron, Joshua and Caleb, all because they saw life, but Israel was in love with death. Recently, I had to pray for a friend of mine because she had a rare attack on her body; she became suddenly deathly ill, and for days lived life from a life support machine. She had an acute rare illness that caused an autoimmune response to her body's system, and the body began eating up the body. Cells began to kill off other cells, and organs began to fight against one another. Here in this instance, Israel had spiritual illness, and they were fighting against themselves, working against themselves, and it all surfaced through them lifting their voices in a murmur.

Kenneth C. Haugk in his book, "Antagonist in the Church", refers to people that murmur as antagonist. "Antagonists are individuals who, on the basis of no substantive evidence, go out of their way to make insatiable demands, usually attacking the person or performance of others. These attacks are selfish in nature, tearing down rather than building up, and are frequently directed against those in a leadership capacity."(Kenneth C. Haugk, Antagonist in The Church: How To Identify and Deal With Destructive Conflict, Augsburg Press., Minneapolis, p.21-22) Consider some of the traits of antagonist/murmurs in the church.

- Antagonist/Murmurers will often demonstrate a change in how they interact with you when they don't agree with you.
- Antagonist/Murmurers often come with general concerns of others which at times may be interpreted as their own anger.
- Antagonist/Murmurers will often ask questions about detail, and often want to know about financial matters to the penny, and about details as it pertains to the next move of the ministry.
- Antagonist/Murmurers are often very manipulative in harnessing support around their issue. They are often charismatic, and have a way of attracting people that feel as they feel.
- Antagonist/Murmurers will often gather secret meetings, spread rumors, and attack vision

without having factual or exhaustive information about what they are meeting on.

- Antagonist/Murmurers will often criticize leadership and the direction of the ministry openly, and will protest quietly but loudly with their withdrawal from activities and other important moments in the ministry.

(Haugk, p. 81-82).

The sole intent of the "murmurer" is to disrupt harmony, disassociate themselves from hope, and discombobulate those that are willing to help. The intent of the murmurer is to defy God's order for accomplishment, and persuade as many others as they possibly can to do the same. We will find ways to handle the "order violator" later in our text,

A Violation of Order Is Manifested When It Seeks To Usurp Leadership

One of the dangers of trying to get people who are out of order to get in some order is that there are times when they will blame you- the leader for the past situation, the present situation and even debunk your suggestion for future resolve. If there has been an issue that has been silenced, swept under the rug, not acknowledge or not addressed for quite some time and a leader shows up to address it or bring some attention to it, it should not be a surprise if attack is soon to follow. When the murmurers did not want to possess the land, they surfaced and sought to remove Moses from his pastoral responsibilities. It is one thing when people who defy order do not desire for you to lead them, but it is another thing when erroneous, divisive, unethical and ungodly attack occurs in the attempt to unseat the leader that is sent to establish order. Ronald Heifitz and Martin Linsky gave validity to the idea when they stated, "You appear dangerous to people when you question their values, beliefs, or habits of a lifetime. You place yourself on the line when you tell people what they need to hear rather than what they want to hear. Although you may see with clarity and passion a promising future of progress and gain, people will see with equal passions the losses you are asking them to sustain". (Walter Earl Fluker,

Ethical Leadership-The Quest for Character, Civility, and Community, Fortress Press, Minneapolis, p.8).

And they said one to another, "Let us make a captain, and let us return into Egypt." The very obvious difference between the call of Moses to leadership, and the call of the congregation's captain is that Moses was appointed by God and the congregation's captain was appointed by themselves. If you are going to serve in leadership while "doing church", it is most important that you position yourself not to be the object of the issue that is being denied or protested against. For example, imagine a church where the pastor may have a vision to do outreach in a community that is infested with the sale of drugs, gripped by gun and gang violence, and is the hot spot for police calls and ambulatory presence. Yet there is a delegation in the church that may rise in protest and issue a vote against the pastor, because they refuse or don't have the desire to deal with the real issue of community decay that is around them. The issue for the pastor is the community; the issue for this church is the pastor.

In my own pastoral experience with the conflict I mentioned earlier in this writing, the issue for me was the misuse of power and financial accountability, but the delegation that sought to usurp my leadership made "me" the issue. While the group will make you the issue, you can't make you the issue. "When you take 'personal' attacks personally, you unwittingly conspire in one of the common ways you can be taken out of action- you make yourself the issue". (Ronald A. Heifetz and Marty Linsky, Leadership On The Line: Staying Alive Through the Dangers of Leading, Harvard Business School Press, Boston, Mass., p. 191). The action is the issue that you want to address, and a good leader knows how to keep it on the issue, and not make it about himself or herself. This is what Moses did when Moses went to God; he became an intercessor for the people that were seeking to stone him. [19]*Pardon, I beseech thee, the iniquity of this people according unto the greatness of thy mercy, and as thou hast forgiven this people, from Egypt even until now.*

I believe that a real measurement for whether one is walking in mature leadership or not, is the leader's ability to rise above chaos, confusion, and calamity, and still perform the ministerial task for which they have been called. Do not make the attack personal; this is not about you! This is about the will of God, and the place where God is trying to take his church. In the game of football, when the defensive line is viciously seeking to hit a swift runningback, the runningback can't take the hit personally. But the running back has the ball, and he must understand that part of the penalty for carrying the ball, is that every now and then you will get hit. It's not personal it's just the way the game is played. This is the mindset that you must have, because you as the leader carry the ball, and there are times when the game will require you to be hit.

If you, as a leader, ever have to face this kind of conflict in your ministry, it is important to hold on to some essential qualities as leaders that will aide you in your authority. Order is often maintained when the leader maintains three qualities in particular: Integrity, Empathy, and Hope as cited in Ethical Leadership by Walter Fluka.

The Leader With Integrity

The Chinese symbol for integrity is Te. While this could also mean virtue and goodness, the best interpretation for this is character that comes straight from the heart. (Walter Earl Fluker, *Ethical Leadership-The Quest for Character, Civility, and Community*, Fortress Press, Minneapolis, p. 66). Thus integrity is that which comes straight from the heart. The leader's integrity is important because it informs actions and behaviors. Whenever there is the lack of order in any church, more often than not, the problem can always be traced back to some issues around integrity. People who come up with schemes in the church, plan deceptive forms of operation, circulate gossip, disrupt meetings, and intentionally mislead others, while they suffer from a spiritual sickness, at the root of their actions is also an issue of integrity. For the leader, integrity must be practiced in what the leader says, does, and how he or she behaves. Integrity must inform the leaders choices, guide direction, and serve as a thermometer for emotions.

Howard G. Hendricks reminded leaders of the importance of integrity when he stated, Vision without integrity is not mission-it's manipulation." (Roy B. Zuck, The Speaker's Quote Book Speakers, Kregal Publications1997, Grand Rapids, Michigan, p. 212) It is most important to note that integrity and character must become the foundation and basis for effectiveness in ministry. It is interesting to me that the adversaries of Moses attacked his vision, but never accused him of living a life void of integrity. If there had been an integrity issue with Moses like infidelity, embezzlement, lying, cheating, and stealing, then these issues would have taken precedence over their fear for possessing the Promised Land. In other words, the issue of integrity would have served as a smoke screen to cover the real issue of fear to possess the Promised Land. While no one is perfect, perfection as a leader must be your aim. You will make errors while leading, but let it be an error that is made while trying to make the kingdom better, rather than an error that is made for self-indulging and manipulative means for private gain. Lord Macauley declared, "The measure of a man's character is what he would do if he knew he would never be found out". "Character is what you are in the dark, and reputation is only what others believe you to be."(Vernon McLellan, Timeless Treasures, Hendrickson Publishers, Peabody, Massacusettes, 1992, 2000, p.33). Moses did not allow his integrity to slip into a place he wasn't familiar with; Moses reverted to prayer. The integrity of Moses led him to not only pray for himself, but to pray for his murmurer's. This has to be foundational for the leader. You can't lead them if you hate them.

The Leader with Empathy

While integrity is more about behavior, empathy is more about emotions. The reason that the leader must possess empathy, particularly while addressing issues concerning order in the church, is because empathy has a way of helping the leader to put himself or herself in the place of the people who may be expressing disgust and the lack of cooperation. Moses must have had empathy for the people, because it is out of his empathy that he begins to pray for God to spare their lives. Empathy has a way of hearing a person's story differently, and understanding in some way why they may refuse to receive the newness God has to offer, but rather choose to hold on to the past.

While it is important for the leader to have empathy, the leader must be ever cautious of not negotiating what God has commissioned over what they are feeling. In other words, the leader's empathy is not an excuse for not executing the assignment God has already given. In other words, pastor/leader listen to the congregations stories, hear how passionate they are about their past, enter into the world of the sensitive, and the things that mean something to them. However, while you are empathizing with their history or their desire, it is incumbent that you always return to your world of what God commissioned you to do. 2 Timothy 4:2-4 says, *"Preach the word; be persistent in season, out of season; reprove, rebuke, exhort with all longsuffering and doctrine. For the time will come when they will not endure sound doctrine; but after their own lusts shall they heap to themselves teachers, having itching ears;* [4] *And they shall turn away their ears from the truth, and shall be turned unto fables".* This is what Jesus did with the woman who was caught in adultery. His empathy led him to dismiss her charge and not stone or judge her, but his divine commission to her was to go and sin no more. There must be balance between what you empathize with, and what you know you are assigned to correct and direct.

The Leader with Hope

Nothing can hinder your creativity and diminish your optimism like people in the church that refuse to follow proper protocol and do things the right way. Nothing can affect the flow of peace and unity like a disgruntled "church doer" that only desires for things to be done his/her way, and no other way. Nothing can disturb the sacredness of church work, like someone who does not have a healthy perception of himself or herself, and has to depend on his/her title to garner importance and significance. However, even though there are times when the leader will encounter these challenges, it is important for the leader to always exemplify a ray of hope. James Gustafon describes hope as confidence in our future. He stated, "Hope is carried by confidence that life is more reliable than unreliable, that the future is open, that new possibilities of life exist" (James M. Gustafon, *Christ and the Moral Life*, Chicago and London: Chicago University Press, 1968, p.250) This must be the reality that every leader must hold on to, if that leader is serious about leading people who do not have hope.

The leader must be serious about confronting the despair that disgruntled people bring, with the hope that leaders have a right to anticipate. Hope is not just being optimistic, or having a positive outlook on the situation, but hope is rooted in the faith that says even when things don't look quite optimistic, we can still passionately believe and follow. Hebrews 11:1 says, "Now faith is the substance of things hoped for, the evidence of things not seen". Before any radical transformation is to happen in the lives of people who resist change, they must be empowered by hope. The pastor/leader must make them feel that if we lose everything in our attempt to get to the Cannan land, we will still have our hope. George Fredric Watt, a Victorian era British artist, in his painting "Hope", depicts a woman playing a harp while sitting on top of the world. However, the world she is sitting on is wracked with trouble, confusion, despair, and vicious malignancy. This woman is sitting on top of the world with her head bandaged, but though wounded, she is playing a harp with one string left to play. The obvious question one would ask is, "Why is she playing a harp with one string, while sitting on top of the world?" The one string left remaining on the harp gives the impression that as long as she has one string left, she can still play one more tune, one more note, and one more song.

The message is clear. Regardless of the attack that comes to rock your world, you must remain determined to keep playing the string you have left. The hope is that if everybody doesn't see your vision, you can learn how to expand your vision with the ones that do. If some turn away and leave, the hope is that there are some who will be determined to stand by your side. The hope is that even when wayward people come against you and seek to vote you out for another "captain", God will never allow the weapon that is formed against you to prosper. This is the hope that we must herald. This is the message that we must minister. This is the fate that we must place our faith in. Hold on to the hope.

The Leader with Security

It is vital for any leader seeking to implement a vision, to be certain about where his or her security lies. The security for the leader cannot be in the succession of leadership, or in the success of the person you have followed. Security is not necessarily in how many years you have served, or in how much you have invested. There are countless occasions in which leaders have served for years, and ended up holding an empty bag. Nor is our security found in the people that serve on our security ministries, and those who sense that they have a call to protect you. Therefore, the security of your position has to solely be in God, and not in any governing board, denominational discipline, or any man or woman. God alone who will plant you, and God will keep you.

This is so apparent in Moses' experience, because even though the Israelites decided to defy order, God did not. The Israelites desired to select another leader, a move that would have threatened Moses' security. But Moses did not have his security in them; his security was in God, and even when they wanted to defy order, God never seconded their motion. I know this because in Numbers 14:4, they elected another leader, but in verse 11 it is evident that God never pays attention to their selection, because verse 11 clearly shows that God still spoke to Moses. In other words, God's order will never be secondary to humanity's order. What I am trying to convey is that when God establishes you as a leader, and ordains you to a place, your security has to rest in the fact that God ordered you to be there.
Though there are times when murmurers can change their plans, they can never change God's order. If by chance human will and human manipulation would lead a group to get rid of you, or

remove you from your leadership post, just remember God will provide and take care of you and the ministry He has placed within you. I once heard a notable preacher say, "It is my job to jump, and it is God's job to find me a place to land". This is the security of the leader. Your leadership must possess confidence, optimism, drive, and zeal. You can have these attributes when you learn where to put your trust. God has not called you to lead in fear, looking over your shoulder wondering whether or not you will be the order of the day at the next church conference. You must lead while trusting God, Isaiah 54:4a says, "Fear not; for thou shalt not be ashamed: neither be thou confounded; for thou shalt not be put to shame…"

Practical Tips For Leaders Under Attack

1. It is important for the leader to understand that disgruntled members love to have meetings. Look out for this request, and be open for meeting when you feel that it is the right time. In this meeting spend time gathering information and discerning the root of the problem.

2. When the meeting is called it is important for you to establish the location. Do not fall into the temptation of meeting on their territory for this is certainly not "holy ground". Make certain the meeting is either in your office, in your place of choosing, most preferably at the church. Try to avoid lunches, walks in the park, or golfing adventures with people who are disgruntled. This creates an environment of friendliness that may compromise discussing the real issue at hand.

3. When the leader is meeting with a disgruntled member, there are times when having a witness with you is helpful. We are living in a day where fallacies are used to oust a leader, and if your spirit leads you to have a witness by all means do so. If a witness is not available, if possible leave the door open, or have someone close by if you fear physical harm. Also note that there are

times when a witness will elevate the matter and make the issue more important than it really is.

4. Avoid keeping secrets. If there is any information that a disgruntled member would like for you to share with them, always let them know that you will be willing to share it with a committee or the entire church body if necessary. You are accountable to the church, not one disgruntled member.

5. When meeting a disgruntled member, always be mindful of your Christian posture, but remain firm. Make certain that you arrive before time, since disgruntled members often arrive early, because they can't wait to get the issue off of their chests. In the meeting, let them talk first, and do not affirm what they are saying with either a yes or a no. You will have your opportunity to speak; just listen. Take good notes as a record, and use the time that they are talking as a gathering moment for you to organize your talking points.

6. When responding to a disgruntled member, keep your answers short and your words very selective. Remember, even though they are not writing, doesn't mean they aren't taking notes, or either "secretly" recording the conversation. Never say anything to a disgruntled member you can't repeat in open court. In your mind, you should always anticipate that the matter can get to that level, and if it does you want to be able to repeat whatever is said.

7. If a disgruntled member desires for you to maintain confidentiality, you must remember to do so if it is a personal matter. However, if what they are discussing is a church matter, it automatically becomes a public issue. This is where you draw the line with confidentiality. You are accountable to the church, and therefore, are

obligated to inform the church regarding matters that are critical and important.

8. When addressing disgruntled members always expect the unexpected. Do not let anything surprise, but learn to anticipate the worst action. If it happens simply, learn to say, "I knew you would do this, so God and I are well prepared".

Where Is the Order While Doing Church?
While it is important to note that the Israelites were out of order when they sought to defy the plan of God, the truth of the matter is that this reality happens often as we seek to "do church". It is imperative that the body of Christ recognizes what God wants from the church today for the church to be in order. When you study the government of the demonic; the rule and the reign of the satanic, you will find that it is organized, systematic and on assignment to do just what John 10:10 says, "The thief cometh not, but for to steal, and to kill, and to destroy….". Ephesians 6:12 reveals the order of the satanic, when it says [12] For we wrestle not against flesh[b] and blood, but against principalities, against powers, against the rulers of the darkness of this world, against spiritual wickedness in high *places*". Principalities come from the Greek word *arche*, which means demonic establishment, executive authority or governmental rule. *Arche* is where we get the word archive. These demonic influences are keepers of the old, traditionalism, and religious routine that seek more to please religious establishment than they do God.

Powers comes from the Greek word *exousia*, which are demonic forces that have been given the right to execute the plan of the principalities. The powers are responsible for inspiring corrupt church practices, deceit upon deacons, and trickery among trustees. Some attribute the work of drug cartels, gross poverty, plagues, terrorism, and other heinous crimes against humanity to this level of spiritual operation. Rulers of darkness are the armed forces of the demonic, and they come with spiritual wickedness. Spiritual wickedness comes from the Greek word *poneros*, which means to antagonize or to cause a malicious act in the way of witchcraft. Witchcraft is control and manipulation, and it comes from the Greek word, *python*. A python is a snake that squeezes the life out of living organisms. Therefore, spiritual wickedness is about controlling and manipulating the church by destroying the life of the church.

Thus in the kingdom of the demonic there is order. And their order is established to cause disorder in the church and in your life. Consequently if there is order in the government of the satanic, then there must be order in church. I Corinthian 14:40 declares, "But all things should be done decently and in order". However, before we seek to illustrate ways to establish order, it is essential that we consider ways that order is defied in the church among clergy, leaders, officers, volunteers, and laity.

When Clergy Are Out of Order

- Clergy are out of order when their ministry is centered around destroying with their tongue and targets other ministries instead of focusing on the development of their own ministry.
- Clergy are out of order when they participate in the destruction of other bishops, elders, pastors, and clergy. All clergy are on the same team. If you don't always agree on methods of ministry, that does not mean you have a right to destroy other clergy. "What goes around comes around".
- Clergy are out of order when the pulpit is used to preach their insecurities and personal hang-ups, and not to center on the hope that is found in Christ. The pulpit should be used to pull people out of their pit, not put them in a pit.
- Clergy are out of order when they get to the point in their preaching that they only get happy off of their own preaching. There is something to learn from every sermon even a bad one. If you hear a bad sermon that you just can't get happy off of, get happy every time they mention a book in the Bible that you are familiar with. Find something to affirm.

- Clergy are out of order when relationships are developed with the members which can hinder their ability to minister truthfully and accurately with the integrity that is found in Christian living. Always remember, whomever you sin with has the potential of sinning against you.
- Clergy are out of order when their human desires and out of the pulpit lifestyles are such that shame is brought to the church and the body of Christ. Clergy should always be mindful of their image, and the representation of their ministry. A good measure for this is to raise this question, "Can I explain what I am doing, if by chance I get caught?' If you can't explain it without shame, you do not need to engage in it.
- Clergy are out of order when they elevate themselves with titles they did not earn. It is a violation of a spiritual law to make yourself an apostle, a bishop, a "doctor" or even a prophet or prophetess. While these are legitimate titles for ministry, these titles must be affirmed by a representing body of faith that can witness the evidence of these titles, and can share in the validity of you becoming and receiving this title placed upon your name. Know that the Lord did not say He will make your title great, God said that He will make your name great. You have a great name without a title.

When Associate Ministers Are Out Of Order

- Associate Ministers are out of order when they solicit or invite themselves to preach in a pulpit. There is a difference between being ready to preach at all times, and presenting yourself as a salesperson of your gift. Just be faithful and available and your gift will make room for you.
- Associate Ministers are out of order when they say, "I know what's on the program, but the Lord told me to say this….and that. If he or she did not get permission from the pastor to alter any part of that program, the minister is out of order. If the Lord told you, the Lord will also

confirm this with the pastor; therefore, get permission from the pastor first.

- Associate Ministers are out of order when they visit the hospital on behalf of the pastor and the church, and never mention that they are there on behalf of the pastor and the church, which allows the minister to get the credit for visiting and not the corporate ministry.
- Associate Ministers are out of order when they leave a ministry to start a ministry without having a conversation or dialogue with the pastor they are presently serving under. Leaving without getting the blessing of that ministry can be detrimental to the future of the newly founded ministry. Therefore, do all you can to communicate your move, and by all means do not seek to build your ministry with members where you presently serve.
- Associate Ministers are out of order when they pray or read scripture longer than the preacher preaches. Always be mindful of the fact that there is power in brevity, and that it doesn't take a long time to do anything for the ministry to be blessed.
- Associate Ministers must always do what they are asked to do. If you are asked to pray, that does not mean read a scripture or sing a song first and then pray. The request was to pray. Obedience is better than sacrifice. If you are asked to a read scripture, it does not mean the entire chapter, it simply means the relevant pericope unless otherwise printed or stated. Use common sense when leading a congregation in worship.
- Associate Ministers when leading worship must be mindful of the difference between worship leading and preaching. It is inappropriate to slip in a sermon because the choir has the congregation motivated. Your job is to be like John the Baptist, you are to simply prepare the way for the designated preacher. Not too many churches can handle two preachers "whooping" in the same service.

When Officers Are Out of Order

- Officers are out of order when they expect to perform their duties and responsibilities without the passion for Christian study and biblical understanding.
- Officers are out of order when they place secular rules and regulations over the establishment of God's word for governing the ministry.
- Officers are out of order when they see their position as autonomous, and fail to realize that their position exists for the good of the church, and not their personal agenda.
- Officers are out of order when they believe that what they do in their secular jobs, qualify them for spiritual tasks. Just because you are an accountant doesn't mean your spirit is right to count church money.
- Officers are out of order when they have a place during worship on the front row, but use the front row to sleep, murmur, or satisfy their need for importance. If you are on the front row, you should catch on fire before the worshipers on the back row.
- Officers are out of order when a vision is set for the ministry, and they refuse to show physical or financial support for the effort the church has chosen to embrace.
- Officers are out of order when they foster an ill spirit among the congregation, and foster division among the members about operations or pertinent church matters. The proper time to convey this information is during formal meeting times and organized church settings when the matter can be addressed in order at the proper time.
- Officers are out of order when they confer issues that they are not happy about to the Court of Law. While there are some operations in ministry that may require legal guidance, referring church issues to the Court of Law is not the best policy for handling God's business. Do all you can to reason out the matter, and seek peace in all of your ways.
- Officers are out of order when they collect the tithe, but don't leave a tithe. Or worst than that, steal the tithe.

When Choirs and Praise Teams Are Out of Order

- Choirs and praise teams are out of order when they do not possess a spirit of worship, and do not have an attitude that is representative of the church and the Holy Spirit.
- Choirs and praise teams are out of order when they only attend worship or participate in worship when it is their time to perform. Choirs and Praise Teams must show reverence for worship and not just performance.
- Choirs and praise teams are out of order when they seek to lift their singing ability over other ministries in the church. Just because their position is highly visible does not mean that their ministry is more significant than another. The church is one body, with many parts.
- Choirs and praise teams are out of order when they are out of dress code. If the dress code is black and silver, that means the choir member that shows up in black, silver, and orange is out of order. It is important that order is represented in the decorum, which has a way of strengthening unity.
- Choirs and praise teams are out of order when they mount the choir stand late, or begin the worship late. God deserves our best effort, and it does not speak well of excellence to be late. If you are late, there should be an appointed time for late members to mount the choir stand, certainly not in the middle of a song or if the choir is already singing.
- Choirs and praise teams are out of order when they cannot adapt to the change of the Holy Spirit in worship services. Just because you rehearse a song, and the song is printed on the program does not mean it must be sung. The Holy Spirit may direct the worship in another direction; the choir and praise team must be open to the move of the Spirit. "I didn't get to sing my song". Technically, it is not your song; the song belongs to the artist who recorded it. If you don't own the copyrights, it's not "your song".

When Ushers Are Out of Order

- Ushers are out of order when they do not visibly show a spirit of hospitality while performing their responsibilities. If there is any ministry that should demonstrate the fruit of the spirit, the ushers should possess it.
- Ushers are out of order when they are out of dress code, and do not exemplify order with the uniformity of the dress attire when necessary.
- Ushers are out of order when they point people to their seating, and not take the time to lead them.
- Ushers are out of order when the church is filled to capacity, and they are sitting while there are guests standing.
- Ushers are out of order when they are not paying attention to directives from the pulpit, or the adjustments that need to be made in the worship service.
- Ushers are out of order when they constrain people that are shouting, aggressively shake people who are slain in the Spirit, and do not keep emergency matters at a level of calm.
- Ushers are out of order when they walk, talk, or pass out programs during the time of prayer, scripture reading, and especially during the preaching moment.
- Ushers are out of order when they get to church late, and leave before benediction. The usher should be one of the last persons to leave the church. It would be helpful to check the pews for paper, gum, and any obvious trash before leaving the sanctuary.
- Ushers are out of order when they lead the tithe but don't leave a tithe.

When Staff Workers Are Out of Order

- Staff workers are out of order when they deliberately violate the confidentiality of church business affairs, or concerns of the membership.
- Staff workers are out of order when they manipulate their staff position to possess power and control over the membership who pay their salary.

- Staff workers are out of order when they take the ministry for granted and do not provide adequate reporting; come to work late, do not offer their best work, and give the church less than a high level of excellence.
- Staff workers are out of order whenever they rebel against a directive from the pastor, and show any form of disrespect towards the position of the pastor or any member of the first family.
- Staff workers are out of order when they discuss the travel schedule of the pastor or share private information concerning the pastor or the pastor's family with anybody in the church or outside of the church.
- Staff workers are out of order when they develop 'cliques" with the members, and develop secret relationships that can compromise their integrity to function as a staff member of the church.
- Staff workers are out of order when they join a contentious group that may be against the vision or the direction that the church desires to move in.
- Staff workers are out of order when they get paid from the tithe, but won't give a tithe.

When Volunteers (Sound and Video Technicians, Parking Attendants, Security, Kitchen Workers, Van Drivers, and Other Volunteer Ministries) Are Out of Order

- Volunteers are out of order when they do not have the highest respect, honor, and regard for God with their service.
- Volunteers are out of order when they arrive late to provide their service. Volunteers are still expected to be on time.
- Volunteers are out of order when they do not have a spirit of hospitality, and serve with an attitude that is not pleasing to God.
- Volunteers are out of order when they make a commitment to serve or lead a committee and do not follow through on their commitment and refuse to follow directives that are given to them.

- Volunteers are out of order when they do not understand that their volunteerism is under the direction of pastoral leadership, official boards, paid staff, and those who are appointed to serve over them.
- Volunteers are out of order when they do not take the time to study God's word, learn their areas of service, and stay in their lanes when providing their services.
- Volunteers are out of order when they find areas of improvement in the ministry, and openly discuss their frustrations among the other congregants and visitors.

When the Congregation Is Out of Order

- The congregation is out of order when it does not submit to the leadership of God, and the vision God desires for that church.
- The congregation is out of order when respect is not given to the pastor at all times, and honor is not extended with highest respect for the office.
- The congregation is out of order when it openly rebels with malice, vengeance, contriteness, and a spirit to do its own will and not the Lord's will.
- The congregation is out of order when it comes to church late, does not participate in the worship, does not adhere to the directives of the worship leader, does not touch their "neighbor" when asked, and sees church as an option and not a necessity.
- The congregation is out of order when it does not financially support the church but benefits from its services and everything else the church has to offer.
- The congregation is out of order when it does not come to Bible study, give the tithe, give time, and offer its talent to be used for the glory of God.
- The congregation is out of order when members are not mindful of their hygiene in worship. While there are some who have no option about good hygiene before coming to church, for the most part, good physical stewardship is making certain that you bathe, brush your teeth, put on deodorant, and for breath freshness, a piece of mint in your pocket.

- The congregation is out of order when it does not attend bible study, but will show up for church meetings to cause confusion over issues that it does not agree with.
- The congregation is out of order when it does not put faith in God, to bring the vision, ministry efforts, and the resources that are needed for the church to be effective.

Steps for Implementing Order In The Church

Organization Is the key to Order and Vision Implementation
One of the greatest atrocities that pastors/leaders make as it pertains to vision implementation is to believe that vision is implemented automatically. The implementation of vision not only requires an announcement that there is a vision, but vision requires organization and a plan for putting the vision in place. C. Peter Wagner, researcher and statistician of church culture, observed that only five percent of pastors ever come up with new ideas, concepts or observations. Another 15 percent of pastors are what he calls, "innovators", which means they are innovative enough to follow the template of ideas demonstrated by the five percent who create great ideas in ministry. This means that 80% of pastors are what Wagner calls "programmatic", which means this group rarely comes up with anything new to do in ministry. As a matter of fact, if something is suggested, they need very detailed steps to actually implement what has been placed before them. *(7 Steps To Transform Your Church*, Baker Book House, Grand Rapids, MI, 1997, Bill Hull, p.39).

Regardless of where you find yourself in Wagner's research, it is important that as a leader you get organized. The lack of order is often caused by the lack of organization on the part of the pastor/leader. Therefore, to mobilize any group of people to accomplish a task, it is necessary for the vision to be made clear. For a pastor who is trying to accomplish a vision, it may be helpful to write the vision, and make it plain. Writing the vision today can be done by writing on an old fashion chalk board, or with technology like Power Point, Internet technology, architectural three dimensional designs, or a phone tree system that can communicate with your members while they are in their home. Some churches are even making good use of text messaging and emailing to communicate ministry ideas and opportunities.

One of the greatest attributes of my ministry has been my using one Sunday out of the year to have what I call "The State of the Church Address". During Sunday morning worship in the month of January, I will present the vision of the ministry for that year to the church. This is a Power Point presentation, with all of the church leaders sitting in a body. During this worship service, I review our performance as a church from the previous year, and then unfold vision and goals for the new year. There are five categories that are discussed: worship, Christian education, evangelism, finances, and physical development. Each category should have very clear and defined goals. The presentation should encompass pictures that will enhance what you are introducing. Once you introduce these ministry goals for the year, you must then organize committees, volunteers, and staff to make certain they come to pass. My advice to any pastor or leader is that if you are not a good organizer, get people around you that are. Because once you announce that vision and goal to the church, you are also responsible for making certain that it comes to pass.

This practice has been very effective for me, because it keeps me praying for fresh vision, but also it shapes my drive for the year to make certain that what is announced to the congregation actually becomes a reality. Don't forget, you have to explain the next January why it did or did not come to pass. What a system of accountability!

Organization involves writing the vision, researching the feasibility, knowing the pros and cons of the ministry idea, having a knowledge base of the resources that will be needed to make it happen, gathering the people that will assist in the ministry implementation, establishing benchmarks, budgeting, networking, and remaining steadfast until it happens. Most of the time, if the organization is there, the order is there. This is not to say that the order will not be tested, but with organization the areas in question are much easier to address.

Re-Design Ministry Focus with Information

Most of the time whenever a pastor or leader is confronted with opposition there is a need to make some changes. If you are seeking to re-design a concept of ministry, it is important that you make changes with information. The primary source of information for any ministry re-design should be the authority that is presented in the scriptures. When presenting a new direction, or the need for ministry opportunity, show where the vision or the idea is theological, biblical, and has good grounding with God. For example, our church just purchased an ice cream truck to aide our efforts in doing evangelism. An ice cream truck is not in the Bible, but reaching the lost is the fundamental purpose for Jesus' coming. So in presenting the ministry idea, I focused on evangelism, not the ice cream truck. Today we have the gospel ice cream truck in operation, and we have numbers to show that we were able to put ministry tracks in the hands of thousands as a result. While sharing Christ, the truck drives around the community with a big song that says, "Our Ice Cream is Blessed and Highly Flavored". This slogan is reflected on the truck along with the advertisement of Praise Pops, Blessed Nutty Buddies, Comfort Chocolate, and Sanctified Strawberry Ice Cream Sandwiches.

Information is not only found biblically, but books and Internet research have been proven to be extremely helpful. Also, exposure is another form of gathering information.

If you are seeking to introduce your church to new ways of "doing church", exposure to information is a major benefactor. There are times when sharing the vision or ministry idea via technology is not enough. There are times when an actual site of what is desired is the best example. This form of gathering information is demonstrated by tours to various churches, locations or sites where what you desire as a leader is already established. For example, if there is a certain style of church that you have a vision about leading your church into building, it would be most helpful if you found churches that exist in that style, and take your leaders there. While this may cost you financially, look at it as an investment. Once the delegation actually witnesses what you have been envisioning, their excitement alone can help convince others that this is the move the ministry needs to make.

Gathering information requires you putting aside your hang ups about denomination, megachurch vs. small church, whether it is a White church, Black church or Latino church, in town or out of town. These factors are not important; what is important is that if it exists, then you want to see it.

Once this information is gathered, how it is presented is also important. Regardless of how you choose to present the information, make certain that there is order in the presentation.

Direct What You Expect

Directing a ministry plan involves preaching, teaching, demonstrating, and explaining what you as a leader expect every opportunity you get. Expectation is not mentioned in the way of being dictatorial, but expectation in the sense of raising a standard. Directing a ministry plan involves delegation. If a vision is to be implemented with order, you must be secure enough to delegate responsibility, and have a system in place to evaluate its effectiveness. A vision is not effective if it only remains with you. However, you can't carry the burden of the vision alone. Directing what you expect does not necessarily mean the leader doing the actual work, but the leader serving in the capacity of a coach, or one who has the responsibility of planning, equipping, motivating, and then letting the players play the game. If a leader does not learn to delegate, it is possible that "burn out", a point of exhaustion mentally, emotionally, spiritually, and physically can soon become a significant matter.

The Fuller Theological Seminary did a study on the stress and strain that goes along with pastoring and leading a church. Consider the following statistics that will reveal the pastors need for delegating authority.

- 90 percent of pastors work more than 46 hours per week.
- 80 percent believe that pastoral ministry is affecting their families negatively.
- 33 percent say, "Being in ministry is clearly a hazard to my family."
- 75 percent have reported a significant crisis due to stress at least once in their ministry.
- 50 percent felt unable to meet the needs of the ministry.
- 90 percent felt they were not adequately trained to cope with the ministry demands placed upon them.
- 40 percent reported at least one serious conflict with at least one parishioner at least once a month.
- 70 percent of pastors do not have someone they would consider a close friend.
- 37 percent admitted having been involved in inappropriate sexual behaviors with someone in their congregation
- 70 percent have a lower self-image after they have been in pastoral ministry that when they started (Fred Lehr, *Clergy Burnout*, Fortress Press, Minneapolis, p.4.)

These statistics reflect the stress and strain that comes with doing church. Because the work is demanding and stressful, it is imperative that as a leader you learn to delegate responsibilities to one you can trust, who is loyal and able.

Directing what you expect takes risk and patience, but in the end the hope is that the aforementioned numbers do not become a reality. If order is to be maintained in the church, it begins with the leader who is well rested and has the health that is needed to lead people in "doing church".

Elevate Expectation with Ministry Excellence

Implementing a vision that has the potential of being threatened by people who murmur, must never be negotiated for the necessity of excellence. To elevate any ministry to a higher standard of operation, the goal should be to first interpret for the members what excellence means to you. It is possible that their expectation of excellence, and your expectation of excellence can be quite different. One wise writer declared, "Excellence is not a skill, but it's an attitude". It is this mindset that makes excellence in ministry achievable for any ministry. If you are in a ministry sitting where the mindset is to do just enough to get by, or that the very minimum will do, remember that excellence is an attitude. So that if a ministry is accustomed to grass not being manicured, the steeple leaning to the side on top of the church, the restrooms having a stench, and the pulpit being cluttered with programs from previous services, there has to be a way to elevate the expectation for excellence. Consider a few suggestions:

1. Make certain the people you lead clearly understand the expectation that God has for the church as you interpret it. While interpreting God's expectation, you also express your expectation for your ministry staff, your ministry leaders, and your volunteers that participate in ministry. Clear expectations can alleviate the lack of order later.
2. Know that excellence begins with the leader. Therefore, as a leader it is good for your members to know that you refuse to settle for less than the best. As a leader it is critical that you be on time as much as possible, and when you show up, you should show up with a plan and evidence of preparation. Always be mindful of your appearance, and show confidence in what it is that God has called you to do. Excellence has to be demonstrated by you, and be synonymous with your name and title.
3. Excellence requires communication and training. There are times when you as a leader must invest in the people you expect to demonstrate excellence. This intimate time with your leaders at retreats, picnics, golf tournaments, or breakfast in the fellowship hall, is critical for your leaders understanding of your level of expectation. You will discover that some major things that are happening in the ministry can be handled with some very minor discussions. Often times it is not that people desire to be out of order You have to take the time to tell them how critical it is that they are in order. Spend quality time, and quality results will follow.

4. Excellence requires commitment of time, talent, and treasure. One of the things I seek to do while building a ministry concept with a committee, is allow them to cast vision without a budget. Often times if you place a budget on a ministry vision, your vision may come out looking like your budget. Now there is a time when budget comes in to play, but let's get the vision out first, then discuss what is affordable and what is not affordable. The leader should aim high, because the people you are leading will often be the ones who will aim low. Never negate the fact that God sent you to elevate the expectation of excellence.

Reclaiming Relationships are Critical for Ministry Transformation

To speak of reclaiming relationships is to say that making relationships is the primary reason for "doing church" in the first place. I have discovered that most of the time people do things that are out of order in the church, whether it is showing up in a different color from the rest of the choir, or acting unbecomingly in a church meeting, or not supporting a ministry goal that is set, it usually stems from a need for connection and relationship.

When people are isolated, they have the tendency not to act or think corporately. Therefore, putting emphasis on relationships in any ministry can be very beneficial for order and ministry success. While leading, you are going to lose some relationships, and you are going to gain some, and the challenge is finding your priority for relationship in the midst of that.

Relationships are essential if you are going to lead any ministry in transformation. Whenever a leader begins to feel that they can function on their own, this can lead to what Heifetz and Linskey call "Heroic Suicide". "Relating to people is central to leading and staying alive. If you are not naturally a political person, then find partners who have that ability to be intensely conscious of the importance of relationships in getting challenging work done...Let them (allies) help you relate to your opposition, those people who feel that they have the most to lose in your initiative." (Ronald A. Heifetz and Marty Linsky, Leadership On The Line: Staying Alive Through the Dangers of Leading, Harvard Business School Press, Boston, Mass.p.100)

Reclaiming relationships also speaks to leaving the ninety-nine and seeking the one lost sheep. In any transition there will be casualties or people who will just drop out of the game. As a Christian leader, do your part in establishing relationships, but in the end, know that it is the choice of every individual to either accept your attempt or reject it. Just make certain that you make the attempt to reconcile matters that are critical for transformation.

The Shepherd's Staff: The Role of the Assistant Pastor[1]

Raquel A. St. Clair, Ph.D.

"…your rod and your staff, they comfort me" (Psalm 23:4c)

The twenty-third Psalm is perhaps the most beloved and memorized scripture in the Bible. It has provided countless people with solace and peace in the midst of difficult circumstances by reminding them of the caring presence of a personal God, *the* Shepherd, who provides, leads, comforts, prepares tables in the midst of enemies, and anoints with oil. However, God is not the only Person depicted as "shepherd" in the scriptures. Isaiah[2], Jeremiah[3], Ezekiel[4], Zechariah[5], Acts[6], and I Peter[7] also refer to the leaders of God's people as "shepherds." Therefore, the terms of "shepherd" and "undershepherd" are often applied to those who serve as Senior Pastors.

The Senior Pastor is commissioned by God to care for the sheep (congregation) in ways similar to those modeled by the Divine Shepherd in this psalm. The Senior Pastor leads the sheep and thereby sets the direction of the congregation as it follows its God given vision. S/he chooses the pasturelands that will nourish the flock. It is the shepherd's responsibility to ensure that the sheep are spiritually fed. The shepherd is also to accompany the sheep during difficult seasons of life, guiding them through valleys of loss and sorrow and comforting them along the way. And in the shepherd's hands are two items to assist with this role—the rod and the staff.

The rod (*shebet*) is an instrument of protection. It is used to protect both the sheep and shepherd from the aggression of wild animals. In addition, the shepherd will use the rod to prevent the sheep from wandering onto dangerous terrain or grazing among poisonous vegetation. When a sheep is wandering into a potentially harmful situation and is beyond the reach of the staff, the shepherd will throw the rod, not at the sheep, but in the sheep's path to divert its course and scare it away from harm.[8] The purpose of the rod is not to hurt or punish the sheep but to protect them from enemies and themselves thereby providing for them comfort. The rod is pastoral not punitive.

The rod is also symbolic of the shepherd's power and authority.[9] Power and authority are two related yet distinct entities. Power is the "ability to exercise control over the behavior of others."[10] Authority is the "socially recognized and approved ability to control the behavior of others."[11] The difference between power and authority is that power is self-evident. It requires neither approval nor sanctioning from others. Authority is socially recognized and approved. It is legitimated power and others must acknowledge and accept it. This distinction is critical. In order for a person to operate effectively within the context of any organization, s/he must know and be able to work with the official (authority) and unofficial (power) hierarchy of leadership. The Senior Pastor, like the shepherd, needs a "rod."

S/he must possess power *and* be vested with the authority to lead the congregation. The shepherd, not the sheep, wields this rod.

The second tool of the shepherd is the staff (*mish'enah*), the long, slender stick with the hook at the end. Whereas the rod is an instrument of protection for both the sheep and the shepherd, the staff functions primarily to support the shepherd. This is the office of the Assistant Pastor. The Assistant Pastor can be defined as "staff" based on the common usage of the word—she or he is an employee who works under the leadership of another, namely the Senior Pastor. However, for the purposes of this article, I wish to explore the role of Assistant Pastor within the context of this psalm and explore the role of the Assistant Pastor as *mish'enah*, the second implement found in the shepherd's hand.

The Fit Between Shepherd and Staff

Shepherds select their own staffs. They are very particular about the sapling they will use to craft it. The shepherd takes great pride in choosing and crafting a tool that is so essential to their profession. The seedling must complement the size and strength of the shepherd. It cannot be cumbersome or difficult to wield. Having selected the young tree that will be used, the shepherd will patiently whittle the wood until it fits perfectly in his hand. The staff is custom fit for the shepherd's use.[12]

Likewise, the Assistant Pastor is the choice of the Senior Pastor. The person selected should be a comfortable fit and complement the leadership style and gifts of the Senior Pastor. During the early years of my tenure at St. James, I initiated a conversation with Pastor Watley about how I might most effectively be of service to him and the congregation. In hindsight, I am deeply grateful that this discussion confirmed his decision to hire me but I would encourage any Senior Pastor looking for an Assistant Pastor and any minister seeking a position as Assistant Pastor to consider these things *before* employment is offered or accepted. These are the three questions that I asked:

1. **What do you do that only you can do?**
   These were the critical items that he needed to have the time, energy, and mental and spiritual focus to complete. To use Stephen Covey's terminology, these tasks and responsibilities represented his "big rocks."[13] They needed to be given priority because if he could not attend to these items, no one else could.
2. **What do you want to do/what are you passionate about doing?**
   These are the areas of ministry that feed our spirits. When we do these things, they energize and uplift us. The joy and satisfaction that comes from participating in these acts of ministry enable us to dream, envision, and be encouraged. I wanted him to include these areas of ministry and place them in his schedule as "big rocks." The answers he provided to question #1 inevitably included some "have to's" that were not necessarily "want to's." The "have to's" primarily benefit the sheep. The "want to's" benefit both shepherd and sheep. The sheep are the beneficiaries of these aspects of ministry but they also benefit from having a shepherd who loves what s/he does. By prioritizing these acts of ministry, the shepherd gains and maintains ministerial passion.
3. **What do you *not* want to do that you can relinquish?**
   Here is the shepherd's golden opportunity to unburden him or herself. Doing the things listed here will lead to burnout very quickly. At the shepherd's level, these items take away passion and give little to nothing in return.
4. **What are the areas of ministry that you wish to create, develop, and/or expand?**
   This question causes the shepherd to focus on the future. His or her answers reveal the next steps of ministry and where s/he has discerned the leading of God for the congregation.

Once Pastor Watley thought through these questions and gave his answers, my role was further clarified:

Question #1: He identified the areas that are his sole domain. There is no need for his assistant to have these gifts or mirror his expertise in these areas. These are areas or particular tasks for which no substitution is allowed or necessary. The Shepherd must do these things to be effective.

Question #2: The ministry passion(s) of the Senior Pastor coincide with the strengths and unique character of the ministry. Once the shepherd answers this question, s/he has ascertained the skill sets that his or her staff will need in order for the shepherd to feel comfortable being absent from the congregation. For example, if the ministry is known for or built upon strong preaching, an assistant who can "deliver the mail" means that in the Pastor's absence, the quality of worship is not compromised. If the Senior Pastor is a strong administrator, s/he should look for someone who has this skill set so that things do not fall through the cracks. If the ministry is known for pastoral care, the Assistant Pastor should have gifts to minister accordingly. This is important because when passion and competence meet, it inspires growth. Powerful preaching creates the need for additional worship services and possibly more worship locations. Excellent administration increases ministry effectiveness thereby multiplying the types of ministry offered by a congregation. Strong pastoral care draws hurting people. Therefore, effective ministry will surpass the ability of the Senior Pastor to do everything at all times, even the things one is passionate about doing. By choosing an assistant with gifts that reflect the key areas of one's church, the Senior Pastor further solidifies the internal strength of the ministry. The assistant need not function at the same level of the Senior Pastor but the overall strength in these areas of ministry need not be compromised or damaged when turned over into the hands of the Assistant Pastor.

Question #3: The items that a Senior Pastor does not want to do and does not need to do are the tasks that s/he should delegate to employees and/or volunteers.

Question #4: The Senior Pastor's answers provide a glimpse of the future course of the ministry. It would be wise for the pastor to choose a staff that not only fits where the ministry is but also where it is going.

After Pastor Watley provided his answers to the four questions, we examined my gifts and passions to see if they coincided with and complemented his list. We began with question #2 to see if my gifts mirrored the strengths of this ministry. St. James is known for preaching, teaching, and worship. In the minds of the parishioners, pastoral leadership executes these ministry services with a certain level of competence and skill. Therefore, the most effective person to serve as his assistant would need to have strong gifts in these areas. Practically speaking, without these gifts, his assistant would run the risk of becoming the second in command in name only. In the absence of the Senior Pastor, these assignments would either have to be performed with a marked decline in ability or "outsourced" to another minister. The result would be that s/he would have the title of Assistant Pastor, but not exemplify the identifying character of the ministry.

Next, we explored what he did not want to nor had to do. We compared it with the areas of ministry he wanted to create, develop, or strengthen. Out of this comparison came the primary role of his Assistant Pastor. Here is what became crystal clear: Pastor Watley is a visionary (no surprise there) and what he did not want to do nor need to do himself *but* required was someone to oversee the day to day operations of the church. In our case, it required someone to handle the business operations and someone to handle the ministry operations. In each instance, he needed a tactician who could catch, implement, and even expand the vision. However, his number 2 needed to be both a strong ministry-minded administrator who not only attended to the details and *liked* them, but could also reflect the core strengths of his ministry. Otherwise, this shepherd's staff would not fit comfortably in his hand.

It is important to note that when a shepherd of sheep picks his staff, there are many trees to choose from. The task of the shepherd is to find one that fits his hand. Indeed, some whittling will be done to customize the staff for his needs. However, a wise shepherd will select a staff that will fit his hand with minimal adjustments. The shepherd does not choose a staff that he must alter so dramatically that none of its original character and uniqueness remains. Therefore, I had already asked myself some questions prior to posing the above questions to Pastor Watley.

My primary task was to get clear about what I was *called* to do and what I *could* or was able to do. It is very important to me that I minister primarily out of my *call* than my *can.* The call is the place of my ministry passions and areas where I desired growth and development. For a good fit on both sides, my call needed to coincide with the ministry need identified in the overlap between the answers Pastor Watley gave to questions #3 (What do you *not* want to do that you can relinquish?) and #4 (What are the areas of ministry that you wish to create, develop, and/or expand?) *and* the strengths/unique character of the ministry because these would be my primary areas of responsibility. If a Pastor's and congregation's needs do not coincide with the Assistant's *call*, then the Assistant will work primarily out his or her *can.* After ministry passions have not been fed or fueled, and a sense of *call* has not been fulfilled *while working full-time in ministry*, the Assistant risks serving at a minimal level or becoming a hireling since the only thing left to consistently inspire performance and growth is a paycheck.

Equally as important is the fact that an Assistant Pastor's competency level in the area of his or her call must be commensurate with or exceed the ministry they serve. A sense of call is no substitute for lack of ability to function within the context of that call. A sense of call enables one to *begin* ministerial training. At the level of the Assistant Pastor, the call should be evidenced and backed by experience in ministry. This is not to say that the Assistant Pastor will not learn as they go. No matter how prepared the Assistant Pastor is, s/he is never above correction. One needs to have a teachable spirit and be open to constructive criticism. However, this is not an entry-level position. The Assistant Pastor should have the highest ordination the denomination gives so that s/he has the authority to consecrate and administer the sacraments. Although some denominations and church bodies do not require it, I highly recommend a Masters of Divinity degree from a school accredited by the Association of Theological Schools. In this information age, the pulpit needs to be not only spiritually, but also academically and professionally prepared to serve.

A comfortable fit between shepherd and staff is important since the staff is seen as an extension of the shepherd. Moreover, it is the only tool used solely by the shepherd and identifies the profession of the one who holds it.[14] The Assistant Pastor is an extension of the ministry of the Senior Pastor. S/he serves at the pleasure of the Pastor just as the shepherd's staff only exists for the purpose of the shepherd and the sheep s/he cares for.

Since the Assistant Pastor is an extension of the Senior Pastor's ministry, s/he, by extension, will often be the recipient of goodwill and assistance from the Pastor's supporters. However, the detractors of the Senior Pastor usually approach the Assistant Pastor in one of two ways. One the one hand, they may transfer their negativity onto the Assistant since s/he represents the Pastor and his/her administration. Therefore, the Assistant Pastor cannot be a people pleaser. S/he has to be able to complete assignments and ultimately do their job regardless of who likes him/her. On the other hand, they may employ a "divide and conquer" strategy. In other words, they will be very helpful and supportive of the Assistant while trying to pit Assistant against Pastor. They will help and compliment while attempting to plant seeds to inspire jealousy, a sense of being under-appreciated or not properly acknowledged.

I remember one instance of this in particular. I was in the receiving line following a Sunday morning worship service. I had preached and God had blessed. Pastor Watley was on vacation but had honored me by slipping in service for the message. As Pastor and I stood shaking hands, a parishioner who we both knew was often negative about the Pastor waited until she had both of our attention to make her comment: "Pastor Watley, you better watch out or else she's gonna out preach you soon." And then smiled in my direction, like she was giving me a compliment. Pastor was gracious and said something like; "She did an excellent job today." While holding still holding her hand, I looked the woman in the eye, smiled sweetly, and said, "There is no competition in this house. Whatever I have learned about preaching I got from this man and the servant will never be greater than the master." Pastor Watley looked at me and then nodded his head. I just shrugged my shoulders, "She is not going to mess up my good quality job with benefits!" And we both laughed.

During my tenure at St. James, I have had not only parishioners but also colleagues try to plant a wedge between the Pastor and myself. Some have told me in not so many words that if they had my credentials and gifts, they would not do my job. In their estimation, I have lowered myself by not being "in charge" and answering to another Pastor rather than a bishop. They have attempted to play on my ego to oust me from my place. Yet, I am clear that God has not called me to the center seat. Perhaps one day, but I must work out my call based on what God is saying today. I have sat close enough to the center seat to know that it will require more than wanting to be in charge to remain there. I am also honest enough to admit that what I do provides enough power, authority, prestige, and status to satisfy my ego needs.

The Assistant Pastor position requires the individual who occupies it to have a strong sense of self and calling to this position. One has to balance the delegated power and authority given by the Senior Pastor with loyalty and humility. One has to always be mindful of the "big picture" and not allow one's ego to get in the way.

The Assistant Pastor is *not* the Senior Pastor. Although this statement should be obvious, it bears explication. Any person considering the position of Assistant Pastor should be clear about their call, specifically if this position is seasonal or vocational. Some people are called to the Assistant Pastor position with no expectation of becoming a Senior Pastor. They are called to minister in this capacity in the same way another person is called to pastor a congregation. For others, this position is training ground for the pastorate. An Assistant Pastor should be honest with him/herself so that they can deal with the congregation and Senior Pastor with integrity. Even if the Assistant Pastor is ultimately called to Pastor and even if the Senior Pastor leaves much to be desired, the Assistant Pastor is not the Pastor of that shepherd's flock. S/he does not have the "rod," the power and authority of the shepherd. The Shepherd has delegated whatever power and authority they have, to them. As the Assistant Pastor functions in this position, s/he does so in solidarity with, not in opposition to, the Senior Pastor. Absaloms need not apply. If an Assistant chooses to Pastor, s/he needs to get a rod, staff, and flock of their own.

The Function of the Staff

The job description of each Assistant Pastor will necessarily vary. Different ministries require different gifts and skill sets. The job description should take into account the needs of the congregation to be served. However, there are some basic functions that the staff performs. Using the Psalm 23:4c as a model, I will explicate some of the basic duties of the Assistant Pastor.

Support

Ultimately, the staff is an instrument of comfort and support. One of its principle functions is to support the shepherd when weary and when the shepherd is crossing over rough terrain.[15] The staff needs to be strong enough for the shepherd to lean on. This requires a level of spiritual and emotional maturity. The Assistant Pastor should be spiritually mature enough to handle the humanity of the Senior Pastor (even saints make mistakes). S/he should instinctively know the conversations that should only be had with God. The Assistant Pastor's relationship with God needs to be at the level where their trust and faith is ultimately in God. S/he should respect, support, and assist the Senior Pastor, not worship him/her.

Ministry is not always easy, and that is an understatement. The weight of ministry on the shoulders of the Senior Pastor can be unbearable. The Assistant Pastor's role is to lessen not add to the load. The work of ministry should not be greater with the Assistant Pastor than without him or her. During the difficult moments and seasons of ministry, the Assistant Pastor needs to bear up under the load and assist the Senior Pastor in reaching the next destination. The staff should not crumble under pressure. Every Assistant Pastor needs a "game face." It is not about being fake or phony, but exercising grace under pressure. At some point in ministry, all of us have a "He may not come when you call Him, but He'll be there right on time" testimony. So until, God comes, the Assistant Pastor needs a stiff upper lip. The Assistant Pastor may also need to carry the mantle of faith and encourage the Senior Pastor until s/he can take it up again.

Another aspect of supporting a Senior Pastor is knowing how to take a "hit" and keep on going. There are times in ministry in which the Assistant Pastor supports the Senior Pastor by taking the blame or flack that comes from members. The reality is that people need to esteem their Pastor at a certain level. So if something falls through the cracks or something is overlooked or someone's feelings are hurt, the Assistant Pastor may need to step up and take responsibility so that the shepherd does not fall in the eyes of the sheep. This is not to suggest in any way that an Assistant Pastor is called to compromise his or her integrity but only to acknowledge that supporting the Senior Pastor and serving a congregation means that we do not always have the luxury of looking good. Sometimes, it is enough for us to *do good.*

An Assistant Pastor has to be able to follow and support vision even in the valley of the shadow of death. The staff, although in the hands of and walking with the shepherd, does not always know exactly where the shepherd is going. The Assistant Pastor must be able to accept the fact that he/she is called to follow and lead others as they follow by faith. The Senior Pastor is not obligated to tell the Assistant Pastor everything or anything. If an Assistant Pastor cannot support the Senior Pastor by faith, then s/he needs to consider whether or not they need to recues themselves from their post.

Several years ago, I was working on a project for the Pastor. He had gathered a small group composed of another staff person, a few officers, and myself. I was working with one of the officers on a proposal for an aspect of the church's ministry. We met and planned and completed our assignment. The presentation made logical sense and was a good idea. However, after the Pastor heard it, he said that he did not feel right in his spirit about it. The officer began to question him and I listened. I asked a couple of questions for clarity but when I saw that his mind was made up, I stopped. Later, we spoke privately and all he said was that something was not settling right in his spirit about it.

For the next few days, the officer kept calling me, trying to convince me to use my influence to change the Pastor's mind. She felt that he was being shortsighted and not giving the proposal a fair hearing. The reality is that she was frustrated by the fact that he provided no concrete reason for refusing to move forward. I remember sitting on my bed after hanging up the phone and I heard the Spirit say to me *very* clearly that if I did not trust the Pastor enough to follow him by faith, then I needed to go somewhere else. If I could not respect his judgment when I did not understand it, then He would remove me because I would not be allowed to be a hindrance to that ministry. Whatever piece of a thought I had about broaching the conversation with him, left never to return again. And whenever I do not understand where the Pastor is leading, I remember what the Spirit said to me that day. Unless the Assistant Pastor is asked to do something illegal or in contradiction to the word of God, s/he is to support the Senior Pastor, *regardless* of how one feels "led." If s/he cannot do that, then they need to serve somewhere that they can.

Let me pause here to say that the Assistant Pastor will not always agree with the Senior Pastor. Differences will arise. However, all differences and those things that may be perceived as differences need to be handled in private. An Assistant Pastor, or any minister for that matter, should never even ask a question or make a comment that may appear to show a lack of support of or loyalty to the Pastor. This does not mean that the Assistant Pastor can have no independent thoughts, ideas, or questions. On the contrary, the Assistant Pastor needs to have both the wisdom and maturity to know the proper time and place to voice one's concerns. Part of the Assistant Pastor's role is to provide the Senior Pastor with perspective and insight. S/he should make the Pastor aware of any potential landmines or issues that may not have been considered or known. In my role, I come into more one on one contact with the ministry leaders, certain staff persons, and ministers than the Senior Pastor. Indeed the shepherd knows his flock but I am sometimes privy to information by virtue of being the day-to-day person.

When the Assistant Pastor thinks that s/he has information or insight, s/he needs to express it with a level of humility. The Assistant Pastor should be mindful that the view from the driver's seat is radically different than the one from the passenger's side, even if one is helping to navigate the trip. In addition, the Assistant Pastor should always seek to present alternate views and considerations in a way that allows the Senior Pastor to contemplate the options and even change his/her mind without being made to feel small or stupid. However, once the decision is made, the Assistant Pastor is to lay aside every hesitation and move forward. If it does not work out, the Assistant Pastor needs to be the first person on the clean-up crew *without* an "I told you so" attitude.

Pastoral Care

The shepherd's staff is the only instrument the shepherd has that is solely utilized for the care of the sheep. Other professions use the rod. Therefore, the staff should be as much a fit for the sheep as it is for the shepherd. When one looks at secular leadership models, the Assistant Pastor is comparable to the senior or executive level of employees. Although there is overlap in terms of the skill sets needed (organizational management, interpersonal skills, administrative skills, finance and budgeting experience), the primary difference is that the Assistant Pastor cares for the "sheep." By nature of the audience served, this position requires *pastoral* skills. The Assistant Pastor needs to be adept at exercising leadership within a Christian, not corporate, context.

In this position, one has to have a heart for people, not simply accomplishing a task or completing an assignment. The bottom line is not the dollar, the program, or the task. The bottom line is the sheep. And the sheep and the assignment are not mutually exclusive. The goal is to get it done, whatever the "it" may be, without casualties. The care of the sheep should be the focus of every assignment, project, and task. One does not have to be praying, preaching, teaching, or counseling to extend pastoral care. Working well with others, encouraging people, even correcting someone with love is an opportunity to care for and nurture the flock and employees who may not be members of the congregation. Attention to detail, understandable directives, and clear organization allow others to participate in ministry and learn as they serve. As the Assistant Pastor attends to his or her daily responsibilities, people should feel cared for and respected, not as pawns manipulated to get things done.

The staff is the instrument the shepherd uses to guide the sheep. He will place the staff alongside the sheep to steer them in the right direction.[16] In similar fashion, the Assistant Pastor must be able to walk alongside the flock, without forgetting that s/he is the staff and not the sheep. There must be a balance between familiar closeness and professional distance. The Assistant Pastor is a spiritual leader and cannot become so "common" that parishioners no longer see them as such. The staff has to guide the sheep in the direction that the shepherd is leading, not simply walk with them. The Assistant Pastor must exercise leadership while modeling followship.

As leader, the Assistant Pastor should never ask people to do what s/he is not first willing to do. We lead by example not command. Being a leader also means that one takes the compliment last and the criticism first. Whenever I make a decision, I am prepared to take responsibility for its failure and share the praise of its success. Therefore, the people who work with me never have to fear being left out on their own. They can walk with me without having to watch their backs.

In order to walk with the sheep, the Assistant Pastor must like people and have the patience to work with them. Most importantly, the Assistant Pastor should be able to disciple them, to help them mature in the faith. It is helpful to be able to discern their gifts so that one can assist them in finding their places in the life of the congregation. If the Assistant Pastor has employees or volunteers serving under him/her, it would be wise to invest in them, develop them for the ministries that they lead so that they can pour into the ministry workers. This guiding function also includes the ability to supervise and hold others accountable. The Assistant Pastor should be able to work with both volunteers and paid staff. S/he should have the ability to put the right people in the right places.

The shepherd also employs the staff to keep the sheep together. There are times when lambs are separated from the flock or from the mother sheep. The shepherd will use the staff to pick up the lamb and place it next to its mother or pull the straying sheep back into the fold.[17] The Assistant Pastor should be a unifying, not divisive, force within the life of the congregation. S/he should have a finger on the pulse of the congregation and try to avert dissension when possible.

The pastoral care that the Assistant Pastor imparts to the membership should also be applied to oneself. The job of an Assistant Pastor can be very lonely. Usually the Assistant Pastor has no "in house" colleagues. The Senior Pastor is above and the staff, both lay and clergy are below. The familiar closeness and professional distance must be extended to those whom the Assistant Pastor supervises, oversees, and helps to shepherd. It is therefore critical for the Assistant Pastor to find appropriate social outlets that allows him or her to be "off duty." S/he should seek to have interests outside of the church that have little connection to organized religion. As Christians, we are to take Jesus with us everywhere we go and let our lights shine. However, we are not obligated to carry the church on our backs. Everyone needs a break from his/her jobs, even the minister.

Finally, the Assistant Pastor must nurture his/her own spiritual life. One should not neglect his/her daily devotional life of prayer, scripture reading, and worship. Daily devotional time is not sermon or Bible study preparation or ministry planning. It is the time that the Assistant Pastor brings him/herself before the Lord. It is "me time" in the presence of the Lord so that one can minister out of the overflow not an empty cup. I would also encourage regular seasons of fasting to encourage physical and spiritual discipline and submission. The Assistant Pastor needs to be a tither. Tithing is first and foremost a spiritual discipline that reflects our relationship with God. It is a reflection of where our hearts are.[18] The bottom line is that no church needs cursed people exercising leadership.[19]

The reality is that the Assistant Pastor worships *and* works on Sundays. Sunday is not a Sabbath day for clergy. Therefore, the Assistant Pastor should set a weekly Sabbath day.[20] The Sabbath should include both worship *and* rest. It does not have to be a day of corporate worship but worship should happen. It should occur once every seven days but not necessarily on a Sunday. One should guard this time and only allow true emergencies to interfere with it. There will always be more to do, which is why we are commanded to observe the Sabbath. The Sabbath reaffirms our faith in God and makes us mindful that God really is in charge of the church and He is the only indispensable part of it.

Administration

The final function of the staff is to count sheep.[21] This is comparable to the administrative function of the Assistant Pastor. The Assistant Pastor should be able to manage resources effectively and efficiently. This includes the management of people and the skills they bring as well as financial/material assets. The Assistant Pastor should be able to create and manage budgets and assist those whom they supervise in doing the same. In all things, the Assistant Pastor should be a good steward of the resources entrusted to him or her including the intangible assets of time and trust. S/he is to complete assignments in a timely fashion. When unable to do so, the Assistant Pastor should take initiative in making this known and seeking an extension by communicating what additional time is needed and why the task is still undone.

Creative management is another component of this job. Sometimes the Assistant Pastor will need to "make brick without straw." S/he should be proactive in generating, soliciting, and seeking out what is needed for ministry. By treating every aspect of one's ministry as an act of pastoral care, the Assistant Pastor creates a potential resource base for times such as these. People are more willing to give back and help when they have been the recipient of care and concern. However, people cannot give or assist when administration is so poor that it cannot concretely communicate to people what is needed.

Multitasking is par for the course. The Assistant Pastor must execute the vision of the Senior Pastor. S/he must ultimately implement ministries, programs, and events without confusion. Therefore, the Assistant Pastor must possess organizational skills. S/he should be able to coordinate people, assignments, and resources to do ministry. This should be done in a way that people can understand and follow vision. A good Assistant Pastor will also develop leadership in the process.

The administrative skills of the Assistant Pastor should exceed maintenance ministry mode. The Assistant Pastor is not the keeper of the status quo but an instrument for growth. Therefore, the Assistant Pastor needs to be a visionary in his or her own right. Although s/he does not set the vision for the congregation, s/he should be able to catch the vision of the Senior Pastor and cascade it to the ministries and members of the church. The Assistant Pastor should be able to assist the congregation with the practical implementation of the vision and help them chart a course to its completion. S/he also needs to be able to see the implications of the vision to maximize opportunities for growth and avoid pitfalls. The Assistant Pastor must see beyond the moment, and like a shepherd's hook, this staff needs to be able to pull back people and projects from the dangers that can stifle or stop vision.

A good Assistant Pastor is not only capable of identifying problems but finding solutions. Within this position and person, creativity and organization should converge. Once s/he identifies a problem, they should develop a course of action to respond to it. The Senior Pastor is never brought problems without options for remediation.

Conclusion

The Assistant Pastor is indeed the staff of the Senior Pastor and should function as such. Yet, we should forever be mindful that we are staffs in the hand of an even greater Shepherd. Therefore, we are to exercise ministry in ways that ultimately are a reflection and an extension of the Good Shepherd who purchased the sheep with his blood. It is in response to His call that we serve and our prayer is that we be found faithful, so that we may "dwell in the house of the Lord [our] whole lifelong."[22]

---

[1] This article examines the role of the minister who ranks second to the Senior Pastor. For the sake of simplicity, I will use the traditional title of "Assistant Pastor" throughout this article although different congregations and denominations use other titles such as Executive Minister (my title) and Executive Pastor.

[2] Isaiah 56:11

[3] Jeremiah 3:15; 10:21; 12:10; 22:22; 23:1, 2, 4; 25:34-36; 50:6

[4] Ezekiel 34:2, 7-10

[5] Zechariah 10:3

[6] Acts 20:28

[7] I Peter 5:2

[8] Phillip Keller, "An Excerpt from: A Shepherd Looks at Psalm 23," http://www.antipas.org/magazine/articles/shepherd_psa23/shepherd_7.html. December 29, 2009.
[9]Shlomo Riskin, "Shabbat Shalom: Parshiot Matot Masei (Numbers 30:2-36:13)" http://www.ots.org.il/parsha/5764/matotmasei64.htm. December 29, 2009.
[10]John J. Pilch, "Power," in *Biblical Social Values and Their Meaning: A Handbook*, ed. John J. Pilch and Bruce Malina (Peabody, Mass.: Hendrickson, 1993), 139.
[11] Bruce J. Malina, "Authoritarianism," in *Biblical Social Values and Their Meaning: A Handbook*, ed. John J. Pilch and Bruce Malina (Peabody, Mass.: Hendrickson, 1993), 11.
[12]Keller, "A Shepherd Looks at Psalm 23."
[13] Imagine an empty glass jar that is filled with large rocks. In the empty spaces, smaller rocks and eventually sand are poured in until all available space is taken. If one were to dump the jar out and put the sand and smaller rocks in the jar first, the big rocks would not have fit. The idea is to put the "big rocks" or important items in first and arrange the smaller, less important things around them. Stephen Covey, A. Roger Merrill and Rebecca Merrill, *First Things First* (New York, N.Y.: Simon & Schuster, 1994), 88-89.
[14] Keller, "An Excerpt from: A Shepherd Looks at Psalm 23."
[15] Keller, "An Excerpt from: A Shepherd Looks at Psalm 23."
[16] Ibid.
[17] Ibid.
[18]"For where your treasure is, there your heart will be also." Matthew 6:21.
[19] "Will anyone rob God? Yet you are robbing me! But you say, "How are we robbing you?" In your tithes and offerings! You are cursed with a curse, for you are robbing me—the whole nation of you." Malachi 3:8-9.
[20] Romans 14: 5-8 says, "Some judge one day to be better than another, while others judge all days to be alike. Let all be fully convinced in their own minds. Those who observe the day, observe it in honor of the Lord. Also those who eat, eat in honor of the Lord, since they give thanks to God; while those who abstain, abstain in honor of the Lord and give thanks to God. We do not live to ourselves, and we do not die to ourselves. If we live, we live to the Lord, and if we die, we die to the Lord; so then, whether we live or whether we die, we are the Lord's." Therefore, I believe it is biblical and acceptable for clergy to choose a Sabbath day that allows them to rest.
[21] Keller, "An Excerpt from: A Shepherd Looks at Psalm 23."
[22] Psalm 23:6.

LEGAL ABC's for MINISTRY

Paul Martin

The legal system touches each and every aspect of our lives whether it is our home life, our education, our employment or our businesses; our churches are not exempt from the long arm of the law. In fact, in a society of excessive litigation and governmental regulation, the Church is regulated internally and externally. Internally, the Church must adhere to its denomination's rules and regulations and corporate bylaws. Externally, churches must comply with federal, state and local laws and regulations including such agencies as the Internal Revenue Service, zoning boards and state charity bureaus. Ministers and church leaders are forced to have a general understanding of the legal system regarding what a church can and cannot do.

Pastor's Responsibilities

The pastor of today's church has the same responsibilities as a Chief Executive Officer of any for-profit corporation. The pastor is not only the spiritual leader of the congregation but additionally has many secular duties. The pastor must coordinate and supervise church staff (employment contracts, health insurance, employment taxes, harassment policies etc.), execute contracts on behalf of the church (leasing office equipment, rental of space, insurance, mortgages and notes, etc.) and maintain financial stability of the Church.

Although a pastor should have the calling from God, he or she may not be equipped with all the tools necessary to handle the sometimes daunting task of running a business. Make no mistake: running a church is running a business. Each pastor must recognize his/her limitations and seek out individuals who can assist in areas that may require professional expertise. A pastor must utilize each and every tool at his/her disposal whether that is the Internet, the denominations tools (Book of Discipline, by-laws) or individuals within the church that posses specialized talents.

Legal Status of the Church

Many pastors take for granted the legal status of their church. When a pastor comes to a new church, the pastor should review all the legal documents associated with the church. The pastor should have the legal documents make easily accessible and should be knowledgeable of its contents. The following papers should be in a secure fireproof location: certificate of incorporation, by-laws, IRS 501 (c) 3 designation letters, deeds for all real estate owned by Church and Employer Identification Number. A copy of the documents should remain in the church office for access on a day-to-day basis. Pastors should review the incorporation papers to insure that the church's name; address and denomination are correct and properly listed.[1]

The documents should also be reviewed to insure that the legal name is correct on all documents.

In many states corporations are required to file yearly status updates regardless of whether they are religious corporations, for-profit corporations or not-for-profit corporations. The federal government requires religious corporations to file with the IRS informational returns. You should inquire of your local legal counsel and/or accountant as to whether your state requires the filing of such documents. The failure to file the required documentation with your department of state may result in the corporation's legal status being revoked or marked inactive.

Church Internal Regulations

A church is a corporation. A corporation is an association of individuals created under the authority of law, which has a continuous existence. A corporation continues to run despite change in management and workers. A corporation is run pursuant to the article of incorporation and bylaws. The bylaws are the rules and regulations that govern the internal workings of the corporation. The bylaws define the positions and responsibilities of the individuals that work for the corporation. A series of checks and balances are outlined within the bylaws to insure that the corporation runs efficiently. No one person should make all the decisions within a corporation (church). There is an appearance of impropriety when one individual makes all the decisions and controls all the money. At the very least there is an opportunity for the abuse of power and misappropriation of funds.

In order to write checks from the church's bank account at least two signatures should be required on the check. Each church should establish a policy and procedure for taking on debt, notes and/or mortgages. The authority to execute legal documents that bind the church should rest with more than one person other than the pastor. Usually these duties and responsibilities rest with the trustees and or stewards of the church under the direction of the pastor.

Subsidiaries

The mission of the church apart from its theological obligations is its social obligation to feed the hungry, clothe the poor and educate the masses. In the past, these responsibilities have been taken on under the church's name. In today's litigation heavy and over-regulated society, it is recommended that a separate Not-For-Profit Corporation (hereinafter "NFP") handle each of the church's outside programs that are social service based. By having separate NFP(s) handle the social service arm of the church, the church protects its asset (church building) from liability, as well as other assets owned by the church. The NFP also is able to apply and receive federal and state funds where churches would be precluded from receiving such resources based upon the doctrine of separation of church and state.

Once the church establishes an NFP, the NFP should be a separate corporation. The NFP should function as a separate entity, have its own board of directors, its own executive director and maintain its own books and records. The NFP is a separate corporation that should be self sufficient and separate from the church, but still have a common direction and mission as the church.

It is a common misconception that the NFP cannot make a profit; a NFP is able to make a profit and function as a successful business. The difference between a NFP and a regular corporation is that the NFP does not distribute its surplus funds to owners or shareholders, but instead uses them to help pursue the goals and mission of the NFP. The NFP corporations should be managed as a for profit corporation; a NFP must have a clearly defined vision, an internal system that evaluates operations and employee productivity and checks and balances to insure integrity.

Social service programs such as feeding the hungry, clothing the needy and, providing youth services can usually be organized under one NFP corporation. A separate NFP should be organized for educational organizations, i.e. day care, kindergarten, primary school, etc. If the schools are housed in separate buildings, managed and directed by separate staff and the purpose and goals are different, establishment of separate NFP corporations are strongly recommended. Transportation services should be established under separate corporations, as well as elder care services.

In recent years, with the push of government to support faith-based and community organizations, churches have established community development corporations (hereinafter "CDC") to address economic development in their neighborhoods. With the economy in such a state of flux, these CDCs have tried to fill the void where government once provided assistance. Churches have found a need to develop economically deprived areas whether in inner cities or rurally depressed areas. Where government and private industry have pulled back in funding projects and business, the CDC has come forward. To the extent that government provides tax incentives for the CDC(s) to invest and operate in depressed areas, the CDC has provided an excellent vehicle to assist churches in helping the community. These church sponsored CDCs have been active in building affordable housing (workforce housing [2]), senior citizen housing, providing job training and establishing partnerships with for-profit businesses to increase employment for individuals from the community.

Whether they are social service corporations, educational organizations or community development corporations a board of directors, like for-profit corporations, manages these church subsidiaries. The duties and responsibilities of a director are to make "major decisions" as it relates to the corporation. A director has a duty of loyalty to act in the best interest of the corporation and in good faith. This duty of loyalty remains whether the corporation is for profit or not for profit.

Appointing directors to the church's not for-profit corporation should not be viewed as a popularity contest or a political move. The appointing of directors should first and foremost become an opportunity to put qualified individuals on the board to insure the corporation's success. Appointments are made to insure the vision and direction of the pastor. The individuals appointed to the board of directors should have the same vision as the pastor and understand the mission and purpose of the NFP. There is no requirement that the directors come from the church membership. In fact, when appointing directors you should think of individuals outside the church, keeping in mind political considerations, banking considerations and networking. Appointing directors to the church's subsidiary corporations is an excellent way of networking with influential business professionals, banking executives, politicians, lawyers and accountants in your community. By reaching outside your congregation you expand your church's circle of influence. This influence is crucial when you are looking for bank loans, access to political figures or professional services.

In order to get the best qualified individuals for your board of directors the church must provide protection over the decisions of the board. An individual may want to assist you in promoting the social good of your NFP corporations but if sitting on your board could cause the individual board member to open himself/herself up to personal liability, the possibility of getting qualified individuals is little to none. Each NFP should provide director insurance to protect your board from liability.

Employee Management

In managing a church in today's world, a pastor has to supervise the pulpit staff, administration, security, bookkeeper and custodians. Depending on the size of the church, there may also be other ministries that must be managed i.e. credit union, kitchen staff, media personnel, and music staff to name a select few. Many churches find themselves in trouble with governmental authorities for not paying the required employment taxes (Federal and State). Outsourcing your payroll to a reputable established payroll company is efficient and cost effective and could save you bookkeeping headaches in the long run. These outsourcing companies keep excellent records; they also tabulate and forward all required taxes, and take a heavy burden off of your staff.

Employee Manual

A standard of conduct for all church employees is a requirement whether you have one employee or fifty employees. An employee manual puts your employees on notice as to what conduct is prohibited and what is expected of them. The employee manual is a statement of the policies of the church, the expectations of the employees and what the employees can expect from the church. The employee manual is a contract between the church and the employees. It is important that the employee manual is clear and unambiguous. Any misstatements or misinformation may cause potential liability for the church. The courts have decided that the employee manual is a legally binding contract between employer and employee. In the event that there is a dispute between the employee and the employer, the employee will look to the employee manual for direction. The employee manual can be a sword for the employee or a shield to the employer. The employee manual must be carefully worded and reviewed by an attorney to protect the church. The employee manual should include the following; Equal Employment Opportunity Statement, Attendance, Confidentiality, Substance Abuse Policy, Sexual Harassment Policy, Compensation and Benefits.

Protecting your Assets

Churches are no longer immune from being targets of lawsuits. Incorporating[3] is one method of protecting church property. A church must also have adequate liability insurance. You MUST have liability insurance. As America becomes more litigious, churches become attractive targets for plaintiff's attorneys. Churches own property, have assets that are easily identifiable, and are usually quick to settle in order to keep any appearance of negligence or misconduct of the ministers and/or staff quiet from the public at large. Litigation can be very costly, whether it is a major case or a frivolous lawsuit. The insurance policy limits should be enough to protect the church under the worst scenarios. The church should at a minimum, carry one million dollars of coverage per incident. In the event that the church has purchased a umbrella policy it should be reviewed to determine whether there is adequate protection for automobile accidents, slip and fall coverage, and other negligent actions such as food poisoning, board/director insurance, and a sexual harassment rider.

Background of Employees

In order to protect your church from future claims of negligent hiring thorough background checks on all employees, especially ones that come in contact with children (i.e. Sunday school teachers, bus drivers, etc) is a must. Each employee should fill out an application for employment. Any references should be followed up with written documentation reflecting that the references were contacted as well as the substance of their opinions.

Criminal background checks should be conducted on all employees. These criminal checks can be done at any local police precinct for a minimal fee. Searching the Internet can identify a number of providers that can do background checks which not only let you know a person's criminal history but also their credit history, where they have formally resided, children's names and bank account information.

Under the legal theory Respondent Superior, employers are responsible for the actions of their employees. In the event your employee commits acts of negligence within the scope of their employment, the church as the employer can be held liable. If the church's employee commits acts of sexual harassment or sexual misconduct, the church can be held liable for these acts and be subjected to very expensive lawsuits.

Professional Services

There are issues for which most pastors will have to seek guidance from a qualified professional. It is important that a pastor has access to an accountant and an attorney to address potential issues before they become actual problems. What are potential issues? Common sense and erring on the side of being cautious should be your guide. This said, here are some examples of when you should seek guidance from a qualified professional: purchasing of real estate, review of contracts, year-end audits, forming and/or dissolving of corporations, when the church is served with legal documents.

When choosing an individual to perform professional services you should use the same criteria employed when choosing someone to represent you personally. Ask necessary questions at the initial interview to avoid any misunderstandings in the future: Have you represented religious corporations? Can they provide references? Do they have a working knowledge of the state and federal regulations dealing with religious corporations and not for profits? How do they bill? Hourly or flat rate? Once you have decided on a qualified professional, ask for a retainer agreement outlining the work to be performed and all fees.

Conclusion

If protecting the well being of the church suddenly appears more complicated and convoluted than it did before reading this chapter, do not be alarmed. There was nothing presented that you cannot manage or direct to the right person. Please use the information provided in this chapter as a reference tool. It is not a substitute for the advice of competent counsel. The key is to make sure that you are up to date concerning the church's legal status, potential legal liabilities and where to quickly access assistance. It is pivotal to recognize when a professional should be consulted since this chapter only scratches the surface of legal issues with which a church may be confronted.

---

[1] In some states certain denominations are exempt from submitting approvals from regulatory agencies for the sale or lease of church property.

[2] Workforce housing is affordable or low cost housing intended to appeal to gainfully employed, essential workers in the community, i.e. police officers, firemen, teachers, nurses and medical technicians, office workers, etc.

[3] IRC 501(c) (2) refers to corporations organized for the exclusive purpose of holding title to property and collecting income.

DOING CHURCH:
the expanding vision

Vision for the Small Church

William Phillips DeVeaux

Introduction

Small churches form the backbone of Protestantism across the United States and Canada. The primary characteristic of these churches is usually that the congregations number one hundred and fifty (150) or fewer members. They derive their mission statement from the words of the Great Commission of Jesus, *go...and teach all nations baptizing them in the name of the Father and of the Son and of the Holy Ghost.*[1]

While the mission statement is vitally important, the vision statement is equally significant as it explains precisely *how* the small church plans to fulfill and implement the *Great Commission's* intent. Specific ministries and other tasks are then added as guidelines influenced by a local church's environment and unique settings.

The purpose of this paper is to analyze the elements in a vision statement for small churches. In this context mission means the reason and purpose of the church. Thus the *Great Commission* of Jesus is always the starting point. On the other hand, the vision statement expresses where the church is trying to go and what it intends to accomplish within a certain period of time. Developing a comprehensive vision statement will require some review of the special features that are exclusive to the small church.

After Pentecost, the Christian Church grew as groups of churches established by zealous and passionate bands of apostle-planted churches. These men and women were inspired by the Holy Spirit to travel throughout the known world. They developed support systems and established models for insuring the transition of leadership. In addition, they created rules of behavior and liturgical participation that have survived until the present time.

These New Testament churches were founded with the clear purpose of active evangelism and growth. They often were drawn together because of ethnic and cultural similarities. When barriers to the spread of the gospel were created because of racial and even religious differences, discussions were held and compromises were made. For example, the Jerusalem Council's manner of dealing with the issue of circumcision in Acts 15 is an instance of how conflicts were resolved. In addition, leaders made visits, wrote letters and dispatched the second generation of Apostles to extend the work of kingdom building. Some of these churches grew to be massive congregations that required several leaders and a cadre of persons in supporting roles. However, other congregations remained modest in size, yet extremely critical in carrying out the teachings of Jesus.

Background

Similar to biblical times, today's small churches were established in at least three different ways:

- First, some are newly formed institutions created under the same zeal as the early apostle-planted churches.

These churches have not had time or opportunity to increase in membership, but they still anticipate substantial growth.

- Secondly, there are churches that once enjoyed large congregations whose membership has now substantially decreased. The decrease may have been brought on by economic difficulties, demographic changes through population shifts, or internal church conflicts.
- Thirdly, there are churches that have been in existence for a long time and who make an intentional choice that their membership not exceed the standard of 150 parishioners or fewer. These churches have found their place in the community and are content to be *neighborhood, niche or special mission* genre so as to perform their distinctive role.

The means by which small churches developed may vary, but they share certain common elements including but not limited to:

- They are generally close-knit communities with strong family ties.
- There is a support community readily available in times of personal or corporate crisis. Members who choose small churches want to feel connected to and known by their pastor and fellow members.
- A strong sense of unity based on common goals and values is a vital element in the life of small churches.
- The perception that the members care about one another provides reassurance and support.

The Small Church Brand

Carl S. Dudley explains the special quality of small churches as follows: *Smaller congregations distinguish themselves by the quiet character of their faith, the importance of Christian fellowship, and the urgency for the church to respond to the people in need. While, as we have noted, churches with larger congregations emphasize clear vision, program diversity, and process efficiency.*[2]

Fellowship, unity and mutual support are among the positive features of life in small churches. Yet, having a small congregation also means experiencing serious disadvantages. Clearly one of the major areas of concern is related to the issue of family orientation and unity. The small church community can be extremely supportive and uplifting. However, at the same time, it can be nepotistic and highly insulated.

John M. Koessler summarizes the dangers some small churches encounter this way: *Another hidden disadvantage of the small church's family is the difficulty it poses for the assimilation of new members. Small congregations are closely knit. Their members are not only part of the same church, but also belong to the same extended, physically related family. New attendees may feel that the only way to gain acceptance is to marry into one of the family clans. These ties can produce a subtle bias that causes a small church to sabotage its own growth. Members feel threatened as they watch the congregation's size increase. As a result, they become suspicious of the motives of the newcomers. Their frustration increases as attendance expands because the church seems less familiar.*[3]

The problem of integrating new members into church fellowship has existed since the New Testament Church. There will always be some tension between the need to remain comfortable in fellowship and worship and the mandate to make new disciples. This classic conundrum can be described as *maintenance versus mission.* Most members are at home in familiar settings with people who look and act like themselves. New members can mean change and change can bring discomfort.

A vision statement for the small church should address the relationship between maintaining congregations and the command from Jesus Christ to expand his church. Small churches are not alone in the need to resolve this dilemma. However, failure to address the problem signals a lost opportunity to strengthen churches and fulfill Christ's mandate.

Building Capacity in Small Churches
Adequate capacity is simply defined as having the requisite human and material resources to support and sustain the church. For small churches the crucial issue in building capacity is acquiring, sustaining, supporting, and strengthening qualified pastoral leadership. Some ordained ministers view their assignment to a small church as the entry-level step in their career development or at best, a temporary assignment. It is seen as a necessary professional obligation that must be fulfilled. The members of the church may also be hesitant to commit themselves to a pastor who they perceive *to be just passing through.*

This is often the case when members react the same way toward a new pastor as they relate to new members. If the pastor is perceived to represent change, some members will create a negative environment. Conversely, other churches may view, *training seminary students as part of their purpose.*[4] These churches are invaluable because they are *helpful in humanizing young pastors beyond any education our seminaries can offer.*[5]

The optimism shown by Professor Dudley is tempered, in part, by his realistic appraisal of the current state of affairs in small churches. Small churches have a will to live- against all odds.

Consider the forces aligned against the proliferation of successful small churches. The phenomenal growth of their opposite, the *megachurches* comprised of several thousand members, has dominated the religious landscape. Judging from reports in the media, it is hard to imagine that anyone is available to join small churches. At the same time, denominational organizations, once central to small church self-identity, have declined in total member, financial support, and influence, reducing a once crucial lifeline of aid and encouragement.[6]

The situation Dudley describes is a serious problem common to most small churches. In fact, it can lead to a rapid turnover in pastoral leadership, as pastors cannot serve for extended periods with limited incomes while their professional and family obligations increase. Thus the small church's long term plans, mission and vision statements are often delayed or even set aside as congregants may be unwilling to envision a new future when they believe their pastor's tenure is limited.

Furthermore, anticipation of losing a pastor and the resultant anxiety of finding new leadership are seen as reasonable excuses for inaction on expanded programming and the creation of new ministries. Solving the problem of short pastoral tenures is common to all three types of small churches (as described earlier). However, stable small churches will be the most amenable to developing vision statements despite the absence of a long pastoral tenure.

The judicatory bodies responsible for small churches can help ease this predicament in several tangible ways. Denominational leaders' involvement should be predictable and consistent.

- First, they can carefully screen persons to match the personality characteristics that will fit best into small congregations.
- Second, they need to provide the requisite training and orientation for pastors prior to their assignment.
- Thirdly, a compensation package should be required and supported by the governing denomination.

The local denominational leadership can also contribute to the health of small churches by seeking pastors who possess the personal qualities cited above along with the ability to generate some portion of his/her own financial resources. One strategy would be to choose a *bi-vocational* minister. These pastors would combine the compensation as well as benefits derived from another occupation with the salary provided by the church. They are men and women called to serve the church but not in a full time capacity.

Such ministers have a passion to work in all areas of the ordained ministry but have chosen to also exercise their call while also engaged in secular vocations. They do not require significant financial remunerations for clerical duties, as their motivation is to serve as ministers on a part time basis unlike full time clergypersons who are totally supported by their church.

Richard H. Bliese in an article entitled *A Small Church Redefines Its Mission* offers and indeed expands the argument for effectively using *bi-vocational or worker-priest* in small churches thusly: *A growing number of congregations have been using this model of worker-priest... some churches have even abandoned the idea of having a full-time resident pastor in favor of having specialized leadership teams of three to five bivocational ministers. One carries the responsibilities for preaching, another for the teaching ministry, a third for pastoral care and a fourth for distraction, with perhaps a fifth responsible for evangelism and mission. The combined compensation for the team, including reimbursement for expenses, is usually less than the amount required to pay a full-time resident pastor.*[7]

Reflection on Current Issues

The issues facing small churches are universal. However, it is helpful to investigate specific examples of what these churches face. For example, the African Methodist Episcopal Church (AME) in the state of Georgia has over 530 churches. Of that number at least 250 could be classified as small churches. These churches are generally unable to provide for a full-time pastor. They may also be a part of two or three church *circuits*. Circuits are characterized by having one pastor assigned to conduct worship services on a rotating basis throughout the month and year. The circuit is considered as one church for reporting purposes and relationship to the Annual Conference.[8]

The concept of circuits while rooted in Methodism is a practice shared by many denominations. The term *Circuit Riders* or traveling preachers, in the tradition of John Wesley, pays homage to the founder of the Methodism. Like Wesley, the typical circuit rider traveled and ministered wherever people migrated during the early days of American expansion. African Methodists adopted this concept with zeal as the black population grew after the Emancipation Proclamation and surged from the south.

A. M. E. Bishops Paul Quinn and Henry McNeal Turner are perhaps the best-known advocates of this form of church leadership. Quinn moved the A M E church across the Mississippi River toward the western states, while Turner concentrated his efforts on the former slave states in the south. They were circuit riders that inspired others to follow their example. The legacy of these early bishops and pastors can be seen in the large number of small churches that remain today.

As more people joined these churches, the members would petition the denominational leadership to become a *station* rather than a circuit. No longer would there be a three or two-point circuit but rather one station church, which had the capacity to meet its financial obligations solely. The membership may have remained small but the churches had reached a degree of stability that called for one minister at each church even if he/she was not full-time.

Small Church Self Esteem and Inclusion

Several issues impact smaller AME Churches in Georgia. The first area of concern is related to economic resources but has wider ramifications. It has to do with congregational and clerical self esteem. The members and pastors of small churches often express a sense of alienation and lack of respect from the larger ecclesiastical body. Clearly, assessments and financial support for denominational responsibilities are usually less for small churches than the large ones.

However, the parishioners in small congregations frequently feel that their contributions are not fully appreciated. In addition, they also feel their participation in activities representing the denomination is seriously limited. Consequently, small church ministers and members view leading pastors and congregations as setting the agenda for the Conference and District[9] priorities while they are marginalized.

The lack of input can lead to a feeling of being assessed without full representation. For instance, decisions that result in additional financial obligations and time commitments do not always take into account the needs of small churches. Questions such as *are we really wanted and what are we receiving as members from the denomination; what makes our participation worthwhile* are often raised. A feeling of neglect, lack of appreciation, and alienation has led to diminution of participation at all levels. The first of which is usually financial contributions. Church officials and judicatory leadership should be extremely sensitive to the emotional, psychological, and even spiritual distance that small churches can feel from the larger churches as well as the denomination itself.

Economic Realities

A second problem often experienced by small churches occurs in the rural areas where pastors are sent to serve. The more attractive opportunities for service are perceived to be in urban settings. It is increasingly difficult for even *bi-vocational and second career pastors* to live in rural communities. Often their jobs are located in larger urban areas. Educational programs for their children and employment opportunities for their spouses are not available in a small town. Retaining pastors is a critical issue in building strong congregations; however, there are a number of other reasons why small churches have experienced declining membership.

The economic crisis, the failure of adult children to return to rural areas for work after educational training, the demise of the family farm and the loss of jobs due to factory closures are clearly significant. AME Churches are now facing a serious problem with recruiting and retaining pastors. Persons seeking ordination as itinerant elders, those that are fully ordained, and traveling pastors must graduate from an accredited seminary or school of religion.

The reality is that most ministerial candidates borrow funds to finance their education. After they graduate, their first assignment is usually to a small church whose compensation package is seldom sufficient to repay the loans incurred as well as support living expenses. For this reason, such pastors are anxious to move as quickly as possible to a church that can provide additional financial support.

Pastoral Accessibility and Its Concomitant Dangers in Rural Churches

Often pastors serving small churches have difficulty traveling long distances to carry out their duties particularly in rural areas. If they are able to meet their basic liturgical responsibilities, they are usually unable to commit to extended periods of time in the parishes to which they are assigned. In other words, clerical leadership is not always available for immediate pastoral needs and community crises. The absence of the pastor creates a vacuum that is either filled by lay leadership or by representatives from other denominations.

This limited access to their pastor and the failure to hear consistently from official church representatives leads to the erosion of doctrinal and theological standards. Therefore, congregants will seek ministerial guidance without regard to denominational affiliation. Television and radio preachers may also begin to set the theological and even social agenda for church members who believe they have lost contact with their pastor.

The AME Church has already experienced a decline in the comprehensive understanding that members have of its polity and basic beliefs. This is especially true in small churches where there is limited clerical direction and supervision. Pastors and properly trained church leaders are needed to insure that Bible study, catechism training, Sunday school and confirmation classes are properly conducted. When pastors are in short supply, religious education, stewardship instruction, and church polity are often neglected.

Small Urban Church Concerns

Small inner city churches experience problems similar to those affecting their counterparts in rural settings. Economic problems, isolationism, lack of respect and pastoral retention are also part of the inner city church experience. However, there are some issues that are unique to urban settings. Escalation in crime, deterioration of communities, gentrification and flight to the suburbs has impacted the ministry of inner city churches.

Moreover, urban churches are often in historic or older edifices that require continual renovation and reconstruction of facilities because maintenance has been deferred due to limited funds. Parking is generally insufficient. Security is a special problem especially during evening and nighttime programs. None of these problems is insurmountable, but they can be very costly and serve as barriers to church capacity building and outreach.

The Way Forward: A New Definition of Ministry

Reduction in resources critical to the small urban or rural churches leads to considering alternative means of doing ministry. If the traditional model is not working well, especially in the small church, then another paradigm may be needed. Alternative styles in ministry such as *bi-vocational ministers, worker-priest* as well as pastors serving two or three point circuits have been suggested. Bliese claims that these new models of doing ministry are absolutely necessary. He maintains that small churches like the ones he has served must... *let go of clericalism and convert the members into ministers . . . (and) leave behind traditional notions of church in order to focus on the congregation's mission on the margin.*[10]

Bliese underlies the need to broaden the concept of who does ministry. He is really addressing a practical application of the concept of the priesthood of all believers. His church had a *bad case of clericalism.* The congregation believed that... *we need a charismatic leader to turn things around . . . But it discovered that small churches could turn things around only if people take ownership of the church's administration and ministry.*[11]

The work and mission of proclaiming the gospel, teaching and drawing people to Christ is far too important to be left only to the full time ordained clergy. The expansion of ministerial duties will require a new mindset and in some cases, revision of church policy. The critical needs facing small churches provide the impetus to explore new arenas of service. An innovative approach is called for if effective ministry is to flourish in times of change and scarcity. There will always be a need for the fully trained, seminary trained ministers, theologians, and teachers of religion. However, the future of small churches depends on a ministry that is less formal in its structure, but effective and accessible.

An Increased Role for Laity

Lay ministers will be needed to augment the work of professional pastors, worker-priests and bi-vocational ministers. These lay ministers must develop proficient ministry skills so that they can represent the Christian Church as well as their denomination. The task of training this fresh cadre of Christian workers and facilitating their integration into the life of the church will not be easy. However, their full participation is crucial to the life of small churches especially those in rural areas.

The Process of Visioning: An Opportunity to Determine the Future

Involving the Entire Congregation and Community

Participation, input and feedback are integral to the visioning process. Fortunately, size is the major advantage that a small church enjoys in fashioning a vision statement. Since rural or suburban small church members live in close proximity, reaching out to the entire congregation can be easily accomplished. As for urban small churches, worship service, church events and other forms of communication might be utilized to a greater extent. No matter the method of garnering involvement, each member of the small church must feel that their views have been solicited, voices heard, and that their opinion matters.

Preparing the congregation to embrace the process is much like planning and arranging a political campaign or upcoming special event. Therefore, it is important that clergy, and lay leadership alike market the visioning process, and have an opportunity to decide the future of the church, and *determine what the church will look like in the coming years*. Again, the intention is to foster enthusiasm, anticipation and support for the process. As mentioned earlier, small churches can be resistant to change and this kind of advance publicity will help allay misgivings as well as thwart most negative reaction from opponents.

The advance publicity should be conducted over a period of time prior to the date that the actual process begins. This groundwork has several beneficial outcomes including:

- Enables the congregation to be well informed
- Allows the congregation to feel comfortable about the upcoming process
- Encourages forethought and introspection about the future
- Encourages involvement
- Creates excitement and *positive buzz*

Stakeholders in the community should also be involved in this process so that they can share with the small church family proposed municipal initiatives that might affect what the vision statement will entail. Such stakeholders who should be invited to address the small church family would include:

- School officials who could provide information on planned new buildings or closings etc.,
- Transportation officials who could provide information on new roads or bypasses and/or closures
- Chamber of Commerce representatives who could provide information on new businesses and/or closures
- Department of Health officials who could provide information on immunizations, prevention and treatment of illnesses
- Other local government officials

The value added benefit of having officials address (and seek input from) the small church family is an affirmation of self worth and contribution to the larger community. More profoundly, information from these stakeholders can trigger or drive revenue-generating opportunities for the small church.

For example, the small church family is informed that adult education classes in their community will cease because a school's space will be needed to accommodate more kindergartners. Perhaps the church has available space that it can *rent* to the municipality thus solving its problem as well as providing a resource stream for the church.

Self-Assessment

Self-Assessment is the essence of the visioning process and is the opportunity to review past accomplishments while focusing on positioning the church for its future. Total church involvement ranging from Sunday School youngsters to the sick and shut-in (assuming that they are able) is key. The point is to solicit a response to two key questions:

- What have we done well in the past or what are our proudest accomplishments?
- What do we want our church to accomplish in the next year, three to five years and in ten to twenty years?

Every church member who is able should be expected to offer his or her response to the questions above. This goal can be achieved through various means that can be validated as well as utilizing today's technology including:

- Open Church Forum or meeting
- By letter
- Via email or text
- Skype

Once the responses have been gathered, discussed and recorded, a consensus on priorities should be reached to enable drafting of the vision statement.

Elements of the Vision Statement

A vision statement is an expression of the goals a church has set for itself to be accomplished within a designated period of time. It will vary depending on the specific needs of individual churches. However, there are some common ingredients that will be helpful to most small churches. A successful small church must include in its vision statement a plan for increasing its capacity to survive by:

- Maximizing its strengths
- Addressing its weaknesses.

A vision statement for small churches should begin by defining its purpose as well as projections for the future. The example below would serve as a prototype:

- This church will create an environment that encourages sacrificial service, outreach to the community and Christian fellowship. It will create programs that nurture and lead people to a richer spiritual experience and a closer relationship with Christ.

In order to achieve this vision over a specified period of time, key goals must be identified and a plan of action for achieving must be developed. The goals should include but not be limited to the following elements:

- A creative stewardship program should be instituted that will help bridge the gap between economic scarcity and adequate funding.
- New means of generating resources for small churches must be developed, as very few can survive in the 21st Century on tithes and offerings alone.
- Special attention must be devoted to creating, practical and efficient ways of insuring that

members are served by qualified ministerial leadership.

[1] Biblical Reference to Matthew 28:19, KJV.
[2] Carl S. Dudley. *Effective Small Churches in the Twenty-first Century* (Nashville, TN: Abingdon Press, 2003), 137.
[3] John M. Koessler. "Dynamics of Small Church Ministry," http://smallchurch.com/articles/dynamics-of-small-church-ministry-92/. (accessed November 2009).
[4] Dudley. *Effective Small Churches in the Twenty-first Century*, 138.
[5]Dudley. *Effective Small Churches in the Twenty-first Century*, 145.
[6] Dudley. *Effective Small Churches in the Twenty-first Century*, 9.
[7] Richard H. Bliese. "A Small Church Redefines its Mission," http://www.religion-online.org/showarticle.asp?title=2878. (accessed November 2009).
[8] Methodist Annual Conferences are the gathering of churches within a certain geographic area which meets once a year under the supervision of a bishop to discuss business, make pastoral appointments, ordain ministers, etc.
[9] A District consists of several Conferences under the leadership of a Bishop.
[10] Bliese. "A Small Church Redefines its Mission".
[11] Bliese. "A Small Church Redefines its Mission".

BIBLIOGRAPHY

Bliese, Richard H. "A Small Church Redefines its Mission," http://www.religion-online.org/showarticle.asp?title=2878. (accessed November 2009).

Dudley, Carl S. *Effective Small Churches in the Twenty-first Century.* Nashville, TN: Abingdon Press, 2003.

Koessler, John M. "Dynamics of Small Church Ministry, http://smallchurch.com/articles/dynamics-of-small-church-ministry-92/. (accessed November 2009).

Team Ministry

Alfred A. Owens Jr. and Susie C. Owens

What an astonishing privilege it is to be chosen by God Almighty to serve and toil in His vineyard. Moreover, it is a phenomenal honor to be called and promoted to the Pastorate office. Truly the orchestrated hand of God that moves in this manner over an individual's life is a manifested display of His mandate and favor.

To be entrusted with the spiritual nurturing and careful cultivation of God's human creation is a tremendous endowment as well as an enormous task. When you consider God, the supernatural creator and overseer of the universe, and embrace the immense role of leading, influencing and imparting to His people, a true leader and called vessel willingly respects the fact that such an auspicious assignment is not to be entered into lightly. Therefore, pastoring is not something that one merely chooses to do. It is not a decision you make. Quite the contrary, it is a calling you accept. 2 Peter 1:10 states, "Wherefore the rather, brethren, give diligence to make your calling and election sure: for if ye do these things, ye shall never fall."

Comprehending the realization of being chosen by the omniscient, omnipotent, omnipresent, omnibenevolent God brings about an abundance of humble appreciation. One who has been chosen has not been found worthy of this bestowal, yet pliable and profitable for ministry. Jeremiah 3:15 states. "And I will give you pastors according to mine heart, which shall feed you with knowledge and understanding." The call to the pastorate does not come about for the promotion and recognition of an individual, but is bestowed upon an individual by God to fulfill a need in the earth and kingdom.

Ministries and ministry work often begins with the call and appointment. Following the call, a vision from God is granted. A vision is a sight (mentally), i.e., a dream, revelation, or oracle. It is a divine summons or leading from God. As the pastorate is embraced, launched, and begins to take on an operational form, a vision is imperative for meaningful and purposeful direction. According to Proverbs 29:18a, "Where there is no vision, the people perish." Vision motivates, gives direction and terminates aimless effort.

The designated pastor/leader is at the helm of implementing the vision. He or she prays, plans and positions him/herself and the flock to approach, produce and effectuate the vision. As time passes in the life of a progressive church, the obligations of ministry become vast, the operational visions become plenteous, the work multiplies and the needs of the congregation become insurmountably demanding. As the progression heightens, it is advisable to monitor closely the stacking responsibilities and deeds of the leadership and identify when the pastor's need for aide and assistance is imminent.

Throughout the development of an emergent church, internal auxiliary/ministry leaders and evangelistic leaders are often designated in an effort to aid the pastor in his or her ever-increasing role. Depending upon the number of internal ministries and the broad level of service a church seeks to provide, the pastor's role and function of leading sub-leaders, shepherding the flock, reaching lost sheep, and overseeing the day-to-day operations of the church can be vast and at times overwhelming. As the ministry reaches new plateaus of escalation and expansion, the need for the development of team ministry increasingly grows.

For the cause of promoting the continued success of and balance for the pastor, team ministry can be implemented if and when God grants that directive. If such a mandate is ordered, the Pastor may promote the First lady to Co-Pastor and/or another proven and qualified leader to the role of Assistant or Associate Pastor to share in carrying out the leadership responsibilities.

Prior to such an implementation, it is prudent for the pastor to enter a period of prayer and serious consultation with God to ensure the appropriate person(s) are appointed and the element of proper timing is in effect. Having the God ordained people in the appropriate God-mandated positions is critical to the continued advancement, endurance and overall survival of the ministry.

The development of a team ministry can be extremely advantageous when it is properly instituted, carefully maintained and consistently and reverently executed. Such an execution can ensure that the needs throughout the congregations are being appropriately addressed. This addition to the leadership can also leverage the work of the pastor in an effort to alleviate some of the stresses that accompany his or her role. Additionally, this strategic restructuring can redeem time for the pastor, enabling him or her to have the necessary quality time to seek God for supplementary visions and tactical plans for further propelling the church and kingdom at large. This can be one of the many ways God puts into action Philippians 1:6. "Being confident of this very thing, that he which hath begun a good work in you will perform it until the day of Jesus Christ." Team ministry is one of the tools God uses to perfect the work that has possibly begun under the leadership of one.

When we consider team ministry, and those guiding the congregations, whether they are male/female husband and wife teams or a team of leaders not joined in marriage, the key fact to remember is that God has used team ministry to bring comfort, hope and healing to many congregations.

These next few pages will primarily focus on team ministry from the makeup of a husband and wife ministry team. While it may appear that this concept became prevalent in the modern day church, when we research the scriptures we find biblical references that give way to such a practice in the days of the biblical disciples.

Act 18:18-19 tell us, "Paul, having remained many days longer, took leave of the brethren and put out to sea for Syria, and with him were Priscilla and Aquila. They came to Ephesus, and he left them there. Now he himself entered the synagogue and reasoned with the Jews."

Priscilla and Aquila are biblical examples of a husband and wife ministry team. They were co-laborers of Paul, in the ministry of Jesus Christ. Paul refers to them as "my fellow workers in Christ Jesus." Romans 16:3-5 states, "Greet Priscilla and Aquila, my fellow workers in Christ Jesus, who for my life risked their own necks, to whom not only do I give thanks, but also all the churches of the Gentiles; also greet the church that is in their house."

Paul left these fellow workers in the city of Ephesus undoubtedly to continue the work they started together. Scripture gives us every reason to believe that Paul's departure was not merely a separation or parting of ways, but more likely he left them in the city of Ephesus as ministers under his apostolic supervision. As a husband and wife ministry team, they lead and provided guidance for a church that gathered in their home. Scripture references their joint tutelage in operation. In Acts 18:26 we read, "And he [Apollos] began to speak out boldly in the synagogue. But when Priscilla and Aquila heard him, they took him aside and explained to him the way of God more accurately." Paul says in Titus 1:5, "for this reason I left you in Crete, that you would set in order what remains and appoint elders in every city as I directed you."

Other biblical examples of husband and wife teams doing the work of the ministry can be found amongst the lineup of Apostles. Jesus' brothers (James and Jude), and Peter traveled conducting the work of the ministry and their wives were with them during some of their journeys where the gospel was shared. In 1 Corinthians 9:5 Paul asks, "Do we not have a right to take along a believing wife, even as the rest of the apostles and the brothers of the Lord and Cephas?"

Were these wives merely the traveling companion of their husbands? Acts 2 could prove to be a guiding resource aiding us in deriving at the conclusion that this was plausibly another citing of team ministry in action. In Acts 2 the Holy Spirit fell upon both male and female and it was Peter who quoted from the Prophet Joel saying, *"this is what was spoken of through the prophet Joel. And it shall come to pass in the last days, saith God, I will pour out of my Spirit upon all flesh: and your sons and your daughters shall prophesy, and your young men shall see visions, and your old men shall dream dreams: and on my servants and on my handmaidens I will pour out in those days of my Spirit; and they shall prophesy."* (Acts 2:17-18) "Prophesy" means to speak forth by divine inspiration, to teach, to refute, to reprove, to admonish and comfort others.

It is doubtful that Peter, who saw the Holy Spirit fall on both male and female, who spoke the fulfillment of the prophecy of Joel, who understood this prophecy, and who was fulfilled that day through the outpouring of the Holy Spirit would then minimize the accompaniment of their wives and have restricted them from fulfilling that which was spoken, thereby constricting their ability to minister and prophesy.

Team Ministry has not only become popular and more prevalent in mainstream churches over the last two decades but more importantly it has been strategically ordained and blessed by God for the edification of the people and the up building of His Kingdom. Consequentially, it has become acceptable and embraced by many thriving congregations.

It takes a spirit filled and spirit-led pastor, yielded to the auspices of God, that will for the greater good share his or her authority and embrace a joint entity that can capably spearhead the rearing of a church. Arriving at this juncture can prove challenging as the enemy who seeks to steal, kill and destroy will launch an all out attack to ensure that such a force is never birthed. Vices of pride, intimidation, a refusal to share in authority and the like may need to be denounced and eradicated. Once human weaknesses that can hinder are brought under subjection and the forward movement toward this gift from God is in place, there are some fundamental principles that will need to be adopted and encompassed into the operational scope.

Spotlighted below are some essential principles that can be applied in a variety of teaming components engaged in team ministry. Note, this list of principles may not be conclusive, as we are mindful that ministry must always remain relevant to the times, and, therefore, there may never be any one set of rules to conquer the challenges that shared authority may pose. Yet, when a team is driven, focused and dedicated to the primary God ordained goals and committed to ministry and ministering, there are some elements that should always remain as an integral part of the set standards.

Bring a Strong Marriage into the Team Ministry: The affects of ministry can have an impact on the strongest marriages. Husband and wife teams are especially challenged in team ministry as one family and household is doubly affected. Therefore, it would be beneficial to periodically take time out and consider the affect the ministry is having on one's life, the life of one's spouse and the overall marriage. We encourage exercising wisdom by evaluating where we are and where we may need to improve in our marriage. At times that may call for adjustments in ministry. God did not intend for team ministry to have an adverse affect on marriage. Therefore, a thorough examination, an honest evaluation, proper maintenance and needed adjustments when and where appropriate should be performed. A team ministry cannot survive and progress unless the marriage is strong, viable, and true to the sacredness of the union. Flexibility, cooperation, understanding, respect, appreciation and love are all the components necessary for a healthy marriage and are also the components needed to provide a base for good ministry teamwork.

Approach Team Ministry as a Partnership: When this happens, the efforts and responsibilities are shared. Thus, both spouses are busy performing their duties. In team ministry, the ministry becomes a representation not only of God, but also of the individuals who are providing the leadership to the ministry. Therefore, your relationship with your spouse must continually flourish, thrive and be connective. God's design must be established and on display in the lives of those He has entrusted the ministry. If there is no harmony in the marriage, the ministry will be lacking. If there is no love, communication, or kinship the ministry will suffer. Team ministry must display unity. Unity is a whole or totality of combining all its parts into one. Unity is harmony, agreement, and the oneness of mind.

Diversity with Harmony: A great benefit that is reaped by churches and its congregations is having the advantage of a team leadership that is diverse in creativity, all the while functioning in harmony. In the event of a partnership comprised of dual leadership, when it comes to decision making, varied points of view, opposing perspectives and the like, the promoting of a harmonious working relationship is vital. Therefore, diversity should be viewed as an asset and not an adversarial factor. A key step to take in an effort to avoid dissention during times of differences would be for both partners to willing look through the lenses of the other spouse.

Designated Head: There is a risk of friction when there is dual leadership, especially if both parties are strong leaders. The role of headship in a pastorate in and of itself can be challenging and therefore, minimizing the potential threats with pro-active preventive measures is advisable. It is obvious that if team ministry is going to succeed, one of the partners must be recognized as primary leader. Respecting the designated head, one would want to avoid any arenas that have the slightest hint of competition. It is helpful to constantly reflect upon the teaming component as one that has been established to enhance and complete but never to compete. As a ministry team you want to send a clear message to the congregants that the pattern of authority is unwavering, and the shield sustaining it cannot be penetrated. Establishing this safeguard protects and leaves no room for manipulation. A firm marriage commitment and oneness in ministry goals are prerequisites for the stability of team/partnership ministry success. Competition and dissension should never be a part of team or partnership ministry.

Defined Roles: Team ministry partners will have *shared* responsibilities as well as *individual* responsibilities. It is important that the roles are made clear in an effort to avoid overlapping and promote a working structure that allows each partner to have a sense of responsibility for their defined area. When the various gifts, talents, abilities and anointing that each team partner brings to the team is acknowledged and welcomed, such acceptance fosters the path to liberty in the work and service that each is to render. Matthew 25:15 reads, "And unto one he gave five talents, to another two, and to another one; to every man according to his several ability; and straightway took his journey." Each partner must respect each other's abilities and not be threatened or intimidated by them. As husband and wife teams join in ministry, you must know and trust each other's strengths and spiritual gifts. One must acknowledge and respect that each member of the husband and wife ministry team has his or her own ministry strengths and manifestations of spiritual gifts.

As we walk as a team in ministry we not only must know each other's strengths and spiritual gifts, we must trust them as they are in operation and are being manifested in ministry through our partner. If we do not have this trust we are susceptible to being used as a hindrance to the move of the Holy Spirit through our partner. Partners must proactively choose to trust the Holy Spirit and His operation through our partner. Additionally, while defined roles are necessary for ensuring that all assignments are being performed, one of the many advantages of team ministry is having a back up, fill-in or substitute should the need arise. As it is with a pilot and co-pilot, although the co-pilot has a certain job description; the co-pilot must have the skills and knowledge necessary to assume the responsibility of the pilot, if necessary. In these instances, the co-pilot is still referred to as just that, co-pilot, second in command. Being seated physically in the pilot's seat and assuming the responsibility of the pilot does not change his/her occupational title.

Realistic Expectations: The expectations of team ministry partners must be realistic and feasible. Although we are careful not to put limitations on God's ability to perform the supernatural, we must be mindful to manage our individual expectations within a realm that is plausible for the capabilities and callings of the partner. It is helpful to examine each partner's strengths and weaknesses so that they can be taken into consideration when expectations are established.

Perpetuate Balance: Balance is another key component that must be prevalent and an element consistently worth striving for. A life of ministry has many seen and unforeseen sacrifices. This includes a sacrifice of time, talent and finances. As a team, one must be open to the yielding of the Holy Spirit to help balance a sacrificial lifestyle. It requires commitment, compromise and patience. There will be times when it appears as though the ministry has taken first priority.

As needs, events, and engagements surface, sacrifices will have to be made. Schedules will have to be changed and roles overhauled. As needs change our approach must change. Keeping fundamental principles operational will be key to fostering stability in the midst of instability.

Communication that Fosters Synergy: Communication is key in any personal and working relationship. Communication is a sense of mutual understanding. Synergy is the combined effort being greater than the parts. It is the working together of two or more, especially when the result is greater than the sum of their individual effects or capabilities. Communication is at its best with both relaying and receiving or talking and listening are in motion and taking the proper affect. Communication is often talked about, but one of the least understood areas of human behavior and one of the most challenging to implement. Superior communication skills would unquestionably enhance the interaction and harmony of any ministry team. To spend time and effort to discern posture, tone, facial expressions, the temperature of the atmosphere, feelings, etc. takes a great deal of effort and can often miss the mark and lead to misunderstandings and misinterpretation. Ministry teams should abolish operating in the unspoken and be forthright in verbally sharing with the team partner requests, wishes, expectations, feelings, thoughts, etc. There is a sense of ease, peace and clarity that comes with relating, relaying and releasing. Ministry partners are encouraged to capitalize on the benefits of opening up and accurately communicating in a frank, honest and respectful manner.

Mutual Respect: It is imperative in team ministry for partners to maintain mutual respect for one another. This is the shared positive consideration or regard that two people have for each other. To respect each other means to give proper acceptance, esteem, reverence or courtesy at all times, during any situation and in any setting. Each partner honors and embraces the abilities of the other partner's understanding that team ministries will flourish when the partners involved work at it with the sincerest heart. If both partners value the worth of each other, there is no reason to expect anything less than a successful partnership working together in ministry for the glory of God. As God has anointed and appointed, in His infinite wisdom He also has given gifts and talents, and they likely will vary between the partners making up the ministry team. It's just like God to guarantee that those He has called are equipped and thereby offering the congregants a well balanced, diverse, multi-faceted ministry team. Team ministry provides an excellent opportunity for two God-given talented individuals to blend their gifting. It entails one knowing that it will take each partner's individual expertise to make this team assignment work.

Mutual Goals: While diversity may exist among team ministry partners, the foundational goals should be common and shared among them. Therefore, the goals must be determined, centered around a defined purpose, and clearly communicated. There should be no room for error and misunderstanding of what the goals are. If there are opposing goals there could be a splintering that would form a divisive block in accomplishing the God given goals. While team ministry goals must be defined, so it is with personal goals. Each partner may have a set of goals which he or she endears to enhance his or her individual growth and development. This can only be an added bonus ensuring that what is bought to the table by each individual enhances the team.

Shared Values: Values are the worth or importance we attach to different aspects of our lives. In ministry, the spouses' values must be rooted and grounded in the Word of God. The Word is the ultimate authority of our value system. Values speak to our integrity, morals, ideals and what we deem significant or important. There should be some common thread that places a ministry team on the same path if not the same page. Values tie directly to, not only convictions, but also beliefs. As a team ministry, each partner's character must be above reproach.

Commitment: When a husband and wife team accepts the call to operate in Team Ministry, they each have made a commitment to God and a unique commitment to one another in ministry. When God's divine order is in place, the ministry will begin to see the manifestation of God's blessing and favor. A commitment is a pledge or promised obligation; to entrust; to bind or obligate, as by pledge or assurance. Spouses must be committed to each other and to the purpose and goals of the ministry. As sure as the challenges will come to the institution of team ministry, fortifying one's driven commitment to each other is a must. When one pursues and establishes the commitment needed, one is able to jointly and solidly face and overcome the threats that attempt to impede the productiveness of team ministry.

Encouragement: Team ministry partners must encourage each other and motivate courage, strength and confidence. To encourage is to stimulate by support; to promote, foster and cheer. Spouses should be the primary encourager of one another. Outside of God, the supreme comforter, there is no other source whereby a spouse needs look. When joined in marriage and ministry there should be a spoken and unspoken vow to be a place of solace, peace and support for the other. There should be an effortless innate nature to motivate and reassure one's ministry partner.

Compromise: Ministry partners learn that in the partnership of marriage and ministry, there must be a balance created between give and take. This is compromise, and it is necessary for effectiveness. Compromise is a concept of finding agreement through communication, through a mutual acceptance of terms. Maintaining a focus on the original goal and desire can aid in stirring the human will toward compromise. Compromise may be associated with concepts of balance, tolerance and flexibility. While it could be perceived that in the process of negotiating, in order to arrive at agreement, someone is destined to be unhappy or disappointed. This does not necessarily have to be the case. There are many benefits to relinquishing one's preference if the more profitable outcome is yielded in the end. This process also supports sharing, acts of selflessness and sacrificing. There is a way to compromise without surrendering your objectives or principles. We don't always have to agree but we should not be disagreeable.

In closing, we will share some summarizing principle guidelines that we've developed, and held in high regard throughout our team ministry tenure:

Principle 1: No one person's way is right all the time; know that you will see many things differently. That doesn't have to be a deterrent. Simply respect each other's point of view, and understand that no decision has to be absolute. In other words, you can change your mind without penalization. Be flexible, versatile, open, and agreeable.

Principle 2: Know your strengths and weaknesses and learn to give and accept constructive criticism. Always look to make each other better, and have each other's best interest at heart.

Principle 3: Keep an attitude of mutual submission. Never take each other for granted and never dominate your partner. Affirm one another regularly. Never throw off on each other in public. Support one another's ministry. Become each other's number one fan. Know that each partner is valuable to the ministry team regardless of his/her position.

Principle 4: Leave the heated discussion for the drive home not the church boardroom or pulpit. Reinforce each other publicly. Never put each other down openly or privately. Always let the congregation see you as one. We NEVER correct or question one another publicly – we discuss and debate the issue when we are alone.

Principle 5: Pray together habitually and pray for each other on a daily basis. Remember that the team ministry that prays together stays together.

Principle 6: Compliment each other on jobs well done. Always acknowledge the accomplishments of specific goals and tasks. Let no milestone or accomplishment go unrecognized.

Principle 7: Assign certain duties and tasks to each other. Know there are things to be done separately, as well as together. Offer help when a job is overwhelming for the other partner.

Principle 8: Communicate with each other any change in plans. Never keep your partner in the dark. Make sure that each partner is fully aware of all important details that pertain to the church and the ministry.

Principle 9: Keep home and church separate. Never allow the membership to wedge a gap between the two of you. Your spouse's happiness is your number one priority. Use love and support as valuable tools.

Principle 10: The partnership is equal. There is no superior position. Remember that roles are interchangeable – one can be a servant leader, the other affirmed helper, and vice versa at any given time. Love and respect are the keys to real balance.

Ministering as a team will require working through situations, not giving place to the spirit of competition with one another, bringing self under subjection, and yielding to the Holy Spirit who will be the ultimate teacher and leader. As you seek to lead the people in a harmonious fashion, it is crucial to keep outside forces in their proper place. Never allow other leaders, the membership or family to place a wedge in your partnership. You must safeguard your marriage and ministry team from such vices that could breed division, as they will come to unsettle your united position. During the process of team ministry, human flaws will surface. Couples are encouraged to readily identify these frailties when they flare up. Detection is the first step to properly countering and dismantling them expeditiously. Remember it is a process and with each process there must be progress. The key is not to become stuck on or in any of the issues. This will take determination, perseverance, patience and love. These are all vital in an effective Team Ministry.

Team Ministry will call for you to be role models to your sub-leaders and the membership at large. You are constantly under a microscope, consistently on display for the perusal of scrutiny, and objects of judging, questioning, second-guessing, criticism, accusations, and ridicule. Isaiah 50:7 states, "For the Lord GOD will help me; therefore shall I not be confounded: therefore have I set my face like a flint, and I know that I shall not be ashamed." You must maintain a strong stand and immerse yourselves in the word of truth. Being a role model to your congregants will call for you to show forth your undying faith in the midst of doubt and discouraging situations; your measureless hope in times of hopelessness; your strength in times of weakness; your stamina in the midst of attacks; your faithfulness in the midst of tired bodies and weary minds; your compassion in times of being wronged; your understanding in times of confusion; your generosity in times of personal lack; your patience in times of disappointment; and your belief in the face of opposing realities, and so much more.

As a Ministry Team, you are tasked with being a close, reachable and touchable extension of God's love. As co-shepherds your flock reaps the benefit of two parents who will readily nurture, scold and train. 2 Timothy 2:24 teaches, "And the servant of the Lord must not strive; but be gentle unto all men, apt to teach, patient. In meekness instructing those that oppose themselves." You are like the doctor who is always on call. One of the many blessings of the teaming factor is having someone to share the load of responding to the needs and calls. Your life is an open book that can be read, and the readers are fortified as they glean knowledge that breed's life for their hungry souls. Your open book will call for sharing to the extent that your story will add value to a life that is in need of your report, and the experiences grafted within.

You'll be faced with the need to be transparent and share those private areas of your life that at times you want to reserve and keep private. You must be wise enough to equally understand that there are times you will allow certain stories to remain private for the sake of the greater good and assurance that you are never ever a stumbling block or hindrance to anyone God has entrusted unto your care. You must know the level of spiritual maturity of the membership, and feed your flock with food that would be a benefit and not a detriment to their growth. When sharing could bring about someone's deliverance, healing and restoration, share testimonies of victory as well as those of trials. Always seek to bring a realistic balance to your congregants. This enables them to further understand that God is no respecter of persons, and as you are blessed, so shall they be blessed. As you must face trials and challenges, so all must suffer for the cause of Christ.

Team Ministry will call for you to show your congregants how to work well with others; and how to support, extol, promote, be accountable to and esteem others. Your partnership must be camaraderie and accountability on display, fervently and consistently defying and defeating division, separation, discord and dissention.

Team Ministry will call for you to constantly reassure your parishioners. They will be faced with life challenges and as they gather Sunday after Sunday and week after week, they look to God and their pastors for reassurance. You must be convincing, confident, positive and real. Never trick, mistreat, starve or abandon your flock. Jeremiah 23:1-2 says, *"Woe be unto the pastors that destroy and scatter the sheep of my pasture! saith the LORD. Therefore thus saith the LORD God of Israel against the pastors that feed my people; Ye have scattered my flock, and driven them away, and have not visited them: behold, I will visit upon you the evil of your doings, saith the LORD."*

Team Ministry will call for you to maintain order while guiding the people. Although you are God's chosen team, never position yourself to become the people's God. While you serve as their spiritual father and mother, always point and stir them to the heavenly Father. Even the best parents teach their children to walk, feed themselves, and take care of themselves. As it is in the natural, so it is in the spiritual rearing. Be careful to take your flock safely through the stages of spiritual development. Allow your expectations of them to mirror God's. Never lose sight of the fact that the people entrusted to your care are God's people. 1 Peter 5:3 reminds us, "Neither as being lords over God's heritage, but being examples to the flock."

Team Ministry is a blessing from God and can be a very rewarding experience for those that enter into it prayerfully, reverently and advisably. The benefits that will come to the leadership, the membership and the church at large are significant. This teaming experience can add years to your life and abundant life throughout your years. As with any worthwhile job, along with the benefits, there are challenges, but the good days in team ministry can far outweigh the bad days. Every ministry team can find purpose, passion and peace in the fact that God, who calls and ordains, also anoints, strengthens, guides, maintains and motivates for the assignment at hand.

We admonish all those who will partake in this charge to acknowledge and obey God in all the feats and exploits you set out to do. Maintain a gracious, humble, helpful and God-fearing posture. Entreat the people of God with the utmost Godly care and lastly let the work that you strive to do be purposeful, thereby promoting the greater good of the ministry and the body of Christ at large.

Marketing Your Ministry

By Dr. Teresa Hairston

The Case for Marketing Your Ministry

Several years ago, a marketing slogan became so hugely successful that it swept across America and transcended race, culture, and even cracked the walls of traditional religion. The slogan was "borrowed" from the theme of a book written in the 1800s. Once it caught fire, it created media frenzy, literally spreading the message to millions and simultaneously bringing in billions of dollars through t-shirts, caps, pens, cups, jewelry and every other conceivable piece of merchandise. You probably remember this slogan. It became so popular that people readily identified it by the acronym—WWJD— that stood for "What Would Jesus Do?"

When it comes to marketing and contemporary ministry, WWJD illustrates a two-fold concept: 1) Successful marketing of a

"Jesus" message in a morally rebellious society is possible; and 2) Successful marketing and successful ministry go hand in hand.

For those who frown upon the "concept" of "Marketing and ministry," as exploitation or misappropriation, I encourage you to be open-minded enough to listen to the words of our Savior. In John 12:32, Jesus said, "And I, if I am lifted up from the earth, will draw all peoples to Myself." Jesus knew the Gospel of the Kingdom had drawing power and He was the embodiment of the Gospel.

So, Instead of stopping at the question, "What WOULD Jesus do", let's go a step further and look at "What DID Jesus do?" Today, more than ever, it's easy to get caught up in the popularity of ministry. Television and other media exposure have a way of making people appear "bigger than life." Therefore, we must be careful not to get sidetracked or diverted from the goal of our marketing. It is all about "lifting up Jesus!"

"What DID Jesus do?"

The Synoptic Gospels (Matthew, Mark and Luke) bear witness to the things Jesus did and taught while fulfilling his earthly mission to save the world from sin. Matthew establishes Jesus as the fulfillment of prophecy—the Messiah and Son of God. He clearly records Jesus' miracles, illustrating His dominion over nature (Matt. 8:23-27), sickness (Matt. 8:5-13) and death (Matt. 9:18-19). Matthew also records accounts of Jesus' exemplary lifestyle, character, actions and reactions. Finally, he records Jesus' commission to all of His followers: "Go ye therefore, and teach all nations, baptizing them in the name of the Father, and of the Son, and of the Holy Ghost: Teaching them to observe all things whatsoever I have commanded you: and, lo, I am with you always, even unto the end of the world. Amen." (Matt. 28:19-20).

Matthew's Gospel shows that Jesus spreads (or markets) the Gospel through demonstration, instruction, and branding.

In the Gospel of Mark, we see Jesus as fully human, yet fully divine. Mark records the deeds of Jesus efficiently and effectively. He shows Jesus as an actively obedient servant to people who through teaching and miracles, met needs. He also shows Jesus as generous and caring—He was the submitted Son of the Heavenly Father—who gave His life as a ransom for many." (Mark 10:45).

People love good samples and they like companies that are genuine and generous. One of the critical components of marketing is to show people how companies' goods, services and products can meet their needs—now and in the future. Mark's Gospel effectively illustrates this aspect of marketing.

Luke's Gospel reveals Jesus as the redeemer/deliverer and savior of the world—as such, Jesus' compassion transcended people's race, geographic location and social class. Successful marketing "connects" with a wide cross-section of people and is inclusive rather than exclusive.

From the Gospels, there are five "What did Jesus do marketing strategies" that growing ministries should consider when "lifting up Jesus" for the world to see:

A. Jesus gained customer ***confidence*** by demonstrating His product.

B. Jesus established ***credibility*** by establishing the uniqueness and authenticity of His product.

C. Jesus effectively ***branded*** His product by establishing a clearly identifiable
mission statement and easily distinguishable product (signs and wonders).

D. Jesus created a ***globally viable*** enterprise that had clear goals.

E. Jesus wrote (via the inspiration of the Holy Spirit) an effective ***distribution plan*** for of his product; it was easily accessible and for everyone.

As we look at what Jesus did in relationship to these five areas of marketing, perhaps your ministry will prayerfully consider how to tweak various areas as well as embrace new, creative thoughts regarding marketing during your next season of ministry.

Forty-Five Marketing Strategies for your Ministry

1. Gain Customer Confidence

Matthew authenticates Jesus as the Messiah and Son of God by tracing Jesus' lineage (Matt 1) and through the endorsement of John the Baptist (Matthew 3:1-12) and God, Himself (Matthew 3:13-17).

1. Produce a professionally written/produced Church/ministry history—in print, online and a brief Video

2. Produce a professionally written Pastor's bio – with updated photo—in print, online and a brief video

3. Produce a professionally produced Church Website, which should include photos, church calendar with special events, address, service times and historical photos of the church, and various other events, special guests, etc.

4. Update your website no less than twice/month--frequently change pictures and make sure events (with times and locations) are consistently updated.

5. Include statements of endorsement from your church's denominational covering or ministry covering (include photos)- in printed materials, online and in videos

Jesus demonstrated his power over nature, sickness and death (see above). Nothing demonstrates credibility and shows that you are an "overcomer" like consistent ministry growth and development. Areas of growth may be: numerical, geographical (new location(s), multi-cultural and social (community activities). Use marketing tools to illustrate your ministries' growth:

5. Produce a professional annual magazine (similar to a yearbook)—this is a great tool to image your growth.

7. Produce a special annual video presentation that can be shown during church/pastoral anniversary.

8. Organize a series of member presentations/ testimonials done occasionally in service, from those who are of a different culture, or of unique background.

9.Organize a series of pastoral/ministry staff presentations announcing community partnerships, sponsorships or events that your ministry has co-sponsored. (Cancer walks, mission trips, etc).

10. Share with your congregation stories that are published in newspapers and magazines, and radio or television interviews and appearances. If possible, invite members to attend and support.

2. Establish Credibility

Integrity in your ministry is established when your leadership and ministry exhibits Godly character and preaches and teaches sound doctrine. Here are some strategic guidelines for programming:

11. Offer programs that exhibit strong family values. Whether the pastor is single, married, widowed or divorced, family ties should be authentically and positively exhibited and reinforced wherever possible.

12. Offer programs that exhibit Godly character. Leadership should never be involved with the works of the flesh (Gal 5:19): "adultery, fornication, uncleanness, lewdness, idolatry, sorcery, hatred, contentions, jealousies, outbursts of wrath, selfish ambitions, dissensions, heresies, envy, murders, drunkenness, revelries, and the like…"

13. Offer programs that exhibit the fruit of the Spirit (Gal 5:22): Your leadership must take care to exhibit "love, joy, peace, longsuffering, kindness, goodness, faithfulness, gentleness and self-control."

14. Offer enjoyable, diverse events that meet needs but are based in sound doctrine. From singles ministry to counseling services, take care to present and protect your ministry's reputation! Remember, "Your adversary, the devil, walks around like a roaring lion, seeking whom he may devour…"(1 Peter 5:8).

Establishing credibility in ministry means offering solid teaching that is clear and applicable to real-life issues that members are facing. In Matthew, from the middle of chapter 4 through the middle of chapter 14, we read of the accounts of the ministry of Jesus while in Galilee. During this time, He commissioned the 12 Apostles, preached The Beatitudes, performed miracles and taught lessons regarding: adultery, divorce, giving, prayer, judging, worry and treasures in Heaven. In chapter 13, Jesus uses parables to provide examples. People need ministry that is real, relevant and relatable.

15. Offer good, sound teaching that deals with real-life issues.

16. Offer creativity in your ministry presentations—i.e. video, music, dance, drama, etc.

17. Stay educated as a pastor, consumer and community member. Stay current by reading, watching and listening to know the concerns of your members.

18. Embrace, demonstrate, teach and promote the full authentic operation of the Holy Spirit within your ministry, ministry services and your personal life.

3. Effective Branding

Successfully meeting the needs of your members ("clients"), means establishing a relationship with them where they know what to expect when they come to your ministry. The uniqueness of your vision and mission should be easily identifiable through every presentation of your ministry. Honesty, consistency, good communication, and excellent administration should distinguish your ministry. Your ministry should have a "flavor" of its own. Here are some branding tips:

Branding helps people know who you are and what you're about.

19. Have a vision statement. What did God show you? Your vision statement is your inspiration, the framework for all your strategic planning. A vision statement is timeless. A vision statement should, ideally be no longer than one sentence. Print your vision statement on all ministry materials.

20. Have a mission statement. What will you achieve? A mission statement is a short but complete description of the overall purpose and intentions of your ministry. It helps to focus your activities and priorities. It tells you what you are and aren't supposed to be focused on. Print your mission statement on all ministry materials.

Branding helps people know what to expect from you.

21. Offer musical consistency. Music is one of the top factors in church growth. Musical presentations should be on par with the preaching presentations and should be consistent from service to service. (For example, traditional music paired with contemporary preaching sends a signal of confusion).

22. Offer musical excellence. Gone are the days of sub-standard musical offerings. Update and upgrade your music staff and insist on excellence. You may even consider a CD recording of your choir.

23. Offer musical variety. Although song selections should be "tailored" to the preaching, there should be a mixture of contemporary and traditional music; hymns as well as praise and worship to meet the tastes of all ages and demographics.

24. Offer musical integrity. Make sure that musical lyrics are Bible-based. The minister of music should be accountable for every song presented.

25. Offer professional sound quality. There's nothing worse than a ministry opportunity that is missed because of insufficient sound!

26. Offer video enhancement. Where possible, expand your ministry's impact through video. In today's society, this is an essential, since almost no one that will attend your ministry is unexposed to television and movies.

27. Offer creative dance. A dance ministry is Biblical! (Psalm 150). Establish a dance ministry and invest in training them. Challenge them to prepare special presentations and recitals/concerts.

28. Offer drama. Creativity is the hallmark of God. Don't shortchange your ministry or underestimate the talent pool that may be sitting in your pews just waiting for an opportunity to serve!

29. Make sure that all creative arts performances are timely and done in excellence. Songs, dances, videos or dramatic presentations should not be longer than 5-8 minutes.

30. Offer excellence in your physical location.
    - Make sure restrooms and classrooms are clean, neat, stocked with necessities and fresh smelling. On days when there is heavy usage, make sure there is someone to check them frequently.
    - Make sure your sanctuary is well kept. Repairs and maintenance are paramount in God's house.
    - Organize storage areas and designate rooms for needed functions. Keep these areas well-stocked and well-organized.
    - Heat and cool your facility so it will be comfortable.
    - Make sure your instruments are in good condition.
    - Make sure your parking lot and lawn are kept in good condition.

Your ministries' identity is important. There is nothing wrong with a slogan or a logo to help visitors and members latch on to your ministries' uniqueness. The Gospels give several examples of this with the fish being an identifier of Christians.

In Mark 1:17, Jesus said, "Come after Me, and I will make you become fishers of men." Matthew 12:40 states, "...Jonah was three days and three nights in the belly of the great fish, so will the Son of Man be three days and three nights in the heart of the earth." Matthew 14:17 shares, "And they said to Him, 'We have here only five loaves and two fish.'" Luke 5:6 reads, "And when they had done this, they caught a great number of fish, and their net was breaking." And Luke 24:42: "So they gave Him a piece of a broiled fish and some honeycomb."

As for a logo, the letters of the Greek word for fish (*ichthus*), which are, translated "Jesus Christ, God's Son, Savior" have been used to create a "symbol" or "logo" for Christianity. There are a number of viewpoints on the usage of this symbol, some of which are viewed negatively by church leaders because they intermingle with pagan ideologies; however, the usage of a symbol or logo of a fish to communicate one's belief in Jesus Christ is part of Christian history. Here are some branding tips regarding logos and slogans.

31. Create a ministry logo that is:
    Simple
    - Not more than three colors, but looks good in black and white.
    - Not too cluttered, doesn't use more than two fonts
    - Free of clipart, gradients, drop shadows, reflections, photos and light effects

    Scaleable
    - Can be reduced or enlarged without losing quality.
    - Versatile—able to work on letterhead or on a vehicle.

    Unique
    - Uniquely shaped but easy to recognize,
    - Appealing at first glance (test it out on at least 5 people)
    - Indicative of your ministry's "flavor"—even without words.

32. Create a ministry slogan that is:
    - Unique and expressive of your ministry's "flavor." Make a list of the main characteristics

of your ministry. Underline key (use a thesaurus if you need help). Once you have your comprehensive list, narrow it down to ten or so.

- Creative. Arrange the words in different ways until you come up with something that sounds "catchy" but positively describes your ministry's benefits. Add some action verbs to the keywords you've identified to give your tagline impact.
- Short. Keep your slogan short and simple so it will be memorable. It should be no more than 7 words long. Remember, the more words, the less likely that people will remember it.
- Memorable. After you come up with your top four or five slogan ideas, write them down and revisit them the next day. Sit down with a fresh perspective and review your list. Do any of your taglines really grab you? If it's a good tagline, you should know it right away. Pick the best one and show it to a friend or family member. Ask them what kind of image it forms in their mind? Is it memorable? Does it have impact? If not, it's time to go back to the drawing board.
- Timeless. Only use slogans that fit your permanent profile. Think long term. If you move locations or change staff or grow in other ways, will your slogan become obsolete?

33. Print cards, letterhead, etc that contain your vision statement, logo and slogan. Make the look consistent on your website.

4. Global Viability

Position your ministry for global impact. The goal of the Gospel is to reach all ages, cultures, communities and continents. Refrain from "localizing" your ministry or using terms that only Christians understand or can relate to. Here are some strategies:

34. Establish relationships with people of other cultures, communities and continents. Be selective, but attend events or serve on committees that will expand your sphere of influence. Attend seminars that will enhance your ministry but will offer you the opportunity to network with others.

35. Nurture multi-culturalism in your staff. Versatility in your staff will enhance your opportunities for new thoughts, ideas and relationships.

36. Travel and visit other ministries. Go out and visit other ministries in and outside your culture, community and continent. Expand your personal and ministry horizons! Be deliberate!

37. Use technology. The Internet really is worldwide. Study the ministries of other cultures, communities and continents to learn about those whom you might be able to network with! Use social networking to carry on conversations.

38. Be respectful. Although you may have different opinions and traditions, you may be surprised by how much you learn when you travel or interface with other cultures and communities. Don't be shy about embracing new brothers and sisters.

Distribution Plan

Getting the word out is the core goal of marketing. When it comes to the Gospel, there are literally thousands of ways to teach, preach and live out the Gospel message as Jesus did. His perfect example gives us a successful pattern to emulate; and the Great Commission commands us to do so.

Many churches would be more effective if their members understood their role in spreading the Gospel. In order for this to happen, leaders must educate, inform, inspire and empower. Here are some strategies:

39. Cultivate witnesses. Being a witness means simply believing that Jesus rose from the dead and telling others about what happened; it doesn't mean that a person has to be an expert in apologetics or know all the answers to tough questions about Christianity. Teach members to share their faith by simply telling others that the Gospel is true, Jesus is real and He has changed their life!

40. Cultivate servant-leaders. In order to "disciple" anyone, a person must first be disciplined. A simple life of obedience is the first step. Train people in your church for life-on-life disciplining (starting at home). This means that the leader/leadership team must "pour" themselves into others.

41. Cultivate interactive Internet outreach. Using technology to witness and develop relationships has yet to be formalized in most ministries. Most young people spend a lot of time on the internet and would probably be "helped" if your ministry developed a "digital" witnessing component. Set goals! Encourage and *incentivize* your youth to become "digital" witnesses.

42. Cultivate Online Bible Studies. Reach the world with creative, interactive, structured Bible studies, blogs and discussions.

43. Cultivate non-traditional educational opportunities. Teach the Gospel inside and outside the walls of your church/ministry. Dr. Suzan Johnson Cook, a creative New York pastor, established lunchtime Bible Study in a Wall Street location, and then she took the same concept to Capitol Hill! Where can you reach more people?

44. Cultivate evangelism opportunities in your community. The traditional neighborhood canvassing is still viable. Pass out tracts or gift cards, or whatever is creative and safe. Pastor Taffi Dollar, of the Atlanta

ministry, World Changers took a team of women to share the Gospel in various clubs in Atlanta. They were able to witness to several prostitutes and compel many of them to change their lives!

45. Cultivate love. A loving environment reflects the heart of God. Above and beyond any other characteristic of ministry, people are drawn by love. Activities like hospital or hospice visits, church picnics and new member receptions should remain a part of the ministry agenda. Sharing the Gospel
should always be done with a Spirit of love, unselfish giving, care and concern!

Despite the era of skepticism in which we currently live, effectively marketing the Gospel via your ministry is possible. It doesn't require money as much as it demands creativity and commitment. Nothing is as engaging as enthusiasm. If your church is "on fire" for God, people who visit will join, and people who join will become active and people who are active will encourage others to come, and the cycle will continue to recreate itself. Marketing your ministry is your responsibility, not just an opportunity!

The Use of Technology in Building Ministry

Lance Watson

INTRODUCTION

Things have changed in the twenty plus years that I have served in pastoral ministry. It is necessary before I wax poetic about how technology has shifted the landscape in which we do ministry, to give you a glimpse into my personal context for ministry. Here's a typical week in my technological life:

- Twitter: 150-200 tweets
- Facebook: 250-300 interactions and connections
- E-mails: 300-400 e-mails per day that require a response
- Blogging: 2-3 postings
- Time: 15-20 hours online
- Visits; face-to-face meetings: 8-10
- Emergency hospital visits: 1 in the last 5 years

Granted, the ministry I serve is a multi-layered, multi-staff, multi-campus congregation whose primary demographic is 20 and 30 year olds, and further, I am a self-affirmed connoisseur of all things technological, so it is somewhat second nature for us to use technology to build, maintain and inspire a healthy church community.

However, as we share this exploration today about integrating technology into the life of our ministries, let me first attempt to address several questions that frame the context for how we faithfully shift from the simple and humble life of a carpenter from Nazareth to a contemporary techno-pastor in the 21st Century. In this chapter, I'd like to explore the joys, dangers and pitfalls of technology and congregational life by examining the historical, cultural, biblical and practical bridges that transport us from the simplicity of the first century church to the complexity of the twenty first century church.

THEOLOGY

Theologically, it's important as we study the scriptures that we view Jesus Christ as the most significant manifestation of divinity to ever be expressed in humanity. Jesus Christ is at the center of our faith and he is the basis for our hope. Jesus Christ stepped into the bio-data of the human experience on a mission from God. As a missionary for God, Christ came into first century culture using the language, images, style, form and metaphors of that culture to effectively demonstrate and proclaim his person and work in the world.

In the gospel of John alone, Christ declares 39 times that he had been sent into the world; into first century culture on a mission by God. Later in John's gospel, Jesus tells his disciples, those that decided to follow him, "As the father has sent me, so I send you." Both this admonition and application applies not simply to those that followed him in first century, but to everyone that would follow him in any subsequent century. Purely and plainly, we are to be like missionaries (people sent on a mission) like Jesus, going into culture using every effective means available to us to point to the God of the Bible who loves us with an everlasting love and sent his only begotten Son to rescue, redeem and restore us.

Now, that being said, after his death and miraculous resurrection from the dead on the third day, Christ then issued some parting commands in the Book of Acts to his disciples who were to follow his example; champion his cause and continue his work in the world. The early church was approximately 120 or so persons and Christ gave them final orders saying, "Wait for the promise of the Holy Spirit to empower and enable your ministry and then go forth and be my witnesses in Jerusalem, Judea, Samaria and ultimately to the uttermost parts of the world." Their "home base" was Jerusalem and through this, Jesus was saying to them that inasmuch as any church is able, they were to have an impact at home first, then spread the teaching of God's incredible grace to their region, their country and ultimately to the ends of the earth.

One scripture that has become increasingly important to guide our understanding of how we should function in culture; how we should think about technology; how we should construct worship experiences; how we should determine the language we use in communicating in the context of culture is 1 Corinthians 9. In that periscope, one of the greatest missionaries in the world, the Apostle Paul writes to a church located in an urban center; a church struggling with how to engage the culture that surrounded them and utilize the opportunities and advantages that their culture presented to them to advance the ministry of Jesus.

In 1 Corinthians 9:19, Paul says, *"Though I am free and belong to no man, I make myself a slave to everyone, to win as many as possible. To the Jews I became like a Jew, to win the Jews. To those under the law I became like one under the law (though I myself am not under the law), so as to win those under the law. To those not having the law I became like one not having the law (though I am not free from God's law but am under Christ's law), so as to win those not having the law. To the weak I became weak, to win the weak. I have become all things to all men so that by all possible means I might save some. I do all this for the sake of the gospel, so that I may share in its blessings."*

The practical point of Paul's teaching was that as leaders and servants in the ministry of Christ, in humility, we are to do all we can so that as many people as possible can come into a life changing relationship with Christ. This does not mean we compromise the message, because elsewhere in scripture we are told to contend for the truth. We do not compromise the message, but here we are instructed to contextualize the method by which the message is delivered. This means that we use every possible means at every possible time to reach every possible person with the liberating, life-changing message of Jesus Christ.

Paul demonstrates for us what it means to function in humility with flexibility when he says, *"To the Jews I became as a Jew, I became a Jew in order to win the Jews..."* He was willing and encourages us to contextualize the method by which we deliver the message so that we might be able to reach people with the good news of the gospel. Pay particular attention to his phrase: become all things to all people that I might win some.

A church must have timeless truth and timely methods. It must contend for the truth, but then contextualize it in culture. Churches that only contend are mean spirited, pharisaic, inflexible and rude and churches that only contextualize invariably lose sight of the scripture and lose themselves in contextual ambiguity and both are unfaithful to the call of Christ. The call on our lives is not to be conservatives or liberals, but we are called to both contend and contextualize for the sake of sharing the gospel of Jesus Christ.

Paul's proclamation is that he is contextualizing to as many peoples, regions, groups, cultures and sub-cultures as he possibly could. In verse 23, he says, *"I do all this for the sake of the gospel that I may share..."* Paul says that using every means possible at every possible moment, he wants to reach every possible person with the timeless truth of the gospel; so that in love, we might enable him or her to build a relationship with God through Jesus Christ.

The guiding principle that instructs us as to how we are to approach culture and utilize technology is this—we want to see as many people as possible come into a relationship with God through Jesus Christ. That is the theological foundation that under girds our approach as to how we use technology—it is to be employed as part of the continuing redemptive mission of Christ to reach people with the love of God.

HISTORY

Historically, there are also ramifications to this particular belief. First, we have to recognize that because they were willing to contend for the truth while contextualizing the truth, in the early church, the news of Jesus spread and the church continued to expand in size, numbers, influence and locations. This continued with such veracity that it was necessary for early theologians like Paul and others to write what the scriptures call *"general epistles"* to entire groups of churches scattered across the Asian and African peninsulas.

Paul and others functioned in an apostolic manner to guide and direct a number of churches. Paul functioned in the "office" of an apostle starting new churches while guiding and directing existing churches towards greater effectiveness. In addition, historically there have always been regional networks of churches in the New Testament.

Each church had persons that were assigned to shepherd and care for the congregation; had its own schedule of meetings and gatherings; had its own style and approach to the work of the ministry, but they networked together out of love and unity to have a greater impact on their culture and community.

For example, in 1 Peter 1, we are informed that he is writing to *"churches scattered throughout Pontus, Galatia, Cappadocia, Asia and Bithynia."* From this, we can easily derive that the church is to be networked together across geographic distance.

Furthermore, over time the church saw movements; networks and denominations emerge from this practice that were also linked together in the work of expanding and demonstrating the work of Christ in the world.

This practice continued throughout the history of the church onto the North American continent where the Methodist circuit riders had influence over a wide geographic area. Methodist circuit riders tended to be in their 20's and riding horseback; they would literally go from town to town preaching the gospel, building churches and expanding the kingdom of God. Yet because of inclement weather and the harsh lifestyle that accompanied this evangelistic practice, the average life expectancy of a circuit rider was just 33 years. The message was faithful, but the method was flawed.

CULTURE

Culturally, there have been and continue to be ongoing technological adaptations made by the leadership and servants of the church so that people could be best served and the message of Jesus could be publicized to the greatest extent possible. Incredibly enough, the average person that attends worship or any type of study group in our churches today sits in a chair or a pew, but for the first 1,000 years of the church's history, there was no seating. Benches were introduced into the life of the church in the thirteenth century; pews as we know them were introduced in the fourteenth century, but did not become popular or common until the fifteenth century.

Consider for a moment that for more than 1,000 years, people stood throughout worship and invariably as seats were added, there were people that complained saying, *"We've never done it this way. We haven't been sitting down. Why do we need to sit down now?"* Perhaps there were some that took the desire to be seated as a sign of compromise or laziness contending that if the people really loved Christ, they wouldn't mind standing up for worship. Yet because of the church's willingness to make this change, more people found worship as an attractive place and were subsequently exposed to the gospel and brought into a relationship with God through Jesus Christ.

In 1361, the first pipe organ was permanently installed in a building and it has transformed the worship experience. This insight came from the realization that the organ was extremely popular in local bars and that people gathered around on a daily basis to sing songs and consume certain beverages that will remain nameless for the purposes of this presentation. It was both a cultural and missiological adaptation for the church to take the organ, bring it into the church, then rewrite the lyrics of many of those bar tunes, effectively turning them into hymns of praise and worship and that's how we got some of the most popular hymns in the Christian tradition.

"Amazing Grace" is an adaptation of a bar tune called, *"O Danny Boy."* Now, as widely accepted and loved as this hymn is in contemporary culture, in the time that it took place, it was highly controversial because it was largely viewed as taking something out of the culture and bringing it into the church.

In 1436, Yohand Guttenberg invented what came to be known as the *"printing press"* and that changed everything. Up until that point, if you wanted a copy of the scriptures or any other literature of a Christian nature, you had to pay for a personally transcribed copy that was very expensive. It was, therefore, very difficult to have these documents available to you, especially if you did not possess extraordinary financial resources. However, when the printing press was created, it enabled books to be mass-produced at considerably less expense. One of the first books he published was the Bible. This single act transformed the Christian movement, helping to under gird much of the Protestant reformation by making books and literature available to those seeking to grow in their faith. Today, very few people would argue that books are a bad thing, but at the time the printing press was invented, it was initially viewed with cynicism and skepticism by many in the church.

Admittedly, when it comes to issues of technology, there are aspects that we must reject and at the same time, aspects that we must receive and redeem for the purposes of the kingdom of God. The printing press could have been used to honor or dishonor God depending on what one chose to publish, but from this example, we get a snapshot of redemption—of the church's eventual willingness to embrace this emerging technology for the purposes of spreading the gospel.

In the late 1800's, concert halls began to be constructed permitting people in mass to come together and hear lectures, concerts and other types of presentations. This was in a time where there were no public address systems, speakers, amplifiers and the like, but these halls were acoustically constructed in such a way that large crowds could still benefit from the presentation and that acoustical adaptation emerging from the culture was one that the church received and redeemed for the benefit of the kingdom of God.

In addition, during the 1800's, electricity became more widely available and with its availability, it created the opportunity for places of worship to be heated, cooled and illumined and thereby becoming more attractive to more people because they were able to gather in comfort despite the weather, gather at a variety of times for worship because now they were not limited to daylight hours.

In 1924, the modern version of the loud speaker was constructed and it was refined in 1958 to fit into a box like we commonly know them today. Today, when we walk into church and see a loud speaker, we think nothing of it, but prior to 1958, that was completely impossible—that means that only in our lifetime has it been possible for the church to benefit from this particular technology.

Now if we contrast the use of loudspeakers and microphones with what happened prior to the introduction of those things, it is a markedly different world. An example of that is the popular evangelist George Whitfield. Whitfield was one of the greatest reforming evangelists to ever preach and he would literally go across the nation preaching in "open air" revivals in huge fields and just to be heard, he would have to scream at the top of his lungs for the entire sermon because his voice was not amplified.

Whitefield preached somewhere in the neighborhood of 18,000 sermons live to approximately 10 million people, and 150 churches were planted from his effort. These numbers are not precise, but it's believed that the largest crowd he ever spoke to in these "open air" revivals without amplification was 30,000 people.

Now, the difficulty with this method is that there were very few people who could do what Whitfield did and second, it was reported that because of the way that he strained his vocal cords; he would literally be spitting up blood after almost every sermon, a sure sign that he was destroying the very voice that God had given him.

Now, compare Whitfield's ministry with that of Billy Graham. Billy Graham benefited from large meeting locations that because of the church's willingness to embrace technological advances had seats, electricity, lighting, heating, cooling and sound amplification. Billy Graham preached live to over 210 million people in 185 countries. In addition, he was able to preach on television well into his 80's to estimated millions of people around the globe, sometimes replaying past crusades so that the word could be heard over and over again: that's the impact of technology redeemed. Because of technology, the work of Billy Graham will continue indefinitely on radio, television and the internet long after he has physically passed off the scene.

In 1895, the first radio signal was sent and when it was, it opened up a whole new venue for human communication. By the early 1900's the human voice began to be transmitted on the airwaves and in the history of the church, this was literally transformational because now a person was no longer required to be physically present in order to hear the gospel.

Today, the airwaves are filled with preaching, teaching, counseling, exhortation and encouragement from the Christian community, all seeking to do what Paul suggested in 1 Corinthians 9 to use all available means to reach all available people at all available times, so that we might win some. The adaptation of film has benefited the church.

Thomas Edison is credited with the creation of the movie projector, he was a Christian and sensing the potential of this creation, he attempted to give the patent to his local church, but they rejected it and refused to receive it because they could not see how it would benefit the church. Yet today, the #1 most watched film in film history is an inexpensive film called, *"Jesus of Nazareth"* that was created by Campus Crusade for Christ and has literally been shown around the globe in multiple languages, enabling an estimated 200 million people to make decisions about Christ.

These are illustrations of believers being faithful to the Great Commission of Christ to go into the entire world and preach the gospel and echoing the sentiment of Paul to use every available means at every available time to reach every available person. That being said, what I find interesting is that today there are more movie screens in churches than there are in movie theaters.

Television is another technological advancement that believers have redeemed. In 1927, the first television as we know it was invented and today, there are twice as many television sets in homes as there are people, not to mention the screens that are now available in cars, phones, planes, buses and countless other places. Everything changed in the 1990's when the internet came into existence.

In 1995, the internet went public and it has absolutely transformed the delivery system for the gospel. The point that I'm driving home here is that theologically, we have a reason and a basis for being flexible with our methods of delivering the gospel, even as we are faithful to the message of the gospel.

Historically, the church has been at times on the leading edge and at other times, on the dragging edge of history and that in most cases, that technology has served to advance the cause of Christ.

Therefore, I conclude that any church that is unwilling to adapt the technology of culture is saying in essence, we do not care about a certain people that speak the language of technology. There are tribes of people that are technologically oriented and their numbers are growing and if we don't have anything to offer them other than the traditional way of doing church, which may work for some, but for others is really what Jesus once called *"old wineskins"*—we make ourselves increasingly irrelevant. Theologically, there is strong evidence for being technologically adaptable. Historically, there is a long precedent of example and culturally, there is an incredible need.

Practically, technology is necessary. Consider that 80% of all churches in America have plateaued. 3,500 churches die and shut their doors every year and yet we have the opportunity to embrace these emerging technologies and redeem them for use in the kingdom of God. Permit me now to discuss some of the joys, dangers and pitfalls of technology and congregational life.

JOYS

Technology has a huge upside for ministry for at least 3 reasons: 1) Its personal, 2) adaptive and 3) contextual. Many people today experience personal relationships differently than those who feel that technology seems impersonal, so rather than discount this as wrong because it's different, we need to understand that there has been a shift in how people experience the "personal."

The use of technology allows for the church's ministry to be done with greater adaptability and speed. While efficiency should not be the sole aim of ministry, using technology better focuses much of the structural and planning conversations that need to take place in any church's life.

In the end, one can certainly deny that there is a change in how people interact today, but I think that is a dangerous stand to take. People exist in the world differently and to ignore that fact is an abdication of our responsibility to be a compelling presence in the world. Alongside the joys, let me highlight the dangers.

DANGERS

There are at least 3 dangers that accompany the increasing use of technology in ministry, they include: 1) Isolation, 2) Anonymity and 3) Exclusion. With the ability to connect to pretty much anyone with a click of a mouse, there is a danger that we can avoid communal interactions and discourse. And while this may be necessary at different points in one's faith life, technology must not be used to create more isolation and individualism.

Sometimes anonymity is contextually appropriate. For the most part, anonymous interactions remove some of the potential relationships that can develop. There's only so far you can get to know the other person when solely using a technological medium without being able to trust that the "real" person is present.

Every community excludes groups based on spoken and unspoken rules and realities. Those that use technology at any level are not immune to this. Exclusions can be because of access, proficiency and/or personal preference, but any ministry-hoping to better integrate technology must be aware of and respond to those places where technology divides. Let me share 3 warnings as well.

WARNINGS

Personality - I often think that technology makes it easier for 'toxic' people to spread their toxicity to more people. While that may be true, the benefits of such access must also be acknowledged. I have found that those who communicate with integrity, compassion and thoughtfulness also have a far-reaching impact. In the end, technology is only the vehicle through which we communicate and interact and, just as in face-to-face communication, our personalities flavor those interactions.

Culture - Not everyone breathes this technological air. Some people are NOT, and WILL NEVER be, comfortable interacting through technologies such as Facebook or Twitter. The best use of technology is built upon the understanding that technological realities are not simply a means and a method, but for many people, it is a way of living and being. Understanding this fact is crucial if any use of technology is to be genuine and effective.

Expectations - Technology will not save your church. Period. If survival is your primary motivation and NOT that your community is yearning for technology to be integrated into congregational life, then don't bother. If you do try to force the use on folks who are not truly interested and able to use the technology, you will be faced with a journey of frustration and resistance.

In the end, no amount of technology; used well or not, amounts to a hill of beans if the congregation does not have an understanding of Christ in their individual and communal life. Having an effective mechanism for communication when the message is indistinguishable only creates confusion and the need for unnecessary explanations. The theological question before jumping in must be "What about our community of faith is worth sharing?" If you can answer that question well, then 75.76% of the journey is complete.

Technology can be intimidating because it changes so quickly, so the best way to think about it is to think about technology like you think about health—it is never something you have, it's always something you are pursuing. Let's dive deeper into ways that technology can help your ministry. Technology has the potential to improve every aspect of your church. With limited resources – time and money alike – you should use technology strategically and where it will have the most impact. Although the challenges may be numerous, there are several areas where technology can be deployed for really significant benefits:

WORSHIP

It is possible to use a variety of different applications to enhance a worship experience; from providing lyrics to songs, text for teaching and preaching, video snippets to illustrate or set up messages; to using digital recording devices to capture audio and video that can be streamed immediately or later to the web or downloaded to mobile devices: the possibilities are only limited by one's creativity.

FINANCE

At a time when all ministries are facing increased scrutiny and a heightened demand for stewardship reporting, technology can help your ministry maintain a high level of accountability. It can also help your ministry efficiently manage budgets and spending, and it can help you access reports that enable informed decision-making.

OPERATIONS

Increasing the efficiency of service delivery; optimizing your volunteers, memberships, and sponsorships; and improving your internal processes are all areas in which technology can and will make a huge difference for your church.

RELATIONSHIPS

Technology can aid in building and strengthen relationships between members. By communicating on a personal level, it engages members and keeps them connected to the church. It's possible to recruit servants, train them, coordinate them and deploy them with the use of the right technology.

We're living in a time of change. We are in the middle of a communications revolution. Social networking is changing and will continue to change the way that we live.

Facebook, MySpace, Twitter, Texting, Skype, Youtube, Skype, Instant Messaging, Live Chat, blogs, podcasts, and electronic communications: the technology for how we stay in touch with each other is undergoing massive change and it offers the church some tremendous opportunities if we are open to it.

The internet is a "virtual campfire" around which we gather to tell our stories. Times have changed, but human needs haven't. Most of us no longer live in close proximity to our "tribe" and consequently, we have evolved new methods of staying in touch and learning from each other. Some nay-bobs decries the "depersonalization of society," but it's important to continue to improve that which connects us across distances and busy schedules.

OUTREACH

At Pentecost, we see the Spirit blowing the disciples out of their comfort zone to go where the people were and there they are given the gifts of speaking in a new way. Ever since then, we've sought new ways to reach out, share the story, and stay connected as the Body of Christ as we gather and as we disperse into the world. Many of these new and emerging technologies empower us to do just that; helping to spasm chasms of separation and isolation to reach people with the redemptive love of Christ. These technologies permit us to speak, create community and share more effectively across the barriers of time, distance, and budget and that is our ultimate mission, mandate and commitment.

Managing Church Growth

Donald Hilliard

Healthy churches are growing churches, but the key factor is how this growth is measured. Contrary to the assumption of many, greater numbers and bigger budgets cannot always measure a healthy, growing church. Healthy church growth is not always, nor is it even primarily, numerical. Because the parking lot is full, and you are welcoming new visitors every week, it does not automatically mean that your church is healthy or that it is growing.

Defining true and healthy church growth entails understanding the proper relationship between qualitative increase, which in the case of the church equates growth to spiritual maturity and quantitative increase, which means both numerical and financial growth. Spiritual growth, numerical growth and financial growth are not the same, nor are they interchangeable. Often but not always, they are related. Spiritual growth in a church may or may not lead to numerical and financial growth, but numerical and financial growth alone will never lead to spiritual growth. Increases in numbers and wealth may make a church bigger, but apart from spiritual growth and relevant outreach, they do not necessarily make a church better.

The Christian church is a local community of baptized believers and followers of Jesus Christ. We are bound together by a common vision, and called to proclaim Christ to a lost world and in His name minister to the needs of the sick, the poor and those who are in need, indeed "*the least of these*." Any group of people that does not function in this manner is not acting as a church, no matter what they may call themselves. One can gather masses of people together, call them the Church and yet not be the Church. One can have a multi-million dollar budget and see no growth. One can carry on dozens of programs and remain ineffective. Again, numbers and dollars alone cannot define healthy church growth.

As a church, are we growing in the grace, wisdom and likeness of Christ? Are we demonstrating on an increasing basis, love, piety, and the fullness of the Spirit of God in our lives? Do we exhibit an ever-expanding knowledge and understanding of the Word of God and sound doctrine? Are we translating our knowledge into compassionate acts of ministry and service to the needy around us? Regrettably, many of us have become so caught up in Church work we have forgotten the God who called us to the work in the first place. This loss of passion has caused too many to descend into preaching a cross-less faith where the focus is too often on personal wealth and abundance, as Dr. Gardner C. Taylor suggests, an "authentic understanding of the Gospel".

Spiritual health is the key factor for any church that desires to experience positive and lasting growth. Numerical and financial growth is only significant to the point in which they relate to and are reflections of the church's overall spiritual health. Spiritually healthy churches usually, but not always, experience numerical increase as a result of the life of the Spirit lived openly, honestly and lovingly among a body of believers. These infectious qualities attract people. Relevant and practical ministry draws in new people and new people bring in new money. Therefore, the church grows financially, as well. (It should be noted that geography has a great deal to do with growth also… "location, location, location" is not just for real estate but churches, as well.)

Unfortunately, the bigger is better mentality in America has left many Christians, including pastors, with an unhealthy or unrealistic expectation of church growth. Of course, every conscientious pastor wants to see his or her church grow. Who among us hasn't harbored a hidden desire to be at the helm of our own "major" ministry or some other church whose growth and success we admire? Realistically, however, not every ministry can or should become "a mega church". Churches do not arise in cookie-cutter fashion, identical in every way no matter their location or specific circumstances.

Nevertheless, unrealistic growth expectations imposed by congregations, denominational leadership or even by individuals' own mistaken notions continue to subject many pastors to undue pressure to perform, to demonstrate measurable success in the form of large increases both in members and in tithes and offerings. As a result, an increasing number of pastors are becoming seriously stressed. Some burn out or become depressed because they have been unable to tap into the mega church experience for themselves and the churches they serve.

When it comes to church growth, size is not everything! It is not even the most important thing. The mega church phenomenon is just that – a phenomenon. Dr. Robert Franklin, in his book, Crisis in The Village says, *"Today's mega churches are products of the traditional black church and are beginning to expand and redefine that tradition. Congregations with thousands of members have social, political and economic power that is unprecedented in Black Church history. Unfortunately, a cleavage between the tradition and these innovators has emerged."* Franklin also says, *"Black Churches have been therapeutic institutions fostering a culture of psychological freedom, mental health and self-esteem. Churches promoted a sense of personal pride and value along with the ego strength necessary to face daily assaults on their self worth and dignity. In black churches, everyone could attain status, hold office, wear a title, have responsibility and be affirmed for their contribution. Insiders amusingly observe that there are often more titles than actual jobs to be done. But everyone feels important and that goes a long way when you're trying to nurture personal responsibility, power and moral agency."*

Just because a Pastor labors faithfully for years in a church without seeing much numerical or financial increase does not mean he or she has failed. Neither does it call into question a pastor's calling, commitment or anointing. Jesus Christ is the head of His body, the Church. As the head of the Church, Jesus has a specific will for each body of believers, one that varies from body to body. While the basic commission of the Church is universal- to make disciples of all nations and baptize them in the name of the Father, Son and Holy Spirit (Matthew 28:19), the specific approach to fulfilling that commission varies from one local Church body to the next.

The reasons for this are simple: No two local church fellowships are exactly alike, and Jesus equips each church for its' specific assignment. This is why it is extremely important as pastors to discern the will of God for your own church. One of the greatest dangers to church growth and church health occurs when a church compares itself with another church and ends up feeling invalid and inadequate because it may not measure up to that other ministry church in terms of membership, financial resources or varieties and types of ministries offered. What is right for one church may not be right for yours. You may be called of God to pastor a small congregation, which is just as high and great a calling as the call to lead the largest mega church. The call is the same; only your specific assignment differs. The key is to know and do the will of God for your church. Follow His lead and not your own ambitions. If you follow God's will, there is no reason to become stressed or depressed by lack of financial and numerical growth. You can believe that God will bring the increase in the right time and in the right manner. Always remember it is the Lord's church!!

Understanding Your Motivation For Growth

Motivation is a key factor in determining whether or not a church will experience healthy growth. Our appearance conscious culture tends to focus on externals only, and many churches have fallen into the same trap. God takes a different perspective. He is more concerned with the issues of the human heart. Churches grow when our heart and reason for desiring to grow is right.

The key to managing church growth is first having the right intentions for desiring growth. I contend that too much growth too soon is manifested when you are no longer able to **effectively engage** with your congregation. You know that you have grown too large when there are more areas that look nothing like what you intended and evidence of your spirit in them cannot be found. Here is where you, a shepherd, must stop and reflect on what your motives may have been for specific areas. When you find yourself delegating so much that very little of the ministry reflects your leadership style or your spirit, perhaps you have grown too large, too soon.

Another sign of too much growth occurs when **connection** is lacking with both those inside and outside the Church. As Church people and believers, we must have solid ongoing connections with one another. We must be deliberate about developing and maintaining connections so that everyone feels they have a place to "plug in". People need to feel connected, to feel like more than a number, they need to feel useful; they need to feel that they have a part to play, something of value to contribute. In a growing church it becomes easy for gifts, anointing and talent to get lost in the multitude. Once your church gets to the level where you are able to hire paid staff for certain things like housekeeping, administration, etc., often the mindset becomes, "The staff will do everything the Church needs done" This is dangerous! As a result, volunteerism within the mega-church can hit an all time low. For this reason, it is important for the church to have a well-organized network of people to find their niche. When this is no longer possible, either the church has grown too large or there needs to be an adjustment in the manner the growth of the church is being managed.

In order to manage church growth, you will need to add supporting staff. However, you must make sure that the supporting staff, Pastors, Elders, Ministers, Deacons and even employees, are just as excited about the vision of God and the ministry as you are. As churches grow, the spectrum of people who flock to them broadens. In essence, you never know what you are going to get. People appear wonderful and you may consider them for leadership but often they are only drawn to your growing church because they feel it will catapult them to the next level. It can become the place to be rather than the place to grow.

Growing churches are often used as stepping-stones. For this reason you must not be impulsive when it comes to choosing leaders in a growing church. All church leaders must be trained and well versed in the vision of your house. They must also be enthusiastic servants of God and enthusiastic worshippers. This includes the worship leaders, Sunday school teachers, youth leaders and workers, anyone who has any leadership roles in the church. With a larger congregation, you may have more leaders, thus making it difficult to get everyone in the same place at the same time. You may need to employ online video conferencing, e-mail or telephone conference calling in order to impart to all of your leaders at one time. Managing church growth requires one to step outside of the box and take risks. You must be willing to do things a little differently than when you have 50 to 100 members.

One indicator of healthy growth is whether a church has learned the importance of a unified approach in everything it does. All aspects of a healthy church's work, message and ministry must be designed to coordinate with the church's clearly defined mission and vision.

The growing church in the post-modern era has to fight the urge to be drawn to "the next big thing." While we want to be relevant to the culture and community, everything is not in line with the God-given mission and vision of your particular church. It is amazing how many churches start off well but get caught up in programs and campaigns that ultimately are at cross purposes with their vision. Eventually, they lose sight of these fundamental principles and end up completely off track. The growing church recognizes the self-defeating nature of irrelevant or contradictory programs and has learned to stay on task by measuring each ministry and program against the identified mission and vision of the church. Our executive pastor at Cathedral International, Dr. Bernadette Glover-Williams, refers to this as, "leading and judging with a steady hand."

Ministry AND Entrepreneurship

Anthony G. Maclin

Ten million dollars came to my congregation's neighborhood this past weekend. In fact, an estimated $120 million will come into my congregation's neighborhood over the next twelve weeks of this beautiful fall season. Remarkably, this is happening during the worst economic recession that this nation has seen in my nearly 50-year lifetime. We are currently faced with an unemployment rate that threatens to reach 10%; home foreclosure rates in my county are among the highest in the state of Maryland, and arguably the country; small business shut-down rates continue to skyrocket; and yet – over a 12-week period, $120 million will come through my congregation's neighborhood during the Fall season of this year – very little of it will stay in our communities.

FedEx Field, home of the Washington Redskins National Football League Franchise, is located less than 2 miles from my church. Central Avenue (one of the major access routes to the stadium) runs directly in front of our door. The stadium seats 90,000 people and is sold out through the end of the football season. There are 2 pre-season games and 8 regular season games. There are also at least 2 additional events held there throughout the year -- mainly concerts with nationally known super star artists and maybe some other type of major sporting event. If you total the 12 events held yearly plus the cost of parking and concessions, I conservatively estimate that $120 million comes to the Fed-ex Field venue on an annual basis. For our community the saddest, most horrifying truth is that - very little of that $120 million is going to re-circulate into the neighborhood where my church is located. I have observed during these periods of increased visitation to our county by National Football League enthusiasts that there are no lines at the McDonalds Restaurant, certainly there is no congestion at the gas stations in the area, The International House of Pancake (IHOP) located in the Kingdom Square Mall has no lines or waiting lists, and there is not an increase in business at other neighborhood restaurants and most certainly not an increase in the church attendance. No positive economic gain to neighborhood businesses or the church's offering plate...just 90,000 people using our roads, riding our subway system, creating additional traffic and increasing the carbon footprint in our county.

In other words, during the Fall season of this year, 90,000 people will be enjoying a wonderful afternoon in our backyard (Landover, Maryland) without making any noticeable "positive" impact on the local economy in our community in which we live, work, pray and play. Couple this truth with the existence of Fed-ex Field an attractive venue for sports and sports related economic enterprises, there are very few business in our community, if any, that can carry the designation of being a first rate retail establishment of any type in such a prosperous environment as Prince George's County. As comedian Chris Rock often says, *"That Ain't Right"*.

Having pastored for over 23 years, I continually "kick" myself when I recall all of the meetings I attended and the time I invested engaging in arguments about whether the church should or should not engage itself in the "Economic Commerce" of the society where we are ministers. We have debated about everything from the selling of food (fried chicken, bake sales) or even placing Pepsi and Coca Cola machines on the church facilities to whether or not we should spend the Lord's money on retreats, conferences, banquets, etc., only to leave those meetings and go to a local eatery with church members and spend money while dining there.

Who can forget the age old scriptural argument found in Matthew's Gospel Chapter 21, verses 12-13: "[12]And Jesus went into the temple of God and cast out all them that sold and bought in the temple, and overthrew the tables of the moneychangers and the seats of those who sold doves, [13] And He said unto them, it is written, why MY HOUSE SHALL BE CALLED THE HOUSE OF PRAYER; but ye have made it a DEN OF THIEVES."

Most of us have engaged in the arguments, never fully realizing until recent times that many of our church members are dependent on the small business entrepreneurial mindset in order to feed their families, educate their children, provide for their needs and most of all in order to support our church ministries through "Tithes and Offerings".

I contend that most of us have learned during this recent season of difficulty that one of the last major "Spiritual Strongholds" that the church must face and conquer is the stronghold of economics. One of the ways that we can do this is by identifying the heretofore invisible connection between Ministry and Entrepreneurship.

Most of us would agree that after years of Biblical research and interpretation what Jesus did on that day was not an admonition against the church participating in Economic Development and promoting Entrepreneurship. Many of the things that were being bought and sold in the Temple were things vital for worship (sacrificial offerings), but not convenient for those who had traveled from long distances to bring with them.

It is my belief that Jesus was condemning the dishonesty that was rampant among the merchants while at the same time commanding that there be a compartmentalization that kept merchandising away from worship.

It is from that belief that I caution, as laws will also verify, that any of a ministry's efforts towards entrepreneurship must and should be kept separate and distinct from the church's legal mandate as a 501(c) 3 institution and its spiritual mandate as a house of worship, prayer and instruction for all of God's people.

Every Church that desires to keep current with these economic times has had to engage in a series of teachings in these past two years in order to instruct its members how to survive these difficult financial times. Messages covering topics about debt reduction, credit counseling, savings strategies, foreclosure prevention as well as other topics have suddenly been cast on the church's plate as major issues of the day. Not only are we now engaged in the battle to save souls, families, and marriages, we are now finding ourselves thrust into the battle to save homes, businesses, schools and yes, even some churches!! Perhaps we are now being confronted with an issue that is just as pressing as abortion, health care, same sex marriage and the like.

As many of us will agree, the time has come for the church to take on the issues of Ministry and Entrepreneurship.

Ministry has traditionally been defined as:

(1) The office duties or functions of one who serves

(2) An agency that is instrumental in providing government or leadership in a certain area or arena of life.

(3) Effort(s) that serve to provide vision, instruction and direction in a particular God given calling of life.

I prefer to define Ministry as an act of spiritual empowerment that creates and/or enhances one's relationship with God through a series of teachings and efforts toward a common goal.

An Entrepreneur is defined as:

(1) One who organizes, manages and assumes the risk of a business or enterprise

I personally define an Entrepreneur as one who devises, develops and directs resources in an effort to turn dreams and vision into an economic experience that motivates a revolution of reality.
The Bible is full of examples of personalities who engaged in what we now come to see as Entrepreneurship. Among them are:

Cain & Abel - Genesis 4:1-8
The first entrepreneurs noted in the Bible are Cain and Abel. Cain is highlighted as being a tiller of the soil. His brother, Abel, is noted as a livestock farmer. In fact, there are some who contend that it is the spirit of entrepreneurial competition that eventually leads to the collapse of their brotherly relationship, all for the sake of entrepreneurial acceptance and gain.

The entrepreneurial enterprise of farming was the practice of several well known biblical characters. Among them are Noah, Elisha, David, Solomon and Uzziah.

Zebedee – Matthew 4:19-20; Mark 1:19-20
Zebedee was a well to do fisherman who lived with his wife, Salome and was the father of James and John (two of Jesus' Disciples). We get a brief glimpse of him with his sons in their boat mending their nets. Research shows that the business impacted Bethsaida where they more than likely lived and the region of the Sea of Galilee where he practiced his business.

It is implied in Mark's Gospel that Zebedee's business was successful enough to precipitate his having employees (hired servants).

Lydia – Acts 16:13-15
Lydia was a successful seller of purple garments (fabric store owner) for which her city Thyatira was well known. Biblical research shows that she was a homeowner and a small business employer (she had workers). She is often regarded as being one of Paul's first converts in Europe.

Jesus of Nazareth
Jesus of Nazareth was perhaps the greatest entrepreneur of all time. He identifies 12 men of various backgrounds and enrolls them in a three-year intensive program of teaching and training that has become the greatest Faith Enterprise movement this world has ever known. It's been going strong for over two thousand years. His Faith Enterprise has billions of converts worldwide and is predicted to stay strong, outlasting any world event until time end and eternity begins.

Entrepreneurial enterprise is not that difficult to come by. There are opportunities for extended enterprise all around us. As Vice President of the Collective Banking Group of Prince George's County, Maryland and Vicinity, one of our visionary goals is to aid the African-American Church in the development of efforts towards economic development and business enterprise.

Among these ideas and opportunities are: Barbershops, Bakeries, Towing Companies, Shuttle Services, Mall Ownership and Management, Landscaping and Seasonal Decorating Contractors, Health Wellness and Fitness Centers, Day Care Ownership and Operators, Photography Studios, Limousine Companies, Florist and Gift Shop Ownership, Information Technology Services Hair Salons, Restaurants, Transportation, Automotive Repair, Bookstores, Home Improvement Contractors, Day Spas, Dance Studios, Security Companies, Funeral Homes and Services, Travel Agencies, Law Offices, Dental, Medical, Clothing Stores, Hotel and Motels, Retreat and Conference Center Ownership and Management.

These and other entrepreneurial enterprises currently operate in many of our communities, employ many of our members and have the potential to positively impact the socio-economic culture of an entire generation. Many leaders of our day, including our current president, have concluded that small business and entrepreneurial enterprise are major players in the economic recovery of our nation. So much so that the Presidential directives are now being made to include these small business and entrepreneurial interests in the 2009 American Recovery and Investment Act.

The opportunities that now exist to franchise in several business arenas have now made available countless initiatives that have not existed in the past. The church can and must develop strategies to avail itself as a leader in the community of the many existing opportunities. Never mind the age old argument that by taking governmental subsidies and state loans the church runs the risk of muting its voice as the moral and spiritual conscience of this nation. I contend that by not actively participating in faith based initiatives, the church will eventually be forced into silence by its inability to understand the golden rule of wealth in this Nation "He who has the gold, makes the rules."

Dr. Kirbyjon Caldwell, in his work with Walt Kullestad and Paul Sorensen entitled "Entrepreneurial Faith: Launching Bold Initiatives to Expand God's Kingdom", states that there are four driving forces that will distinguish entrepreneurial ministries from others as you seek to develop an entrepreneurial spirit in your church.

1. The Entrepreneurial Church must be opportunity driven.

2. A lead entrepreneur and a team must drive the Entrepreneurial Church.

3. The Entrepreneurial Church must be stingy with its financial resources.

4. The Entrepreneurial Church must depend on a unified fit and balance between all of its driving forces.

There are indeed many models of entrepreneurial excellence in ministry that can be highlighted across our Nation. Some of them are:

1. The Potter's House Christian Fellowship, Jacksonville, Florida, Bishop Vaughn McLaughlin

2. Faithful Central Baptist Church Ministries, Los Angeles, California, Bishop Kenneth Ulmer

3. Living Word Christian Center, Chicago, Illinois, Pastor William (Bill) Winston

5. The Sanctuary at Kingdom Square, Capitol Heights, Maryland, Pastor Anthony G. Maclin

6. Windsor Village United Methodist Church, Houston, Texas, Pastor Kirbyjon Caldwell
7. The Potter's House, Dallas, Texas, Bishop T.D. Jakes

8. First African Methodist Episcopal Church (F.A.M.E.), Los Angeles, California, Dr. John Hunter

9. New Birth Missionary Baptist Church, Atlanta, Georgia, Bishop Eddie Long

While this list is by no means exhaustive, it does provide a clear glimpse into the types of opportunities that are available and experiences that can be afforded through developing a ministry with a mind towards entrepreneurship. These ministries among others have exhibited the ability to successfully participate in the arena of entrepreneurship while at the same time maintaining their voice as a mouthpiece for socio-economic justice for its people. With the advent of many firms that specialize in accounting, legal advice, corporate and church laws, there is no longer a need to fear confusion about the church's missions as long as these and other specialists are utilized to the full focus of keeping "All things decent and in order."

The Entrepreneurial Spirit

I believe one of the present untapped resources many churches have is "Land." I remember in early real estate investment courses being advised to "Buy land because God is not making any more of it."

Throughout Biblical history many of the wars and conflicts were land related. The same still rings true today. If a church or its members have land resources, you are well on your way to linking Ministry and Entrepreneurship. Listen to the lesson of Acts 4:32-37:

"[32] *And the multitude of them that believed were of one heart and of one soul; neither said any of them ought of the things which we possessed was his own; but they had all things in common.*[33] *And with great power gave the apostles witness of the resurrection of the lord Jesus: and great grace was upon them all.*[34] *Neither was there any among them that lacked: for as many as were possessors of lands or houses sold them, and brought the prices of the things that were sold,* [35] *They laid them down at the apostles' feet: and distribution was made unto every man according as he had need.*[36] *And Barnabas (the son of consolation), a Levite and of the country of Cyprus,*[37] *Having land, sold it and brought the money, and laid it at the apostles' feet."*

Please do not misinterpret the text. This is not an admonition to sell your land as much as it is an admonition to develop your land, revitalize your city, create business opportunities and recycle the wealth resources of your congregation. The end result is that the dollar in your church community will do what it is said to do in the Jewish communities — it recycles itself as much as 7 times before it leaves the community.

Unfortunately, the same cannot be said in the African-American community. In many cases, the maximum number of hands in our community that touches our dollar is somewhere between 1 to 2 times before it leaves, never to be seen again.

The Church: The Center of Economic Influence for the Community

Whether you pastor a congregation of 300 or 3,000 on a weekly basis, you have a captive audience; a core group of people gathered for a purpose that can serve as a center of influence for the community that you serve. For the most part when Pastors and church leaders talk, people listen. It's the E. F. Hutton law at work in the church.

Politicians realized this long ago. That is why they appear before your congregation during seasons of election to try to solicit votes. How can we successfully teach our people Biblical standards of stewardship without including some discussion about the direction in which the "Steward Steers the Ship?"

We must begin to engage our congregations in conversations that:

- Encourage the **planting** of faith-based businesses
- Encourage the **proper management** of faith-based businesses
- Encourage our members to **patronize** our faith-based businesses – we must lead by example
- Encourage our faith-based businesses to **employ** people from our congregations and our communities
- Teach our people the biblical mandate and value of **sowing tithes and offerings into the local church**

The Possibility of Partnerships

All across America there is an increasing number of national "Chain Stores" that have expressed their willingness to enter into dialogue with various faith-based organizations about establishing "partnerships" and offering "franchising" opportunities for the purposes of economic and entrepreneurial development.

Among them are: The McDonalds Corporation, Subway Sandwich Shops, Church's Chicken, Quiznos Sandwich Shops, Papa John's Pizza, Edible Arrangements, Denny's Restaurants, Burger King, Hotel Chains, Grocery Chains

Other opportunities may become available in your particular area. It is wise to monitor the daily business news in your town to stay abreast of business openings and closings that affect your area.

The International Council of Shopping Centers (ICSC) hosts national as well as regional retail trade events that highlight trends, opportunities for expansion of retail businesses as well as franchise opportunities in your area.

You may also consider entering into a "land lease" contract whereby the church or its economic development corporation (or other) designated entity leases its vacant and/or unused land to a particular corporation so that it might locate a specific business on that site.

Another option is to consider the acquisition of various businesses that are "struggling for survival". Sometimes it's just a matter of an injection of people or financial capital that could determine the success or failure of a business. Please beware of over inflated business projections and ill-advised business uses. It is wise to have your economic development team thoroughly research all of the pros and cons of such a transaction. Also, a well-formulated business plan that details just how you intend to revitalize the business and infuse it for a possible turnaround is essential. Be sure to research other time-tested businesses in your community for their best practices.

Be mindful of the potential impact of the proposed "business" on the church's operation and on the community as a whole.

Entrepreneurship and Biblical Teaching

One does not have to go far before he/she encounters the presence of the Entrepreneur in the Bible. Listen to this parable that Jesus speaks in Luke 19:11-27 for the sake of brevity. I will only highlight verses 11-13:

"[11] And as they heard these things he added and spake a parable, because he was nigh to Jerusalem and because they thought that the kingdom of God should immediately appear.[12] He said therefore a certain nobleman went into a far country to receive for himself a kingdom and to return.[13] And he called his ten servants and delivered them ten pounds and said, Occupy till I come."

The widely accepted interpretation of the word "Occupy" means to "Engage in Business." Jesus makes a clear-cut statement about "Business" and "Entrepreneurship". In fact, he later highlights the rewards given to those who are successful in business trading and the punishments meted out to those who refused to do as was commanded. Jesus also uses this parable of business in this passage to illustrate the urgency and necessity of promoting the Gospel.

In Luke 8:4-8, there is an admonition to business enterprise. It highlights the perils of sowing but it also emphasizes the success that can be experienced if only 25% of your sowing efforts pay off.

"[4] And when much people were gathered together, and were come to him out of every city, he spoke this parable: [5] A sower went out to sow his seed; and as he sowed, some fell by the way side; it was trodden down, and the fowls of the air devoured it.[6] And some fell upon a rock and as soon as it sprung up it withered away, because it lacked moisture.[7] And some fell among the thorns; and the thorns sprung up with it and chocked it.[8] And other fell on good ground, and sprung up, and bare fruit an hundredfold. And when he had said these things, he cried, He that hath ears to hear, let him hear."

We fully understand and appreciate this parable because it reminds us if you sow sparingly you will reap sparingly. But if you sow bountifully you will reap bountifully. My advice for any ministry that has a vision for entrepreneurial enterprise is to proceed with caution while at the same time act with the intention of being successful.

For many years, there has been reluctance on the part of many churches and pastors to engage in entrepreneurial efforts. In my opinion, many times it is due to a narrow and often conservative interpretation of scripture. However, once scriptural revelation begins to open itself to the full potential of the church, especially in this post modern society, one can easily see the profound impact that ministry and entrepreneurship can have when blended together to meet the needs of this current society.

Take for example the scripture found in Acts Chapter 6 from which we see the first evidence of difficulty in the New Testament Church. Most scholars agree that it was due to cultural diversity that left some widows feeling neglected in the daily administration of the church. The twelve Apostles after gathering the disciples of the church agreed that it would be unreasonable for the Apostles to leave the word of God to give particular attention to this aspect of ministry. They validate its importance by assigning seven men of high character and qualifications. They were to be men of honest report, full of the Holy Spirit and possessing wisdom. These men were to be appointed over this "Business" while the Apostles gave themselves continually to prayer and the ministry of the Word.

It is highly remarkable that the Apostles did not minimize the importance of the ministry of serving tables. Instead it can be strongly argued that they saw it as a separate and distinct enterprise and business aspect of the church that needed the care and attention of highly trained and uniquely qualified individuals within the ministry. It is from this position of wanting to make sure that this aspect of ministry business was fully carried out to the strength and advantage of the church that this office/enterprise called Deacon was introduced.

In fact, many biblical scholars would agree that the Apostle Paul infamous "uproar at Ephesus" comes about as a result of ministry that challenged the economic livelihood of the silversmiths and craftsmen who made their living making shrines to the Goddess Diana (Acts 19:21-41). It is not until the town clerk speaks up that the mob is finally quieted and dispersed and Paul and his companions barely escape with their lives.

The Issue Of Recycling The Wealth

I contend that the influence of the entrepreneurial spirit can best be seen as it impacts the life of Nehemiah (an officer in the cabinet of King Artaxerxes) who while on "vacation" in Jerusalem, experienced an overwhelming urge to do something to rebuild the broken down wall that surrounded the city. Nehemiah engages in a community revitalization project and in the midst of external opposition, was able to complete the project in the record time of fifty-two days.

His courageous story, found in the biblical book that bears his name, has long since been the inspiration for many pastors and congregations who have taken on building projects and stewardship programs of all shapes, sizes and proportions.
Nehemiah 2:17-18 (KJV) *"[17] Then I said to them, ye see the distress that we are in how Jerusalem lieth waste, and the gates thereof are burned with fire: come, and let us build up the wall of Jerusalem, that we be no more a reproach.[18] Then I told them of the hand of my God which was good upon me; as also the king's words that he had spoken unto me. And they said, let us rise up and build. So they strengthened their hands for this good work."*

The combined efforts of inspired visionary leaders along with the committed support of congregations who agree to pool their resources have risen to great levels of faith that have empowered people to change paradigms through initiatives that are often faith based.

This type of initiative that gives rise to ministries that begin to operate in the mindset and spirit of entrepreneurship has begun to require different labels of identity. These new labels are defining this rising tide of Economic Empowerment, which has been birthed through church ministries across this nation. The title "Pastorprenuer" is now becoming a common title as it is used to define strong congregational leaders who nurture a spirit of church and entrepreneurship involvement and successfully marries ministry to a mindset of marshalling resources in order to influence commerce in their particular community and city.

It is because of this spirit that I believe a sleeping giant has been awakened.

- One that finds its Genesis in the likes of Noah, the ark making/zoo keeping entrepreneur (Genesis)

- In Solomon, the entrepreneur of temple design and sacred worship place construction (Kings)

- In Jacob the well digging entrepreneur (Genesis)

- In King Uzziah, the entrepreneur of underground water works and sewage disposal system.

- In modern day heroes like Dr. Floyd Flake and the Greater Allen A.M.E. Cathedral of Jamaica Queens, N.Y., where millions of dollars have been used in the redevelopment of the communities that surround the church, and has evolved into a major employer of people, and creator of job and housing opportunities in New York.

- Other modern day heroes like Bishop T. D. Jakes of Dallas, Texas, who, while in West Virginia, took a bible study for women and evolved it into a Women's Conference that grew into national prominence. From this lone event a book and stage play were written which led to the creation of a screenplay for a movie that evolved into a multi-picture deal with Sony Enterprises.

- Like modern day heroes Paul and Jan Crouch whose life ministry call has grown into the great entrepreneurial effort of the Trinity Broadcasting Network (T.B.N.) through which we now have Christian Television Broadcasting around the world.

I thank God for the passion He is perfecting in pastors across the nation and people around the world who have caught the vision and are utilizing their ministry gifts as developers, housing counselors, business incubators, community revitalization experts, television broadcast executives, health care providers, senior and active adult community coordinators and the multitude of increasing entrepreneurial ministry efforts that are being birthed.

So be bold, be courageous, be proud and always remember, *"The gifts and the calling of God are without repentance"* Romans 11:29

THINGS TO CONSIDER FOR ENTREPRENEURIAL MINISTRY

(1) Provide goods and services by opening businesses to serve those who are a part of your congregation, your community and your county.

(2) Focus on recycling wealth, reclaiming legacy, and revitalizing communities.

(3) Remember that church people do not go to "Mars" on Sunday Evening. We go out to restaurants. We eat soul food. We buy gasoline. We get our hair done. We shop for personal goods. We engage in entertainment. We are major consumers.

(4) Question yourself daily: How much of the disposable income that my congregation spends is being spent in our community?

(5) Learn to be a good steward, not only over what you spend, but also over where you spend it.

(6) Demand equal reinvestment in our communities for every dollar we invest/spend with national retailers and institutions.

(7) Make sure that we mind (pay attention to) our own business(es).

(8) Don't just focus on controlling crime in our communities. Realize that one of the greatest crimes in our communities is our failure to control commerce. If we monitored the speed at which a dollar leaves our community like we monitor the membership attrition rate, we would indeed be outraged.

(9) Start seeing yourself and your ministry as being above and not beneath. The head and not the tail. The lender and not the borrower.

(10) Focus on serving your people not just on Sunday and "spiritual things" but also throughout the week in "practical things."

I offer basic definitions of various entities that are available that might be a source of direction as you pursue your vision of "doing church." As always, I strongly advise that you solicit the professional help of trained and certified experts in these fields.

COMMUNITY DEVELOPMENT CORPORATION (CDC)
Among the major purposes for organizing a CDC are:

(1) To organize, conduct and/or operate educational, charitable cultural and/or other programs designed to alleviate urban depreciation and to promote the social welfare through programs and activities that qualify under the tax exempt section or the 501(c)(3) Internal Revenue Code.

(2) To organize, conduct or operate social, employment, community development and/or job opportunity programs for economically disadvantaged people.

(3) To expand opportunities for disadvantaged businesses and persons to own, operate and manage enterprises in economically depressed areas.

(4) To make low income housing available to economically disadvantaged persons.

(5) To operate, manage and/or own Assisted Care Housing Units and/or Nursing Facilities.

(6) To engage in any lawful purpose and businesses allowed to a tax exempt organization.

COMMUNITY DEVELOPMENT ENTITY (CDE)
A CDE is a partnership or corporation that acts as an intermediary vehicle for the provision of loans investments and/or financial counseling in low-income communities. Among the benefits of being a certified CDE is the ability to apply to the CDFI Fund to receive New Markets Tax Credits (NMTC), allocations to offer its investors in exchange for equity investments in the CDE and/or its subsidiaries and to receive loans or investments from other CDEs that have received NMTC Allocations.

COMMUNITY DEVELOPMENT FINANCIAL INSTITUTION (CDFI)
The CDFI Fund under the U.S. Department of Treasury seeks to expand the capacity of financial institutions to provide credit, capital and financial services to underserved populations and communities by providing monetary awards to certified CDFIs to help them to build capacity through (1) providing affordable and appropriate financial products and services that positively impact the low income communities they serve (2) being a viable financial institution (3) using and leveraging CDFI fund award dollars effectively. For more info go to www.cdfifund.gov/what_we_do

ECONOMIC DEVELOPMENT CORPORATION (EDC)
Economic Development Corporations are usually 501(c) 3 non-profit organizations that operate under the mission to promote the economic welfare and development of a particular geographical region or area.

LIMITED LIABILITY CORPORATIONS (LLC)
The Limited Liability Corporation is a type of company authorized in certain states, whose owners and managers are permitted to operate while experiencing limited liability and the tax benefits of a subchapter S Corporation without having to confirm to the S Corporation restrictions. Though it bears common similarities to both, it is neither a corporation nor a partnership. The owners are classified as a member and can pass along to the owners, the company's profits, as well as its losses while at the same time protecting its owners from any personal liability from the business debts. Having this type of structure enables the company to operate with greater flexibility and/or ease of managing.

COMMUNITY HOUSING DEVELOPMENT ORGANIZATION (CHDO)
The Housing Development Division, in many states, provides financial and technical assistance to CHDOs for the acquisition and/or rehabilitation of rental housing, new construction of rental housing, acquisition and/or rehabilitation of homebuyer properties, new construction of homebuyer properties and direct financial assistance to purchasers of HOME Assisted Housing sponsored or developed by a CHDO with Home Funds.

Balancing Pastoral Priorities and the Social Justice Agenda

Reginald T. Jackson

More than anyone else, I find my ministry more and more modeling that of Jeremiah, the son of Hilkiah, from the city of Anathoth. In the Old Testament book that bears his name, we get a glimpse of the inner life of this extraordinary servant of God. He had a tumultuous life and ministry. Perhaps his life and ministry would not have been so tumultuous if God had only called him to priestly responsibilities, but God also called him to be a prophet. (Jeremiah 1:5) He made Jeremiah His spokesman, to speak to the powers that be, and the people in His name on issues and matters of that day. Jeremiah is critically important to anyone in the ordained ministry because he reminds us of something very important, and that is that we are called not only to priestly but also prophetic ministry. In this age unfortunately, there are far too many colleagues who are engaged in priestly but not prophetic ministry. There are several reasons for this unfortunate predicament.

First, there are those who do not see "prophetic" ministry or the pursuit of social justice as part of their calling. They are responsive to God's call, but do not see prophetic ministry or social justice as part of that call. There is a legitimate argument to be made that the call to ministry is not always inclusive of a "prophetic" call. The call is solely to pastoral responsibilities. This is particularly the belief as it relates to ministries such as counseling, chaplaincy, etc… However, there is also an argument to be made that even these ministries are inclusive of the responsibility to be the prophetic. Counseling and other ministries require us to speak truth in our interaction with individuals, couples, families, and people in general. Prophetic ministry is not limited to speaking to those in positions of power or public pronouncements; often it is speaking truth in private or behind the scenes.

Second, there are those for whom prophetic ministry and social justice is not important or does not matter. It is not that they have not been called to prophetic ministry but that they ignore this part of their call. Speaking for God on issues of justice that impact the people and communities we are called to serve is not a priority to some. This mindset says that our priority is the "saving of souls" and "winning people for Christ." Much of what we call "social justice; this mindset calls political or secular and is not the concern of the church. Certainly, it is not part of "doing church." It is reminiscent of preachers who during the height of the Civil Rights Movement never preached or spoke out about equality or justice, and never marched or participated in pursuit of rights for Blacks. It's as if, we are not aware of what is going on around us, or even worse, God has said nothing to us to speak to His people. With all that is going on in His world, in our communities and in the lives of His people, God must have something to say, for He does still speak.

Third, there are those who do not speak or act in pursuit of social justice because they are afraid or intimidated. Prophetic ministry requires faith and courage. God when He called Jeremiah said to him, *"Do not be afraid."* (Jeremiah 1:8) Many ministers today are afraid because they are not informed on social justice issues and feel inadequate to speak about them, fear being in the public arena, particularly dealing with the media, or are intimidated by the powers that be and the possible consequences of their speaking out or taking action. This fear and intimidation are very real and the consequences can be hurtful and embarrassing, not only to the minister, but also to his/her family and even the church, particularly if the minister has anything in his/her life which can be exposed.

Fourth, prophetic ministry can make the minister controversial, and for the most part ministers don't like to be controversial. When many see The Rev.'s Jesse Jackson and Al Sharpton, we think of controversial ministers. This is because the media has defined them that way. Truthfully, being prophetic doesn't usually get you in the headlines or on the television. Usually, we speak to local situations that don't cause headlines, but there are times when situations and crises occur that thrust the minister into the headlines and into controversy, but if the minister operates in integrity and doesn't seek to promote him/her self, the crisis and the controversy will pass. Our motivation must always be to speak or act on God's behalf to the situation at hand. It is never about us and we must be careful to always speak and act within God's will to accomplish that end.

Cause for Alarm

We should be alarmed by a seemingly increasing reluctance on the part of the Black Church today to engage in social justice issues. This reluctance is a contradiction of the historic role that the Black Church has played in the forward march of blacks in this country. There is nothing for the progress of Blacks in this country where the Black preacher and the Black Church have not led or played a major role, from the Free African Societies led by Richard Allen and Absalom Jones, the Underground Railroad, founding of the NAACP to the Civil Rights Movement. The Black preacher, in particular, has been the champion of social justice, serving as both the "watchman" and "trumpet" for the people, speaking for those who have no one to speak for them and fighting for those who have no one to fight for them. They organized community meetings, used God's Word to stake out the position on the issue and then led rallies and marches to city hall, boards of education, downtown or wherever they had to go. History books are full of the names and stories of Black Preachers who played prominent roles in the struggle for social justice. We recall in our own time the contributions of Martin King, Ralph Abernathy, Hosea Williams, Adam Clayton Powell, Fred Shuttlesworth and others who now from their labors rest. They were pastors, but they were also engaged and provided leadership in the struggle for social justice. They were about "saving souls" but also committed to social justice. We are still reminded of the prophetic words of Martin King who declared, "Peace is not only the absence of tension, it is also the presence of justice."

But where are the voice and the presence of the Black preacher and the Black Church today on a host of social justice issues that impact our people and community and quality of life. For example, presently the nation is engaged in a major and heated debate about healthcare reform. A debate that has polarized the country, deepened the partisan divide in Congress and caused loud and hostile town hall meetings. The problem is those we are hearing from are those who already have healthcare or are benefiting from the present healthcare system. Most of those in this country who do not have healthcare are Blacks and Hispanics. The question is who is speaking for us? Where is the voice and presence of the Black preacher and the Black Church? There is a deafening silence. If the Black Church organized, it could be a major force and have great influence on this issue.

Healthcare reform for the Black Church is not a political but a moral issue. We believe that in the wealthiest nation in the world, that all its citizens should have access to healthcare. In all of the debate over this issue, the moral imperative has not been raised. The Black Church is missing an opportunity to have a major impact in the Lord's name to ensure that every American has health care. Much of the problem with the Black Church's increasing failure to address social justice issues rest with denominational leadership whose first priority is their "smaller denominational world" as opposed to the "larger world" it is called to save and minister to. In fact, Black Church growth would be aided if the church addressed the issues that directly impact the daily lives of people. People both in and out of the church look to their religious leaders to address these issues.

This is why the pastor in the local church is so critically important. He/she is there where the people live and are impacted by what goes on in their communities. Jesus Himself lifts up the critical role of the pastor when He says, "the good Shepherd cares for the sheep." The pastor's motivation to speak and act on issues of social justice is because he/she cares and is impacted by what happens to the sheep who are under his/her care and who live in the community. When the decision is made to close down the inner city hospital, the schools don't provide a quality education, banks don't lend in low income neighborhoods, whenever perceived injustice is afoot, the people look for the "man or woman of God" to help them get justice.

It is important for the pastor not to underestimate or minimize the role that he/she holds. Far too many, pastors don't realize the important position that they hold. You, as the pastor, are a leader in the community where you serve. By virtue of the fact that you are "the pastor," you hold a position of leadership. Too many pastors abdicate this position. As a leader, you should get to know the political, educational, business and other community leaders and be able to interact with them. You are not just the "preacher," you are the pastor. You are the leader of a congregation and you speak to that congregation every week, probably more than anybody in the community. You influence people. Don't ever underestimate or minimize the role that you play as pastor.

A Lot on the Plate

People expect a lot of the pastor. In fact, they expect us to be everything at all times. They expect us to be the preacher, teacher, counselor, troubleshooter, trustee, chief custodian, a lawyer, doctor, and a prophetic agent for social justice. Most pastors are not fortunate enough to be able to deal with pastoral responsibilities; they have to handle the day-to-day affairs of the church, church finances, interact with the church organizations, etc.... It leaves little time for study, sermon preparation and planning. Notice I did not say anything about dealing with social justice issues. This is because social justice issues are not planned; they just come. Injustice is not scheduled; it just shows up, sometimes boldly, at other times subtly. Whenever a social justice issue arises there is always something else we have to do, or need to be doing, even though the cause of justice demands our attention. This is also when we are put to the test. What is our response to the call for social justice? Do we believe social justice is part of our calling? Are we afraid or intimidated? Do we want to stay away from controversy?

Let me assure you the call for social justice will come. Something will happen in your community, some crisis or tragedy that shakes the community, some injustice which has been building for some time and comes to a head, something which happens to a congregant or family in your congregation, whatever it is, it will come. We will either be called upon or we will respond on our own because of the calling on our lives. Whenever or however it comes, it won't be because we don't have anything to do; a pastor always has something to do. Our plate is always full.

It is important for us to note and remember that the powers that be are happy when we are busy with our pastoral responsibilities. They like it if we keep busy with our "in house affairs," performing baptisms and marriages, teaching Bible Study, and meeting with boards and auxiliaries. If we are busy with our pastoral responsibilities, we won't be able to involve ourselves with social justice issues. The education establishment likes us to be busy with pastoral responsibilities so we can't organize and come to board meetings and speak out about the failure of the schools to educate our children, while the schools have become a pipeline to the prisons. The utility commission likes us to be busy with pastoral responsibilities so we cannot come and speak out about utility rate hikes that place an unbearable burden on low-income residents while corporations receive reduced rates in the name of creating a "pro business environment." State legislators would like us to be so busy with pastoral responsibilities that we won't rally and address them about the violence and death caused by guns in our communities, when it is easier to get a gun than it is to get a driver's license. The powers that be don't mind and in fact are pleased if we are so busy with pastoral responsibilities that we can't give leadership and speak out on social justice issues. They want us to stay in our houses of worship and in fact believe that is us "staying in our place."

The Quest for Balance

Ultimately, the question is not pastoral versus social justice, or whether we believe God has called us to "prophetic" or social justice ministry. The ultimate question is whether we are going to be faithful to the call of God upon our lives. We cannot completely separate one from the other. The "saving of souls" is not exclusive from God's demand for social justice in "His" world. I believe this is what Jesus was getting at in the Lord's Prayer when He prayed, "Thy kingdom come, Thy will be done on earth, as it is in heaven." (St. Matthew 6:10) Our prayer and our ministry should be that God's kingdom comes on earth. That will not happen unless justice is done on earth. And those of us in Christian ministry must always look at justice out of the prism of God's Word and God's will.

Just the thought of "kingdom work" can cause us to become overwhelmed because there is so little time and so much to be done. And the question comes, "How then do we do it all; pastoral responsibilities, social justice issues, and what about our family and ourselves?" "Do I hear somebody crying out, "Help me somebody"? Must have been me.

Hear it is, "How do we balance our pastoral responsibilities and the social justice agenda?" This is the question, and if we can find the answer it will save us from what the hymn writer Harry

Fosdick, calls, "weak resignation to the evils we deplore." It will also make our ministries more effective, productive and relevant, and our governments, communities and people more just. While the kingdom will not come on earth as it is in heaven, where we live will become more like heaven and less like hell.

First Things First

Prioritizing is important, and it is critical that a pastor always remember that his/her first priority is the charge to which they have been called or assigned. I constantly remind myself that the primary reason that I am in New Jersey is because I was assigned to pastor St. Matthew AME Church, Orange, New Jersey. There are a number of major boards that I sit on and important positions that I hold, but the reason that I am in New Jersey is because I am the pastor of St. Matthew AME Church, so my number one priority is and must be St. Matthew AME Church. Far too often, our pastorates suffer because we do not treat it as if it is the number one priority.

There will always be things calling for our attention, many of them important and worthy of our time and attention. We must be careful and mindful however that they do not cause us to become needlessly distracted or stray from what our priorities. As pastors, we have a host of responsibilities that are demanding of our time. I have never understood pastors who have a lot of spare time, and I greatly admire my colleagues, who out of necessity, work another job while pastoring a church. Our congregations expect the pastor to be "a jack of all trades." Usually when I attend a conference or meeting and they ask everyone to introduce her or himself I introduce myself as "the chief custodian of St. Matthew Church." Earlier I alluded to everything people expect of the pastor, but the danger is that too many pastors try to live up to all of their expectations and fail to be faithful to the actual responsibilities of a pastor. The consequence is that our churches are stunted and fail to grow and do not meet the needs of the people committed to our care.

Pastors must be mindful that there are some responsibilities on which we cannot compromise; this includes the call of social justice issues. Better yet, they will aid us as we seek to address social justice issues. First and foremost is the responsibility to preach the word. This requires us to spend time in preparation. Saturday night specials do not serve the congregation well and are irrefutable evidence that our priorities are out of order. We've heard people say, "Open your mouth and God will speak for you" but that does not negate the fact that we should speak to God before we seek to speak for God. It takes hours to prepare a sermon and we must prioritize to "make" time for those hours. Many pastors spend little time in sermon preparation. Preaching includes speaking for God on social justice issues. Additionally a pastor must spend time in prayer. How can we pastor without prayer, without talking to God? Our ministries will be weak and ineffective without prayer. There will always be something to distract us from time to pray, but we have to "make" time to pray. I am constantly amazed about the difference prayer made in the life of Jesus. He rose early in the morning and spent hours in prayer and then proceeded to do great things. The more time we spend in prayer the more power our ministries will have. In prayer we also seek and ask God for direction as we make decisions for our lives and ministry. It will save us from seeking to do things on our own.

We must, and I emphasize must, also spend time in studying the Word of God. The Word of God is not only for our preaching, more importantly it is for our living and serves to inform us as we live today. God still speaks to us out of His Word. Amazingly many of the social justice issues we wrestle with today are addressed in God's Word. It is imperative that His Word be the foundation or source for the positions we take on the issues of the day. As advocates for social justice, we are God's ambassadors, we speak for Him and not ourselves. First and foremost we are pastors and have priorities and responsibilities, and it is important that we have our priorities in order if we are going to be effective as pastors and as we seek to be advocates for social justice.

Finding and Maintaining Balance

Having our priorities in order does not make it easy to keep a balance between our pastoral responsibilities and efforts to assure social justice. Sometimes the issue is so large and the circumstances become so overwhelming, we find ourselves saying, "I need to get a life." Such was the case as I became engaged with the racial profiling issue that developed in New Jersey in 1998. It was a struggle finding and maintaining a balance not only between my responsibilities as a pastor and advocate for social justice, but also between my responsibilities as a husband and father. Let me say a word about the racial profiling issue and at the end comment on lessons that I learned from it.

On April 23, 1998, I had preached at St. Matthew Church and later took a train to Dover, Delaware to visit my parents. During the night on the New Jersey Turnpike near Exit 7A, the New Jersey State Police had trailed and then pulled over a vehicle with four young minority males (three African Americans and one Hispanic). Subsequently, three of the males were shot and the driver was charged with speeding and the State police claimed drugs were in the vehicle. On Monday morning, I stopped in Trenton to hold a press conference at the State House (on what issue I don't remember). At the end of the press conference, a reporter asked me about the shooting on the turnpike that I actually had not heard about. Not wanting the press to know that I didn't know about it, I said I didn't have all the information but that we were going to look into it. I serve as Executive Director of the Black Ministers Council of New Jersey which represents about 600 African American churches in New Jersey, and advocates on issues important to African American Community, so often I am asked about issues. But I had no idea, how great an impact this incident would have on my life and ministry.

Collecting information and talking with other sources, we discovered that the information provided by the troopers was false. The car driven by the four men was not speeding and there were no drugs in the car (only a John Steinbeck novel and a

Bible). It turns out that this was another instance of racial profiling, of Black motorist being stopped not because of any motor vehicle or criminal offense, but because of the color of their skin. We call it "driving while Black." Police had denied racial profiling for years even though there was overwhelming evidence to prove it was real. This instance caused tremendous anger among Blacks and the Black Ministers Council and other groups led a campaign to expose it and end it.

This campaign for social justice became a daily and constant presence in my life. Every day, it seemed like there were new developments, reports, press conferences and meetings. There were threats on my life, pressure from a number of sources, criticisms from some who claimed we were pushing too hard, others who said we were not pushing hard enough, political influences that were backing the State Police and others who supported our cause and investigations at both the federal and state level. This went on for three years and I found it dominating my life.

It was difficult finding a balance between my pastoral responsibilities and my efforts to bring about social justice regarding racial profiling. I found myself constantly having to make decisions between my responsibilities as pastor of St. Matthew Church and my efforts to end racial profiling, my time more and more being consumed with this effort. Meetings regarding St. Matthew were juggled around or cancelled in order to accommodate the racial profiling campaign. I found it more difficult to "make" time for sermon preparation, prayer and study because I was being distracted more and more with the racial profiling campaign. It was becoming overwhelming and I felt the strain and weight of the effort to end racial profiling and those who were fighting hard to maintain the status quo. Thanks be to God, the efforts of the Black Ministers Council, Legislative Black Caucus, NAACP and others were successful. The State admitted that racial profiling was "real, not imagined", State Police were put under a consent decree and reforms put in place, legislation passed and signed making racial profiling a crime and putting oversight of State Police under an independent monitor.

In many ways, justice was won. African Americans today can drive the state's interstate highways with little fear of being stopped simply because of the color of their skin.

From the racial profiling struggle and other issues, valuable lessons were learned as it relates to how we balance our pastoral responsibilities and the ongoing struggle for social justice. I lift up these lessons with the hope and prayer that they will guide and give others direction and assistance as you seek to be faithful to the call of God on your life; the call to not only pastoral but prophetic ministry as you advocate and work for social justice.

1. You Can't Fight Every Pharaoh

The struggle for justice is ongoing. There will always be injustice somewhere; there will always be a cause to fight for, but it is not possible to spend all our time fighting and be effective or productive. As a result of the racial profiling struggle, the Black Ministers Council, as an organization, and I, as an individual, have found ourself constantly being called on to fight for some cause or against some perceived evil. If you are committed to social justice, there is a passion and temptation to join in every struggle to fight for thats right. I found myself about to yield to that temptation, but the Lord put a friend and colleague around me at the right time, to save me from myself. I was speaking to him about all the stuff that was going on in New Jersey and I felt the need to address. I was ready to get engaged, but my friend and colleague, Dr. DeForest Soaries, (Pastor, First Baptist Church, Somerset, New Jersey) pulled me to the side, looked me in the eyes and said, "You can't fight every Pharaoh."

I am indebted to my friend and colleague for telling me not what I wanted to hear, but what I needed to hear. It is good advice for me and for every pastor who is committed to social justice. The fact is that we cannot fight every Pharaoh and be an effective pastor or advocate for social justice. What we will actually do is undermine our own efforts and people will begin not to take us seriously. It will be said of us, "they have something to say about everything." We must exercise discretion in choosing which "Pharaoh's" and battles to fight and remain focused on our priority to shepherd the flock we are called or elected to pastor.

2. People Will Use You if You let Them

Another important and painful lesson I learned is, people will use you if you let them. When people discover you are committed and willing to fight for social justice, they will seek you out whenever they feel they are victims of injustice or have been wronged. I have discovered over the last ten years that "everybody with a problem will call you." Some of their problems are genuine and some are not. In some instances, the people have not gone to agencies and places where they can get help or they have not tried to help themselves. Many people have no regard for you they simply care about themselves, and will try to run a guilt trip on you. They are never involved in helping anybody else or any other cause. Particularly disappointing are colleagues who will not get involved in social justice issues, but when one of their congregants has a problem they tell them to call you. If you seek to respond to every call, you will burn yourself out, become ineffective in your pastorate and possibly jeopardize your health. When you are burned out, sick or worse they will find somebody else. It also sends a message to the congregation we pastor that they are not our first priority. We cannot be everything to everybody and still be there for the congregation we pastor. There is no balance when we try to fight every Pharaoh and solve everybody's problem; it is too far tilted in the other direction and the church will be shortchanged.

3. Maintain Independence

When we speak out and advocate for social justice, it will usually bring us into interaction with political and government leaders. We will either be supportive of some policy or action it has taken or at odds with them. Interaction with political leadership should always be taken with caution. Dependent upon how effective you are, the leaders will either seek to isolate and ignore you or they will seek to woo you and win you over. As pastors and social advocates, it is important that we have principles and ethics, that we not practice expediency or allow ourselves to be compromised. The issue or the cause for which we are advocating must always remain paramount. Additionally, we must keep ourselves in a position where we can speak and act without fear of being threatened or found out. Political leaders may also seek to appoint you to something that would give them leverage over you and enable them to dictate or manipulate you. Independence for a minister is critically important. Ministers must be very careful how we respond when political leaders "summon" or call us to meet with them. They must never be allowed to feel that we are beholden to them or that they control us. Independence for a minister must be maintained. Often the minister has to speak for those who have no one to speak for him or her and fight for those who have no one to fight for them. In the mold of Jeremiah and other prophets, we must be free to speak "truth to power."

4. Remember Who and Whose You Are

We will not have balance in our lives or have a fulfilling life or ministry if we do not remember who and whose we are. These words sound simple but their importance is often lost as we become caught up in our work and efforts. When I have found myself becoming overwhelmed with work and causes that I am engaged in, it is because I have lost sight of who I am. I am the pastor; I am the leader of a congregation and have influence in the community and state, but this is not the totality of "who" I am. I am also a husband, a father, a son, a brother and a friend, and all of these are important. I have a life outside of being a pastor and an advocate for social justice. Remembering who I am and the relationships I have help me to keep balance in my life. They cause me to step back, take a break, relax, laugh, and enjoy the simple things in life. Our lives must not be all work. Do not forget who you are and that you matter to special people in your life.

If we are going to have balance in life it is also important for us to remember "whose" we are. We belong to God. We are in the ordained ministry because God "called" us. In the Black Church, we believe we are "called" to ministry, not recruited or volunteered. We believe our lives are in His hands and we are fulfilling His purpose for our lives. It is not about us, we are His ambassadors, His spokesman and His servants. This gives us security and confidence as we live and serve Him.

In the End

Whether pastoral responsibilities or social justice causes, in the end, our goal is to have God's will done. As a pastor through preaching, teaching, and ministries, we seek to win and grow people for Christ, to "make disciples." As an advocate for social justice we seek to promote God's kingdom on earth. This was Jesus prayer, "thy kingdom come, thy will be done, on earth as it is in heaven." (St. Matthew 6:10) Both will take our lifetimes. Just as importantly, both require our spiritual, emotional, physical and intellectual investment. In the end, both the pastorate and the cause of justice require faith, courage, sacrifice and much prayer. Just as importantly in the end, both the pastorate and the cause of justice take a toll. How we balance our pastoral responsibilities and the social justice agenda will determine how great a toll they take. Not long ago, I went for my regular doctor's appointment. He wrapped the cuff around my arm and started taking my blood pressure. He looked at me and said "Reverend, your pressure is up." I said to him, "I pastor a

Black Church." I can't imagine any pastor of any church without high blood pressure. Ministry will take a toll.

Balancing pastoral responsibilities and the social justice agenda is important not just to be effective and productive in ministry, but also to protect our health; spiritual, physical and emotional. Inclusive in balancing our lives, there will be times when you need to vent and get stuff out of your system. There are a number of ways to do this. One is through worship and praise. Many people under estimate the value and blessing that comes through worship and praise. A second is through prayer, when we ask God for divine intervention on our behalf and trust Him for the outcome. Third is through exercise and working out; it helps to clear the mind as well as relieve stress on the body. Fourth is time we spend with family and friends, and doing things we like to do like going to movies, playing sports, etc…

Balance in life is important in everyone's life, especially those of us who are in ministry. We are irresponsible and in denial if we fail to seek balance, to do our best for God. May we go forward in His name to minister and seek justice, to promote His kingdom on earth, and in the end, may we hear the God who called us, say as only He can say it, "Well done, my good and faithful servant."

Building and Managing a Multi-Site Ministry

Claude Alexander

As I write this article, there is an admission that I must make. Multi-Site ministry was not a part of my initial strategic plan. It wasn't included in the original vision that the Lord gave me upon arriving at University Park Baptist Church 19 years ago. It was not what we saw for ourselves. However, it isn't what you see for yourself. It's what the Lord sees for you. In Him, that upon which you seem to stumble has actually been a part of His plotted path.

During the years of 1990-2000 University Park Baptist Church grew from a congregation of roughly 600 to 3500 members; who went from worshipping once per Sunday, to four times per Sunday. In response to the growth, in 1999 we began construction on a new campus. At the time of its completion in the spring of 2001, while we had doubled the space for worship and education, we were already out of administrative and ministry office space. Coupled with this was a concern about our leaving an urban setting for a more suburban setting, and losing our "community credibility." With this challenge came the first opportunity for multi-site ministry. Keeping the original campus would allow us to maintain a ministry presence in the more urban setting, as well as accommodate current and future staffing needs. The decision was to continue to house our emergency assistance, outreach, and senior citizens ministries at the original campus, which we named 1 University Park, and all other ministries moved to the newly constructed campus named 2 University Park. Each campus required its own administrative and security staffing. Sunday morning worship was held at 2 University Park.

The move to 2 University Park was believed by many to be the final move. After all, we had an 83,000 square foot facility that seated 2500 in worship, with 20 classrooms, and a family life and wellness center with a full gymnasium, fitness center, commercial kitchen, and audio-video recording studio. What more could you want or need? *That's what we all thought.* To our surprise, God thought more. Having moved into 2 University Park in the spring of 2001, by the fall of 2003, we were overcapacity in terms of classrooms and parking, and were about to move from two to three worship services. Once again, we were confronted with the challenge of being at overcapacity in critical areas and approaching *negative growth.* Negative growth is a term used to describe growing to the point where people no longer see a place where they can comfortably and significantly fit. Having prayerfully examined alternatives, the decision was made to establish a congregation on the southern part of the Charlotte area.

At that time, we were located in Northwest Charlotte. A large concentration of African-American congregations was and continues to be located in West, North, and Northwest Charlotte. A significant number of African- Americans, however, now lived and were moving to South and Southeast

Charlotte. Though some were commuting north to worship, others were not. Many of those who did commute were not as actively involved in the weekday ministries. Therefore, we had an opportunity to potentially alleviate overcrowding, provide a more meaningful discipleship opportunity for current members living in South Charlotte, and reach another segment of the population that was underserved.

In October of 2003, we started with a seed group of 100 people who met at one of the high schools in South Charlotte. They were pioneer members of The Park South Church. Through personal invitation, prayer walking, and community engagement, we began to develop a core group of persons who believed in the vision of The Park South. In April of 2004, we were made aware of a church in southeast Charlotte desiring to sell their campus to us. In August of 2004, The Park South Church entered its new home. The Park South now numbers 600 active and committed members.

With the launch of The Park South in 2003, we moved from two worship services in one facility to three worship services in two facilities. This required the development of a worship team for The Park South. Current ministry staff would facilitate the ministry programming. Whereas the launch of The Park South created outreach into South Charlotte, it did not alleviate the overcapacity issues at the main campus. 2 University Park continued to experience its issues. Consequently, in August of 2004, another worship service was added to 2 University Park.

With an eye towards accommodating current ministry growth and facilitating future growth, we purchased the Charlotte Merchandise Mart in November of 2006. Currently, our Counseling Ministry, Job Transition Ministry, Singles Ministry, Young Adult Ministry, and Leadership Development and Deployment Ministry operate out of this site. Plans are being made for the transition to full-time worship being moved from 2 University Park to the Charlotte Merchandise Mart property now known as The Park.

These experiences cause the following considerations to come to mind with regard to building and managing a multi-site ministry. They are in no way an exhaustive list of considerations. They are those basic to any approach to multi-site ministry.

Purpose

For what purpose does one consider multi-site ministry? Is it being considered to solve a problem such as overcrowding or is it being considered as an outreach/growth strategy? It is important to be clear about the purpose so that the goals, objectives, and strategies are clearly defined and communicated to all of the necessary constituencies. In our first instance, the purpose was simply a matter of increasing capacity. In the second instance it was a combination of increasing capacity with outreach to another geographical sector. In the third instance, it is a combination of increasing capacity and growth strategy. In each instance, it was important to be clear about the purpose behind the endeavor so that the goals, objectives, and strategies might be developed and pursued.

Identity

What's the identity of the additional site? Is it a satellite, or a church plant? The two are not the same. A satellite is an extension of the headquarter congregation. A church plant is a congregation being birthed and set apart by the mother church. They have two entirely different natures, purposes, functions, and structures. It is necessary that one think through the identity of the additional site. Those within and outside of the congregation will need to know what the considered work will be. The requirements in terms of funding and staffing are particularly impacted by this decision. A satellite requires less site specific staffing than a church plant. However, with a church plant, there is the possibility of establishing a totally different aesthetic and praxis and greater latitude with respect to experimentation.

Another aspect of identity is the notion of brand. Will it carry the name of the sponsoring congregation? As a satellite, continuity would suggest in favor of carrying the name in some form. A church plant may choose a different name to establish its own sense of identity or it may choose to carry the name of the sponsoring congregation to leverage the power of the existing brand.

Target Population

Who's the primary population that you are trying to reach? Is it the same people racially, ethnically, socio-economically, and generationally in a different part of town, or is it different people in a different part of town? The more clear you are on the target population, the more specific you can be in terms of your communication and strategies of engagement. Depending upon the demographical profile of your targeted population, certain ministry programming may take precedence over others. The scheduling of the programming may be different depending upon whom you are seeking to serve. The worship style and approach may be different. The goal may be the same at both sites. However, the methods and modalities may be different.

Staffing

The question of staffing flows from the aforementioned concerns. Based upon the identity as satellite or church plant, the notion of staffing can begin to be addressed. If it is satellite, then you may employ a central staffing approach where all staff are members of the headquarters church staff and lay leadership teams are developed at the satellite. If it is a church plant, then you may employ an approach where the planting pastor and the leadership team are initially employees of the mother church but eventually become self-supporting and free standing. They are able to develop ministry staff of their own.

The Initial Appeal

What's the initial attraction/magnet? If it is a satellite, is the appeal geographical proximity for current members? Is it the continuity of the pastor and the worship? Is it an alternative in terms of worship style? Is it the opportunity to highlight a minister being considered as a successor? If it is a church plant, is the initial appeal a ministry in an underserved area? Is it the person of the planting pastor, pastoral couple, or ministry team?

Is it the philosophy and approach to ministry? Is it the teaching arm or small group experience?

The initial appeal must be considered in terms of its sustainability. The way that one starts, establishes the expectations of the ministry. Therefore, one should start the way that one wants to continue. Once you've begun and the level of expectation has been set, it is difficult to change in midstream. In the case of a satellite, if it is begun with the senior minister preaching, the expectation is set with the senior minister preaching. It is more difficult for the senior minister to hand the preaching responsibilities off to another. However, if it is started with others preaching, then it is easier for the preaching responsibilities to be assigned to someone other than the senior minister.

Facility and Financing

The choice of a facility is a crucial point in one's strategy. The first consideration is location. Second to that is type of facility. A corollary consideration is whether one chooses to lease or own the facility. There are advantages to both, depending upon one's objectives and financial standing.

Again, these are in no way an exhaustive list of considerations. They are a good beginning. In walking through them, one is able to begin to develop a comprehensive strategy towards multi-site ministry.

Reaching Eutychus: Reflections on Ministering to the Disconnected in the Postmodern Age

Delman Coates

In the twentieth chapter of the Acts of the Apostles, verses 7-12, Luke describes an interesting incident that took place during the Apostle Paul's evangelistic ministry. On the eve of his return to Jerusalem, Paul convened a mixed group of believers and potential converts to preach and discuss his teachings. In the service was a young man named Eutychus who became overwhelmed by the length of Paul's discourse. Eutychus, "who was sitting in the window, began to sink off into a deep sleep while Paul talked still longer." (Acts 20: 9a; NRSV) Apparently, the length of Paul's sermon, which lasted well past midnight (cf.

Acts 20: 7), was too much for Eutychus to handle. I can only imagine that with each hour, his eyelids grew heavier, his head struggled to keep from drooping, and he must have constantly changed his seating position to try and stay awake. But Paul's unending sermon was too much for Eutychus to handle. Overcome by sleep and fatigue, he "fell to the ground three floors below and was picked up dead." (Acts 20: 9b; NRSV)

Poor Eutychus! He was a victim of homiletical homicide. He came to the revival meeting looking for encouragement and inspiration, but he ended up being killed by the preacher and the ministry of the church. Paul does venture to rescue the boy and to seemingly bring him back to life, but the tragedy is that the great apostle seems completely oblivious to what has just happened and why it happened. After helping the boy, Paul goes back upstairs and preaches for another 6 hours. (Acts 20: 11). The church folk at the service seem to be comforted by the fact that the boy is returned to life (Acts 20: 12), and Paul seems to be reinvigorated that his reputation has been enhanced by the miracle, and sails off to continue his missionary travels.

This story, while inspiring to some, is a sad reminder of the way in which churches and church leaders engage in ministry. They ignore the way in which there methods and approach to ministry impacts those whom God has called the Church to reach. As a consequence, many churches are struggling and others dying because of their inability to reach "the Eutychus generation." While it is tempting to castigate Paul, truth is no one is exempt from the tendency to be ineffective in evangelizing this generation. As a pastor in my mid-30's, I thought I was exempt from the charge of being potentially irrelevant to the Eutychus generation. I am relatively young, and regard myself as contemporary and cutting edge, so being unable to reach the Eutychus generation was an indictment I reserved for other church leaders. That is, until I had my own Eutychus experience.

While visiting a college campus some time ago, I prepared a care package for the daughter of a close family friend enrolled there as a freshman. I wanted to surprise her with money and supplies that I thought she needed for school, so I arrived with several items I recalled needing my freshman year in college. The package included notebooks, pens, pencils, a scientific calculator, and a few calling cards so that she could call home to speak with her parents any time she wanted. I even included a CD/DVD player for watching movies and listening to music. Much to my chagrin and dismay, I was in for a huge surprise. It turned out she did not need the notebooks, pens, or pencils because all of the students typed their notes in class using a laptop computer. She did not need a DVD player to play movies because the students had cable television in their rooms and used Tivo to digitally record movies and television shows. She did not need a CD player because everyone had mp3 players to download music from the internet, and she did not need a calling card because she had her own cell phone with an unlimited long distance calling plan.

As my enthusiasm soon turned into embarrassment, I realized how antiquated, outdated, and obsolete my gifts really were. Even the check I handed her almost seemed passé. And so, there I was trying to give this college freshman something she did not need, in a format she did not understand, and in a method she did not want. Here I was giving this woman of future, tools and resources that were products of the past. Certainly, I could have said, "It worked for me, so it should be fine for you." I could have retorted, "These young people today are so ungrateful and don't appreciate anything." But it was then and there that I realized I had done to her what Paul did to Eutychus in Acts 20. I was so focused on myself that I failed to understand the person I was trying to reach. I realized that as contemporary, current, and cutting edge as I think I am, I am disconnected from the lived experience and social world of those whom the Lord has called me to evangelize. That experience was a microcosm of what is happening throughout the body of Christ everyday; well-intentioned church leaders failing to reach the unreached because they are out-of-step with the ways and morays of today's contemporary society.

WHO IS "EUTYCHUS"?

A few caveats are in order when it comes to taking about the Eutychus generation. First, the Eutychus generation falls into two groups. On the one hand, there is the unchurched. The "unchurched" are those who have had no connection to the Christian Church, its message, its ministry, or its God. There was a time in America when the unchurched generally referred to people in foreign lands, but with the emergence of a post-Christian society in America, the unchurched refers not just to those abroad, but to a significant portion of the population here at home.[1] While the unchurched may have attended a wedding or a funeral in a church, they otherwise have not had a meaningful relationship with a particular congregation. Since the church is not the main cultural institution that shapes and defines contemporary social morays and values, the unchurched see the Church as lacking what they have. While the Church views them as un"churched," the unchurch views the "churched" as un"world."

The Eutychus generation also consists of the dechurched. The "dechurched" are those who were at one time a part of a local congregation, but for a variety of reasons have lost that institutional connection. In some instances, the dechurched may no longer identify themselves as Christian. The dechurched represent a rather significant population for church leaders to contend with. According to a 2008 LifeWay Research survey published in USA Today, seven in 10 Protestants ages 18 to 30, both evangelical and mainline, who went to church regularly in high school said they quit attending by age 23, and 34% of those said they had not returned, even sporadically, by age 30. The Eutychus generation, then, includes both the unchurched and the dechurched.

The Church is called to reach these two audiences in the midst of complex and confusing time of great social upheaval and cultural transition. The Church has to reach the Eutychus generation at a time when globalization and cultural pluralism present radical challenges to the way in which the Church has understood itself.[2] Additionally, the digital and technological revolution in our postmodern society has transformed the ways in which people receive, process, and interpret information. The internet, IPOD's, podcasts, blogs, social networking sites (i.e. MySpace, Facebook, Twitter, etc.), smart phones, etc. have become standard features in today's social and technological landscape. These digital and technological innovations have radically changed the way in which the Eutychus generation experiences the world, hears the Word, and interprets the meaning of life. Technology has become so pervasive in our culture that church leaders must resist the temptation to assume that the Eutychus generation consists simply of teens, college students, and young adults. When we speak about the Eutychus generation, we are referring to a cross section of people of all ages and backgrounds. There are seniors who are as technologically savvy as younger people. Therefore, when we talk about "reaching Eutychus" we are not simply talking about how to reach young people. That would be a mistake because those who have been disaffected by the church fall into all demographics and cultural backgrounds.

The tragedy, however, is that in the midst of this great season of social change and technological transformation the Church has been asleep. In many ways, the Church has been like Rip Van Winkle who slept through a revolution. As a consequence, the Church has failed to capture the spiritual imagination of the Eutychus generation, even in the age of the megachurch and media and market savvy ministry. While the Church has been engaged in conventional approaches to ministry, a disconnect has emerged between those in the Church and those outside the church. Some social scientists, cultural commentators, and theologians have described this state of affairs as a collision between the Church and postmodernism. Postmodernity is a term used to describe a variety of cultural discourses and worldviews that question foundational and universal truth, elevate the self over the community, and replace universal cultural narratives with particularized, individual accounts.[3]

REACHING EUTYCHUS

While many books have been written to help the Church negotiate this divide, there is perhaps no resource more valuable than the Bible containing useful insights on addressing this enduring challenge for the Church. Bridging technological, cultural, linguistic, and sociological change is nothing new for the Church and has always been at the heart of the unfolding of God's will for the Church in the earth. When we consult the scriptures with clear eyes we learn that dealing with cultural change has always been at the heart of the Church's founding. So, the question becomes, what did God through the Church do then, that God through the church can do now to help us reach the unchurched and the dechurched?

At its inception, the Jesus movement consisted of a band of Palestinian Jews who believed in the ministry, message, and mission of Jesus of Nazareth. After just a few years of ministry, this group of believers faced the threat of becoming socially, spiritually, and culturally obsolete. This threat existed because up until that time the followers of Jesus only spoke one language, Aramaic. This fact put a barrier of language, culture, and custom between the disciples of Jesus and those who were not a part of the movement. The group was isolated and insulated because its members only spoke one language, and consequently, it created a divide between those inside the community and those on the outside. The particularities of its speech, the nuances of its cultural lexicon, and the idiosyncrasies of its cultural expressions made the Jesus movement socially and theologically irrelevant at a time of great socio-cultural change.

According the Acts 1: 8, this was an unacceptable situation in the eyesight of the Lord. The Lord wanted His Church to have meaning and relevance beyond the geographical and cultural confines of the city of Jerusalem. The ministry and message of Jesus was to connect with those in Judea, Samaria, and the uttermost part of the earth. According to the theology, literary context, and rhetoric of the passage, this could not happen so long as the followers of Jesus only spoke one language. They had to have the ability to speak intelligibly to those who were not a part of the community of faith. So what did God do? Fifty days after the ascension of Jesus, on the day of the Jewish Feast of Pentecost, God empowered this beleaguered group of believers in the upper room with the Holy Spirit, and according to the text they spoke in a language that those outside the faith community could understand (cf. Acts 2: 1-11).

When considered in context, it becomes clear that the theological and narrative thrust of Acts 2 was to provide God's answer for a spiritual movement on the verge of cultural irrelevance. God's method for addressing the growing chasm between the Church and the disconnected was to empower the believers to speak a language (cf. Acts 2: 4) the world could understand. Likewise today, if the Church is to connect with the disconnected, if it is to revive, restore, and renew fellowship with the dechurched, it must make its mission, its ministry, and its message plain by speaking a language the world can understand. This is what the miracle of Pentecost, which inaugurates the founding the New Testament church, is all about.

MAKING IT PLAIN

Fundamentally, that's the charge and challenge of the Church today. In the midst of rapid social change and technological innovation, the Church has to find a way to communicate the message of Jesus Christ with relevance, meaning, and purpose in a language the world can understand. While there are many different views regarding the stance the Church should take vis-à-vis emerging technologies, digital media, and social networking tools, I am of the view that the church must embrace these prevailing modes of communication. Eddie Gibbs writes in his book *Church Next: Quantum Changes in How We Do Ministry*, "Churches cannot stand apart from society and invite people to come to them on their terms. Rather, churches must go to people where they are and communicate in terms that will make sense to them, addressing the issues that shape their lives and speaking in their language."[4] It is important for church leaders to understand that these emerging technologies "are far from being faddish. Instead they are the very essence of how people construct their worlds."[5] Consequently, more and more Americans of all backgrounds will be increasingly isolated from the traditional modes, methods, and modalities of doing ministry, as we know it. What we do know from Acts chapter 2, however, is that doing nothing and decrying change is not an option.

In his book *eMinistry: Connecting with the Next Generation*, Andrew Careaga writes, "The cyber church cannot exist independent of the 'real world' church and neither can the church flourish in the new era without acknowledging the importance and impact of cyberspace in our lives."[6] These are important realities to embrace because there have been times in the Church's history when cultural and technological change has been viewed as antithetical to its mission and message. Around 1440, technological innovations in Germany revolutionized the printing industry. The advent of the Gutenberg press enabled books, including the Bible, to be mass produced in various languages people could understand, and made it possible for the average person, not just the elite, to have access to books that they could read for themselves. Some leaders in the Church, however, did not view this democratization of literacy and knowledge, as a positive development.

The reason church leaders would view such a technological innovation as a threat is because the democratization of knowledge in the mind of some destabilizes the hegemony of power, culture, and ideas that have historically been the province of the Church. No longer was knowledge and information the primary, protected treasure of the clergy. People did not have to go to a priest or a preacher to find out what was in the Word. The technology enabled them to circumvent establish church structures to obtain information for themselves. And I suspect this is the operative underlying assumption that continues to cause some church leaders today to oppose progress, resist change, and eschew the use of technology in ministry because these new technological innovations might cause them to lose the perceived sense of power that believe they possess.

Church leaders should understand that new ministry methods and technologies do not have to necessarily supplant current modalities of doing ministry. Instead, embracing new approaches and tolls can merely supplement and enrich current approaches. Pierre Babin and Angela Zukowski state in *The Gospel in Cyberspace, Nurturing Faith in the Internet Age*, "Church leaders and ministers must avoid the tyranny of either/or, which means we cannot root ourselves in only one means of communication while ignoring the others as irrelevant."[7] To that end, if church leaders want to ensure the current and future viability of their local churches, and if they want to position their churches to effectively reach the unreached and the disconnected, they must remain open-minded about the prospect of using new technologies and ministry tools for the purpose of reaching those who have yet to connect with the church.

"MULTI-LINGUALISM" IN MINISTRY

The imperative to make the message and ministry of the church relevant for the purpose of reaching the unreached in a new era requires further qualification. Returning to Acts 2, when the Holy Spirit fell on the Day of Pentecost, the believers did not simply speak in "a language" others could understand, but rather, they spoke "in languages" that those outside the community could understand. (cf. Acts 2: 4) This is a subtle, but significant distinction. To effectively reach the unreached, the believers needed to speak in multiple languages, not just one language, because the audience they were called to reach was culturally diverse. Acts 2: 5 describes the presence of devout Jews from every nation under heaven who were living in Jerusalem. Verses 9 – 11 then list the places from which they had come. These were people living in the same place, all speaking different languages, and were unable to understand the common language spoken by the followers of Jesus (i.e. Aramaic). To bridge this cultural, linguistic, and potentially spiritual chasm, the Holy Spirit empowered the believers with the ability to be a multilingual community. The assembled believers simultaneously spoke in multiple languages to multiple constituencies in order to make ministry meaningful, viable, and relevant to those on the outside. In the same manner, today's church must have the same multi-discursive ability in ministry if it is to reach the Eutychus generation in our postmodern, technologically advanced society.

The relevance and future viability of the Church in general, and the local church in particular, depends upon its ability to speak to multiple groups, using multiple communicative modalities, styles, and methods, at the same time. The mistake in many contemporary church contexts is to assume that the postmodern audiences God has called us to reach is a cultural monolith, and as a result, tend to essentialize what it means to be relevant to this generation of current and potential churchgoers. The focus of doing ministry in the postmodern era has to be in speaking multiple "languages" or modalities because the unchurched is not a cultural monolith. Technology and cross-cultural fertilization have created a situation in which there is much more socio-linguistic and cultural diversity within, across, and among various demographic groups. No longer can church leaders assume, essentialize and delimit the interests that potential churchgoers in any particular demographic group have. For example, it would be a mistake to assume, as is often done, that most or all teens and college students like hip hop and R&B music, and as such are only attracted to worship services that contain the latest contemporary music rhythms and resonance's. Likewise, it would be a mistake to assume that most or all seniors are not actively utilizing the internet and other digital media.

These flawed assumptions induce church leaders to plan worship, orient preaching, and design ministry around one particular style, focus, or orientation. The decline of many mainline churches over the past 50 years is attributable in part to churches failing "to speak," or design ministry, in multiple discursive modalities. In relegating worship and preaching modalities to Euro-American cultural forms, for example, these churches restricted the potential evangelistic terrain for people who might have responded to the Church's witness if its ministry and worship were more dynamic. This is even the case for predominantly African-American churches and clergy that embraced indigenous African cultural and spiritual forms of ministry and worship over the past 30 years. Replacing one cultural parochialism with another in a pluralistic era eventually results in a situation wherein the local church and clergy leader are unable to accommodate the various cultural needs and spiritual aspirations of increasingly diverse postmodern audiences. The time when people's spiritual sensibilities were generally confined to particular denominations, worship styles, and ideological perspectives is waning. The impact of digital media and emerging technologies have increased the cross fertilization of spiritual interests and desires. Those in our churches, and those yet to be reached, have access to a vast array of theological perspectives and orientations that shape and inform how they seek to satisfy and nourish their spiritual appetite. When we recognize that the churched and the unchurched are dynamic not static, we will seek to develop ministry, worship, and modes of teaching and preaching in a way that affirms the multidimensional and multifaceted composition of the people inside and outside our pews.

LET'S GO FISHING

This means that if church leaders are to more effectively evangelize the Eutychus generation, they must have a thorough understanding of the psychosocial dynamics and orientations that shape those whom they seek to reach. This is an important principle of evangelism that is laid out in scripture, and the ability to effectively reach the unreached depends upon having an acute understanding of the diverse and dynamic audiences we are called to reach. The metaphor of fishing used in Matthew 4: 18-22 to describe the goal of Christian discipleship and evangelism underscores the importance of profiling those whom God has called the Church to reach.

Good fishers know that the kind of bait and/or nets you use depends upon the kind of fish you plan to catch. Therefore, if the contemporary church is to effectively evangelize those outside the church and keep those within, it must conduct a profile of the "fish" God has called it to catch, and church leaders must do so reserving judgment about the psychosocial characteristics of people in this generation. The temptation which profiling today's generation is for church leaders to subject those shaped by present realities to the realities of the past. This kind of approach ultimately leads to stagnation in ministry.

Among the many things that could be said about the Eutychus generation, we can say that they have been conditioned and programmed for instant information and immediate gratification. They are used to multi-sensory experiences and have been shaped by a media and technology culture that provides constant sensory stimulation. As a result, churches and church leaders are challenged to design worship, ministry, preaching and teaching in a manner that accommodates audiences that desire more dynamic styles of worship and approaches to ministry. This can be done with integrity without compromising the substance and content of the Church's mission. With respect to the worship life of the local church, for example, church leaders should give great consideration to developing blended worship experiences as a means of accommodating the vast socio-cultural and spiritual diversity of the Eutychus generation. By "blended worship," I mean worship experiences that incorporate a variety of musical genres, worship styles, and preaching/teaching modalities into the corporate worship service. It cannot be assumed that the spiritual preferences of churchgoers in any demographic are homogeneous. There was a time when churches could confidently boast being "a high church," "a silk stocking church," or "a contemporary, praise and worship church." There was a time when preachers could boast just preaching "prosperity," "faith," or "the social gospel." But the days when churches and pastors could confidently limit themselves to one particular theological orientation, worship style, or preaching modality are gone.

The churches that will be the most successful in drawing, reaching, and keeping the Eutychus generation will have to self-consciously integrate a variety of ministry descriptive markers. While there are isolated examples of thriving ministries with a parochial vision of its worship culture and ministry orientation, the future suggests that these are not sustainable models in an increasingly diverse social, cultural, and ideological environment. If the local church is to be relevant and viable in the future, it will not be able to just speak "a language" that others can understand, but it must speak "in languages" or in multiple socio-religio discourse; incorporating the old and the new, traditional and contemporary, didactic teaching and demonstrative preaching, anthems and praise & worship, hymns and spirituals, etc. Churches that cultivate a dynamic spiritual and ministry culture will be better positioned to reach the unreached in the future. This kind of ministry "multilingualism" is necessary not simply as a tool for intercultural outreach, but for intracultural sustainability that leads to intergenerational, well-balanced, healthy local churches. The diversity about which we speak is not just across cultures, but also within.

WHAT ARE WE CONNECTING THEM TO?

I have attempted to make the case that in order to reach the Eutychus generation; the Church must communicate the message and meaning of the Gospel to multiple audiences utilizing multiple communicative modalities and discourses. But when it comes to reaching Eutychus, church leaders must constantly ask themselves, "What are we connecting the Eutychus generation to?" This must be kept at the forefront of our minds because the subtle temptation in our effort to reach those outside the church is to assume that the goal of ministry is to connect people to "church." In this age of cultural change and technological transition, we must make sure that we do not make connecting people to institutional Christian religion the primary goal of ministry. Clergy leaders must maintain a hermeneutics of suspicion with respect to the array of ministry strategies and methods for outreach, church growth, and evangelism. Many of the marketing strategies, church growth methods, and technological tools used for reaching the unreached tend to connect potential churchgoers to the local church, and in many instances, to the personality of the preacher. In his article, "Twitter This" Tony Morgan states that most of the social media technologies "fuels the self-promoting, banal, narcissistic tendencies of our culture."[8] In the contemporary church, these new technologies have tended to be used to connect people to the institution of the church and the person of the preacher, rather than to the person of Jesus Christ. This is an unfortunate state of affairs because the new tools can be used in so many other ways. If we are to embrace the vast array of emerging ministry methods and tools we must always keep in mind that the goal ought be to connect people to a life sustaining and life changing relationship with Jesus Christ.

Spiritual encounter that leads to personal transformation, spiritual renewal, and social consciousness must be the focus of the Church's outreach and ministry efforts. Consequently, clergy leaders must contextualize and deconstruct popular ministry tools, approaches, and methods because many of the popular tools and methodologies of church growth are based upon corporate principles whose goals are not always consistent with those of the Church. While market driven models that are based upon corporate culture provide useful and helpful principles for excellence in ministry, it must be understood that market driven approaches are designed to create customers whose primary goal is to receive. The mission of the Church, however, is to create disciples who understand their mission primarily in terms of giving. It should be no surprise then that the rush to develop 5-star ministries over the past 10 years has created a contemporary Christian culture wherein people look to be served, rather than to serve. The preoccupation of the modern day churchgoer is on what the church has to offer them. The focus of many modern day churchgoers is on what the local church and the preacher has to offer their children and their family. This in and of itself is not a problem, however, when this is the extent of the concern, it creates a self-centered mindset in which people are primarily interested in cash, cars, and clothes, rather than the cause of Christ. Unfortunately, far too many clergy leaders feed into this mindset, engaging in a host of interpretive gymnastics to twist and distort Scripture as if it is simply a self-help manual.

Market driven, consumer models for doing ministry are insufficient in and of themselves for reaching the Eutychus generation because the principles that inform these strategies are not always rooted in a biblical theology for doing ministry. The emphasis upon accommodating wants and needs, and organizing ministry solely around meeting felt needs, which is at the heart of market driving models of ministry, has led to the commodification of the Gospel and the creation of an entrepreneurial evangelicalism in many churches where the bottom line is in numbers. Despite their perceived advantages, market-driven approaches to ministry distort the way in which churches view potential disciples by embracing the central marketing precept that "the customer is always right."[9] By making the audience rather than the Lord sovereign, market-driven models tend to orient ministry around attracting would-be "customers" by turning the Gospel message into a means of personal fulfillment.[10] Such an approach to ministry ultimately leads to an escalation of demands as church marketers seek to stimulate new needs in order to create additional markets. According to Os Guinness, "Meeting needs does not always satisfy needs; it often stokes further ones and raises the pressure of eventual disillusionment. Modernity has expanded and corrupted the very notion of need by creating a 'need on command' society."[11]

There ought to be no surprise then, that in an era of market-driven, technology and media savvy ministry we have created ecclesial environments in which people want connection to the Church without commitment. The ministry emphasis upon convenience, accessibility, and media technology give people the illusion of connection and a false sense of community. Think about it. The "virtual" world is not real. The "friends" and "contacts" people have on the latest social networking tools are merely "virtual" friends. As church leaders contemplate incorporating emerging technologies and ministry methods, they must make sure not to foster or encourage an environment in their churches wherein people settle for virtual community, virtual worship, or virtual church. Why? Because in the virtual world people get all of the conveniences of ministry without fellowship, service, sacrifice, or commitment. At the end of the day, people want and need to know God, and we cheat them out of a real relationship with a real God and His church when we fail to problematize and when necessary to sanctify secular modalities.

From a biblical perspective, it was not the demands of the crowds that set the agenda for the ministry of Jesus. Therefore, the appropriation of marketing insights has to be viewed with discretion. While it is important for churches to operate in a standard of excellence, operational excellence does not necessarily lead people to an encounter with the Holy. You can have clean buildings, graphically appealing promotional literature, and sophisticated logos, but if it does not lead people to an encounter with God, it ultimately is of no redeeming value. According to George Barna, the Church's reliance upon "greater sums of money, better techniques, bigger numbers and facilities, and more impressive credentials…have failed us; in our efforts to serve God, we have crowded out God Himself."[12]

Not only does the local church have to employ a hermeneutics of suspicion as it relates to the appropriation of corporate models for doing ministry, but it also has to deconstruct ministry models and strategies that emerge from different cultural contexts. The uncritical adoption of ministry models that are products of different cultural contexts can have negative consequences for the local church. Take, for example, the very popular discipleship model of small group ministry that was popularized by the Fuller Institute of Church Growth in the early 1980's. The strategy of introducing people to Christianity through small groups was imported to America from Korea. The Yoida Full Gospel Central Church grew to be the largest church in the world under the leadership of Pastor David Yonggi Cho using a small group, cell-based system of evangelism, church growth, and discipleship. The methods and concepts of small group ministry were embraced and adopted by many churches in America in the last quarter of the 20th century. In his book *Sticky Church*, Larry Osborne surveys the evolution of small group ministry and concludes, "Despite the rhetoric, most small group programs and methods don't work very well."[13] The reason is because the concepts and models of small group ministry are not easily portable in the American context. Cho's model was "designed for a culture that has little or no historical connection to evangelical Christianity."[14] In the Korean context, most people come to Christ by first meeting in small groups in people's homes. In America, on the other hand, many people find it much more intimidating to go to someone's home for a small group bible study, and instead prefer to go to a corporate worship service to be introduced to Christ. According to Osborne, small group models also work best in cultural contexts that have a strong view of authoritarian leadership, where there is limited social mobility, and where people have strong familial ties.[15] While small group ministry is not inherently a bad model, many American churches are finding that its cultural distinctiveness limit its effectiveness in different cultural and ecclesial settings. Churches that adopt strict corporate models for doing ministry or models that derive from different cultural contexts will struggle to reach the Eutychus generation due to a lack of biblical integrity and socio-cultural authenticity.

Churches and clergy leaders would be well advised to shift from a market-driven orientation to a mission-driven orientation. In his book *Leadership Next: Changing Leaders in a Changing Culture*, Eddie Gibbs writes, "there is a growing desire for church structures that are more relational with less emphasis on stage-managed professional performance and more emphasis on doing ministry to one another and mission in the world." Churches and clergy leaders must begin to see themselves as agents of change in a hurting world and seek to relate the Gospel of Jesus Christ and the work of the Church to the myriad of social issues that impact the communities (local and global) within which local churches find themselves. By highlighting the mission of the local church and the social role of the Church in the world, churches will be more apt to capture the hearts and the spiritual imagination of the Eutychus generation. Churches must do a better job of leveraging their resources to address the social ills that confront the people in the pews and in the community. The Church must become a place where people gather for worship to be empowered to go out in mission. This can only happen when people are invited into a life-changing encounter with God through an apprehension of the socio-prophetic message of the Gospel.

The Eutychus generation is looking for the Church to make a case for itself at a time when the culture does not automatically concede authority to religious institutions. This can only be done when churches envision worship, utilize their resources, and appropriate emerging tools to highlight the public witness of the Gospel message, rather than simply accenting matters of personal piety and advancing the personal ministry of the preacher. A tremendous evangelistic opportunity exists for churches to reach the unreached by promoting the public witness of the Gospel and the socio-prophetic role of the local church. In so doing, churches must move beyond the important role of extending charity to those in need to "living adventurously as a subversive movement"[16] that pursues systemic change. The spiritual power and anointing experienced in corporate worship must be related to the pain and the pathos experienced by those outside the church and clergy leaders must look for creative ways to engage parishioners in social justice ministry.

As a pastor, I have witnessed the impact that having a public theology and a public witness can have on transforming the culture of the local church. In July 2007, I was led to organize a campaign to challenge the corporate sponsorship of entertainment images and messages on music video programs that promote drug use, violence, and sexually explicit content to youth and children. The "Enough Is Enough Campaign for Corporate Responsibility in Entertainment" was announced in a Sunday sermon, and included weekly rallies, media research, and advertiser advocacy. The campaign involved hundreds of members in our church and community, including churches and clergy leaders in the New York metropolitan area. The campaign resulted in substantive changes in the music video programs of concern, including the cancellation of several programs, but the unplanned result was that it inspired a broader group of people to get involved in our church who had been disaffected and disillusioned by traditional church life.

To develop a broader vision of the social role of the Church, clergy leaders will need to broaden the hermeneutical framework within which they appropriate the scriptures. The challenge for the contemporary expositor of the Bible is that many of the received tools, methods, and categories for interpreting the Bible are based upon antiquated presuppositions of the "modernist" era. The confidence in science and historical reasoning that have tended to dominate biblical theology in the West over the past 400 years has led to a crisis in the Church, as clergy leaders attempt to use modernist tools and methods to relate the meaning and message of the Bible to postmodern audiences. This will increasingly become a problem as pastors, theologians, and the laity attempt to relate the veritable truths of the Bible to the complex social, cultural, and spiritual issues of our day. This is the case for conservative, evangelical, and liberal Christians alike, as they all in various ways attempt to answer contemporary, postmodern questions using the modernist categories of history, science, and objectivity.[17] What is needed is for Christian preachers to reclaim forms of early Christian thinking that configure Biblical meaning on an alternative epistemological basis; understanding the meaning and message of the Bible in narrative, non-literal and Christological terms, rather than on literal, historical, and scientific terms. It is then that the contemporary church will be able to reach Eutychus.

[1] Eddie Gibbs, *Church Next: Quantum Changes in How We Do Ministry* (Downers Grove, IL: InterVarsity Press, 2000), 27-28. Andrew Walls, "Western Society Presents a Missionary Challenge," in *Missiological Education for the Twenty-first Century*, ed. Dudley J. Woodbury (Maryknoll, NY: Orbis, 1996), 19. Thom Rainer, *The Unchurched Next Door* (Grand Rapids, MI: Zondervan, 2003).

[2]William M. Easum, *Sacred Cow Makes Gourmet Burgers* (Nashville: Abingdon, 1995), 19.

[3] Stanley J. Grenz, *A Primer on Postmodernism* (Grand Rapids, MI: Eerdmans, 1996), and Roger Lundin, *The Culture of Interpretation* (Grand Rapids, MI: Eerdmans, 1993).

[4] Eddie Gibbs, *ChurchNext: Quantum Changes in How We Do Ministry* (Dovers Grove, IL: InterVarsity Press, 2000), 39.

[5]Eddie Gibbs and Ryan Bolger, *Emerging Churches: Creating Christian Community in Postmodern Cultures* (Grand Rapids, MI: Baker Academic, 2005), 20.

[6] Andrew Careaga, *eMinistry: Connection With The Net Generation* (Grand Rapids, MI: Kregel Publications, 2001), 170.
[7] Pierre Babin and Angela Zukowski, *The Gospel in Cyberspace, Nurturing Faith in the Internet Age* (Chicago, IL: Loyola Press, 1999), 19.
[8]Tony Morgan, "Twitter This: Embracing Social Media In The Church," in *Rev! Magazine* (Loveland, CO: Group Publishing, Inc., July/August 2009), 53.
[9]G.A. Pritchard, *Willow Creek Seeker Services* (Grand Rapids, MI: Baker Press, 1996), 242-246.
[10]Pritchard, 256; Eddie Gibbs, *Church Next: Quantum Changes in How We Do Ministry* (Downers Grove, IL: InterVarsity, 2000), 44, 45. See also, Philip D. Kenneson and James L. Street, *Selling Out the Church* (Nashville: Abingdon, 2997), 73, 74 who write, "If the church's goal is to meet felt needs, then the danger arises that the entire enterprise will be shaped primarily by those needs that the consumer desires to have satisfied. This consumer orientation in the church echoes the retailing industry's maxim: The customer is always right. Some Christians might legitimately worry that this emphasis on consumer sovereignty might undermine the integrity of the church's witness."
[11] Os Guinness, *Dining with the Devil* (Grand Rapids, MI: Baker, 1993), 65.
[12]George Barna, *The Second Coming of the Church* (Nashville: Word, 1998), 99.
[13]Larry Osborne, *Sticky Church* (Grand Rapids, Michigan: Zondervan Press, 2008), 140.
[14]Osborne, 140.
[15]Osborne, 145-147.
[16]Gibbs, *Church Next*, 51.
[17]Delman Coates, "Towards A Progressive Christian Interpretive Praxis" in *The African-American Pulpit* (Germantown, TN: Hope for Life International, FALL 2004); Delman Coates, "And the Bible Says: Methodological Tyranny of Biblical Fundamentalism and Historical Criticism" in *Blow The Trumpet In Zion* (Minneapolis, MN: Augsburg Fortress Press, 2005).

The Changing Role of the Bishop in a Post-Denominational World

Dennis V. Proctor

One of the advantages of being born in a Methodist parsonage is that I am, and have been familiar with bishops for a long time! When it comes to the office of bishop, like the old gray mare, *"she ain't what she use to be!"* Or should that be, "he" ain't what he used to be! Lest we spend an inordinate amount of time arguing the theological underpinnings of gender specific assignments within the Body of Christ, let it suffice to say that this post denominational world has ushered in a gender-neutral leadership that renders such discussions, null and void. Neither shall we debate the primacy of Episcopal elevation, whether through selection or election, or the distinction between appointive or suggestive ecclesiastical power. The focus of this chapter is to examine with specificity the changing dynamics involved in defining a bishop's role in today's contemporary context.

The exploration is relevant given this current era where a local assembly can become the summum bonum (final word) of ecclesiastical existence, and a person can don as many titles as their letterhead can accommodate! Such an exploration is not only relevant it is urgent! Day Star, The Word Network, TBN, The Inspirational Network, and the like have introduced us to apostles, evangelists, overseers, pastors and bishops. Oh yes, bishops. Apostolic, Baptist, Methodist, Independent, mail order, internet authorized, you want it, you got it, "Reverend, Doctor, Elder, Founder, Pastor and Bishop!"

The term "bishop" has replaced yesterday's *"Doctor."* No longer is it sufficient to wear chevrons on the sleeve of one's robe, one must now posses the vestments of a jurisdictional or reformational prelate. Cassock, surplus, chimere, ring and cross are all part of the bishop's standard issue. A miter and Episcopal crest designate the scope of authority and clarify the bishop's mission. The processions are regal; the colors are royal, the music resplendent and reminiscent of the grandeur in Isaiah 6 with all of its splendor. But do such appearances a bishop make?

To ignore the changing landscape, liturgy and language of today's congregant, in favor of ancient definitions and job descriptions may cause episcopates from traditional venues to suffer with Barbara Tuchman's concept of "the illusion of permanence." [1] It has been said that had the dinosaurs been willing to adapt, they would not be extinct! A keen understanding of the signs of the time and appropriate adjustments will allow this sacred office not only to survive, but also to thrive with significance and stature.

The bishop is the quintessential symbol of prominence in the church. Such prominence often becomes synonymous with leadership, and leadership at this level should be devoid of three fatal flaws, before attempting to impart lessons to those they lead. The *trifecta* of personality pitfalls is: insincerity, insecurity and indecision.

Insincerity is dangerous because the bishop must be someone in whom trust can be deposited. In a world of smoke and mirrors, live versus DVR, those charged to re-present Christ would do so with a pure heart. Warren Wiersbe writes, "When a political candidate appears on television, the most important member of his team is not the speech writer but the image maker, the media expert who sells the candidate to the viewers. When you find yourself more concerned about your 'image' than your work, you have stopped glorifying God."[2]

Is it any wonder that when Gandhi was asked about Christianity and its life changing power he is reputed to have replied, "Give me Jesus, but keep the Christians. I might have become a Christian, were it not for the Christians I have seen." How sad it is when the content of our character injures the image of Christ. Insincerity so offends God that in Matthew 7:21-23 Jesus says, *"Not everyone who says to me, 'Lord, Lord,' shall enter the Kingdom of heaven, but he who does the will of my Father in heaven. Many will say to Me in the day, 'Lord, Lord, have we not prophesied in Your name, cast out demons in Your name, and done many wonders in Your name?' And then I will declare to them. 'I never knew you; depart from Me, you workers of iniquity."*

Insecurity impairs the profile of the prelate because there is nothing higher in terms of position or prestige the church can offer the person who assumes this office, and if he or she is in any measure dissatisfied with himself or herself, no balm can fill the emptiness in that individual's soul. John Maxwell says, No one can live on a level inconsistent with the way he sees himself…If someone sees himself as a loser, he finds a way to lose. Anytime his success surpasses his security, the result is self-destruction.[3]

Carter G. Woodson spoke to this pathology, "When you control a man's thinking you do not have to worry about his actions. You do not have to tell him to stand here or go yonder. He will find his proper place and will stay in it. You do not need to send him to the back door. He will go without being told. In fact, if there is no back door, he will cut one for his special benefit." [4]

The Rev. Dr. Cameron Jackson says that it is dangerous to have "midgets in the seats of the mighty!" When the position is higher than the capacity of an insecure person, they will whittle it down to a manageable size.

Indecision is a bane of the bishopric. If theocracy (judgments flow from God to the leader) is a legitimate form of governance, then the bishop must accept that "the buck stops here!" Once the bishop has reached a decision inspired by Godly judgment or the urgings of the Spirit, he or she must believe in the assurance of divine dictum.

"When a man realizes that he has been entrusted with a grave responsibility, he cannot act as if it did not matter how he discharged it. Always he feels the spur of another's trust and confidence. To remember that another depends on him, has placed his confidence in him, helps to keep a man responsible and true to his trust.[5]

The thirty-fourth chapter of Ezekiel pronounces a sobering reminder to those who mislead or mishandle the Lord's sheep, due to our issues or infirmities. We pause to ponder the person of the personality, only briefly because it has been rightly stated, "you can't give what you don't have!"

The question before us is "what is the responsibility of the bishop?" The Bible records in Paul's letter to Timothy, *"The saying is sure: whoever aspires to the office of bishop desires a noble task. Now a bishop must be above reproach, married only once, temperate, sensible, respectable, hospitable, an apt teacher, not a drunkard, not violent but gentle, not quarrelsome, and not a lover of money. He must manage his own household well, keeping his children submissive and respectful in every way...for if someone does not know how to manage his own household, how can he take care of God's church? He must not be a recent convert, or he may be puffed up with conceit and fall into the condemnation of the devil. Moreover, he must be well thought of by outsiders, so that he may not fall into disgrace and the snare of the devil."* (1Timothy 3:1-7 NRSV)

There has been much focus on the qualification and as it relates to one's marital status, often to the negation or mitigation of one's ability to impart, to instruct, to equip, to edify, and to train. The experience of trial, trauma and triumph, etches insight into the soul of the episcopate. In everything we do, we teach. The bishop becomes the chief teacher and the archivist of history and mystery of the church and of its Christ. The bishop is the standard bearer for their jurisdiction in the Kingdom. If time makes ancient good uncouth, then it is the task of the bishop to redeem the time, so that "what was" can be understood, appreciated, modified and celebrated as a plank in the bridge that brought others across. In the world in which we live, religious history, church culture and etiquette are almost nonexistent. This malady is resident in the pulpit and the pew.

With pressure upon the bishop to be the connector for a disconnected generation, the role of the bishop is at least three fold.

The Bishop as Model

We all tend to emulate those we admire, and it is almost certain that there will be those who will emulate the behavior and characteristics of the bishop as a leader. Obviously this can be both beneficial and detrimental. All of us, human beings that we are, have negative elements of our personality and behavior that others should shun. This "dark side" that each of us possesses, "like oil in a body of water, will always find its way to the surface and create a mess if it is not acknowledged and redeemed."[6] We all have "raw materials" from our dark side – pride, selfishness, self-deception and wrong motives. These are difficult for us to reckon with because "the unhappy truth is that all too often we are not that interested in probing our motives too deeply for fear of what we might find."[7] The bishop must model this kind of self-examination, among other valuable Christian traits; for in doing so he or she puts on display that kind of accountability that is essential to maturity as a Christian. Thus the bishop is not some strain of "super-Christian" or leader. We all have feet of clay. In fact, as D.A. Carson observes: What is required in some sense of all believers is peculiarly required of the leaders of believers. There is a difference of degree. That is why Paul will be able to say, 'I urge you to imitate me' (1 Corinthians 4:16). Those of us who want to be leaders in the church today, then, must begin by recognizing that there is no special elitist qualification…when Paul in 1 Timothy 3:1-7 sets out the qualifications for an overseer ("bishop" in older English), the most remarkable feature of the list is that it is unremarkable. It contains nothing about intelligence, decisiveness, drive, wealth or power. Almost everything on the list is elsewhere in the New Testament required of all believers.[8]

Others will learn how to exemplify Christian behavior when they see such behavior modeled in the life of the bishop. Bishop Kenneth Monroe once remarked, "The job of a pastor/leader is to teach people how to be Christians." Apple makes computers, McDonald's makes hamburgers, Krispy Kreme makes donuts, and so should the church be known for its product, Christians worth copying! Thus the bishop, the chief pastor, must model for those who follow a life that glorifies God, not a glorified life!

We are dealing with a generation who are impressed with *things* – material success, large honorariums, expensive accoutrements that indicate that one has "arrived." Such manifestations are not in and of themselves sacrilegious, but when they become the motivation for one's employ in the Master's vineyard, we have misconstrued the abundant life, with the abundance of things. Reinhold Niebuhr observes, "Prosperity which once had been sought in the service of God was now sought for its own sake… (We) have congratulated God on (our) virtues and ideals, which have so well merited the blessings of prosperity we enjoy."[9] We must never forget that the Adversary has access to "thingdom" in his kingdom. How else would he have been able to tempt Jesus with it in Matthew 4:8-9?

It seems that we have lost interest in taking account of the dictate and instruction of Jesus when he sent out his disciples to the field of work: "He ordered them to take nothing for their journey except a staff; no bread, no bag, no money in their belts; but to wear sandals and not to put on two tunics" (Mark 6:8-9). Let your sufficiency be found in God and God alone. Learn to see Jehovah Jirreh as being enough, more than enough to supply even our secret desires. Gabriel in the television series "Desperate Housewives" uttered a memorable if not theological musing, "In life I got everything I wanted, only to discover I wanted all the wrong things!" Dr. Kenneth Q. James raised the question in a, lecture, "What happened to the first yes? When our response to the Divine call was simply to let the Lord know that if someone was needed for service, "Here am I, send me!"

The bishop must embody a moral authority and integrity. One who loves God, loves the Church, and loves and serves God's people. Therefore, the bishop must be a model, and a sincere one, for as John Maxwell says, "We teach what we know; we reproduce what we are."[10] The bishop's private prayer should be, "Lord help me to be what you want your people to become!" In this day of "preacher paparazzi" the bishop must desire, "an increasing distaste for things unholy!"

The Bishop as Mentor

A mentor is defined as "a wise and trusted counselor or teacher; an influential senior sponsor or supporter." Bishop Walter S. Thomas in a sermon entitled *"Someone's Got to Do the Dirty Work"* argued that we are experiencing a "generation of preachers who were born without Father's or mothers in ministry." They have become students of sound bites and style. Spiritual superstars of the plasma screen! Ministerial mentoring cannot be maximized or materialized through manipulated media productions. I shall never forget congratulating Bishop T.D. Jakes on never preaching a bad sermon on television. He calmly and sincerely responded, "I can edit my success!" That means there is much more to the sermon, ministry and minister's life than is seen on a thirty minute telecast! In ministry, as in life, some lessons are taught; others are caught! Once more, we find the wisdom of Paul in suggesting that the bishop must be "able to teach" and must not be "a recent convert." Many of us face the trouble as expressed by Eugene Peterson in acknowledging that, "all the models I had were either managerial or messianic."[11] Even when evaluating the deficiencies of a particular mentor, at least there was a structure from which to make an evaluation. Bishop Reuben L. Speaks used to say, "You can't improvise, until you know the scale!" For many now seasoned clerics who disagreed vehemently with the instruction of their mentors, over time, they have come to see the wisdom that was heretofore unobservable. Is there an adult today who now sees the wisdom of a parent or sage who may now be long departed? Time often provides perspective! The mentor must provide lessons for a lifetime, allowing the mentee to adjust the sails to navigate through "every stormy wind that blows!" Alan E. Nelson, in his book *Leading Your Ministry*[12] cites five reasons for what he calls "the leadership dilemma."

Our civilization is undergoing incredible changes. Things are not like they used to be. Change used to be the exception to the rule. It is now the new rule. Change creates stress. During times of stress and change, we seek leaders.

Institutions have not provided for leadership training. Our models of seminary training for persons in ordained ministry dating back to the middle of the nineteenth century have remained much the same, even though society has changed by leaps and bounds.

The fragmentation of society has made leadership much more difficult. We have varying loyalties often in conflict with one another. Our pluralistic society allows for the idea of multiple "truths." Further, the lack of community in our society today ,simultaneous with the breakdown of the family structure ,makes leading harder than ever.

Leadership paradigms have changed. Previous generations provided for more obvious leaders due to the "Great Man" theory – a hierarchical, top down, authoritarian and dramatic style of leadership. [It is interesting to note that in the A.M.E. Church, in the 2008 General Conference, the pastors of the five largest congregations in the denomination did not offer themselves as candidates for the office of bishop. Previous generations looked at the size of one's congregation, budget, and denominational influence as a precursor to Episcopal leadership] In the postindustrial age, leadership is taking on a "kinder-gentler" approach. Twenty-first century leadership is more apt to involve interdependence, sensitivity to people, and sharing ideas and information, calling for leaders to be more relational and less autocratic.

Leaders are feeling greater demands and fewer rewards. Of course, leaders by their very nature tend to receive criticisms and adversarial encounters and must make tough decisions. Most do not receive the pay, perks or recognition that would help create a balance, thus, as crass as it may sound, the payoffs may not seem significant enough to attract the best and the brightest.

This defines the expectation of the bishop as mentor. No leader can lead effectively when the leader has such severe deficiencies that the followers are expected to compensate for this lack with rewards and trophies and trinkets. It will soon wear the people out, or at the very least discourage those who might be valuable to the ministry and grow weary of having to support holding up another's ego. Psychic disfigurement cannot be massaged out of existence! "Leadership is best reserved for those who don't need positions of leadership to validate who they are."[13]

In the age of the "prosperity gospel" when it seems that some enter the ministry for its perceived rewards (and perhaps this accounts for the discouragement some feel, not because ministry is not meaningful but rather because those rewards have not been realized), and gauge their success by the achievement of mercenary standards, someone must guide, mentor and shape the thought and expectation of those who will serve as "servants of the servants of God." This seems now to be an important role and vital function that the bishop must provide. Therefore, it is apparent that in order to ascertain what is the motivation of the preachers and persons assigned to his or her charge, the bishop must be clear about what is his or her own motivation.

One should not seek the office of bishop to gain status, clout or influence. This is why the church has always set forth specific and strict benchmarks for the expectations of what any leader in the church must possess, especially while realizing that "some from the baptized assume the burdens of guidance, teaching, correction, care, and community concern in a way that edifies and calls forth the ministry of all Christians."[14] Because not everyone can know the "story before the glory" it is vital that the bishop not emphasize the benefits before sharing the burdens. Henri Nouwen was correct when he asserted that we are, "Wounded Healers." This is the greatest service of mentoring that the bishop provides, and it cannot be done with insincerity, for the shallowness that lurks beneath the surface of that ministry will ultimately be revealed.

The Bishop as Messenger

Leadership involves vision, and vision, in the words of George Barna, is "a clear, mental image of a preferable future imparted by God to His chosen servants and is based upon an accurate understanding of God, self and circumstances…Vision is a picture held in your mind's eye of the way things could or should be in the days ahead.[15] Making the vision clear means that the message must also be clear. The Apostle Paul says, *"Now, brothers and sisters, if I come to you speaking in tongues, how will I benefit you unless I speak to you in some revelation or knowledge or prophecy or teaching? It is the same way with lifeless instruments that produce sound, such as the flute or the harp. If they do not give distinct notes, how will anyone know what is being played?" (1 Corinthians 14:6-7, NRSV).*

There is some concern that the message of the church today to the ears of the world is muddled, messy or too mysterious, unclear and unsure. This was never to be the way the message of the gospel was to be preached and taught. As the leader, the bishop then must give clarity again to the message of the church. The bishop "sets the tone" for what the preachers in his or her charge will preach each Sunday, as well then as to the type of ministry that is performed in the name of God. And this is the crux of the message – "The Bible seeks people who can and will ask about God. It seeks those who are capable of letting their *little* questions – and which of them is *not* little in comparison – merge in the *great* question about the cross, that is, about God."[16] The bishop as leader, as model, mentor and messenger, must lead in emphasizing and if necessary recapturing this "great question," for as Barth says further,

"The word of God on the lips of a man is impossibility; it does not happen: no one will ever accomplish it or see it accomplished. The event toward which the expectancy of heaven and of earth is directed is none the less *God's* act. Nothing else can satisfy the waiting people and nothing else can be the will of God than that he himself should be revealed in the event. But the word of God is and will and must be and remain the word of *God.* When it seems to be something else, however brilliant, however Christian, however Biblical, that something else may be, it has ceased to be itself."[17] A skillful homoletician may craft a sensational sermon, yet it can remain devoid of transforming power!

The message is the message of the cross, and the church must not diminish, devalue or deny it. It is the task of the bishop today, in this post-denominational world, to bring the church and its preaching and message back to the preaching and the message of the cross. The message of the cross leads one to sacrifice, fully aware that in the end God will dole out the just reward. The old church used to say, "If you do God's work, you'll get God's pay!" It is this attitude that governed the behavior of John Wesley. He wrote to his critics, "Let me ask you one plain question: For what gain will you be obliged to act thus? To live exactly as I do? For what price will you preach (and that with all your might, not in an easy, indolent, fashionable way) eighteen or nineteen times every week; and this throughout the year? What shall I give you to travel seven or eight hundred miles, in all weathers, every two or three months? For what salary will you abstain from all other diversions, than the doing good, and the praising God? I am mistaken if you would not prefer strangling to such a life, even with thousands of gold and silver."[18]

Some have described Wesley's devotion, as being that of an, "obsessive compulsive neurotic," but his zeal was unmistakably heavenward. Isaac Watts would affirm this ideal in the word of his hymn "Am I a Soldier of the Cross" when he writes: "Must I be carried to the skies on flowery beds of ease, while others fought to win the prize, and sailed thro' bloody seas?" He answered his own question, "No I must fight if I would reign: Increase my courage Lord. I'll bear the toil endure the pain, Supported by thy word."

If the bishop is cavalier about this decision to follow and live by the message of the gospel, to be true to its essence and essentiality, that disease will infiltrate its way into the rank and file of ministry from top to bottom, and infect the congregations and churches in his or her charge. This spirit will pollute the process by which appointments are made and rulings are reached, and will sully the sacramental nature of the church of the living God. So, considering all the changes that surround us in the culture and the expectations of leaders, the divergent landscape in which ministry must now be accomplished, and the despair and pain in the environment in which ministry must be conducted, a new evaluation and assessment of the role of the bishop is clearly called for and only those with true courage and unwavering clarity about their call to serve, much less to lead, will seek to make this new understanding come alive.

The bishops of old in their prophetic role were called upon to speak truth to power. Indeed bishops of today bear that same mantle. As never before bishops must speak truth to the powerless—to those who populate the pew and precinct—declaring an end to the celebration of ignorance and indolence. Our message is to become what the late Dr. Samuel DeWitt Proctor would call the "Certain Sound of the Trumpet."[19] We must provide preachers and parishioners with the tools to articulate and navigate through this post modern and, some say, post Christian era. A few years ago, Dr. Gardner C. Taylor, considered to be the Dean of Preachers, questioned whether his classic form of sermonizing would bring people to the altar today. Although we unreservedly said it would (because his character is as powerful as his preaching), we applauded the transparency and audacity to evaluate one's effectiveness in, and integrity to the "High calling of Christ Jesus!"

The bishop has a changing role with a changeless mandate: *"To serve this present age, my calling to fulfill, O may it all my power engage, to do the Master's will!"*[20]

---

[1] Barbara W. Tuchman, *The March of Folly: From Troy to Vietnam,* Ballantine Books, New York,1971, p.126

[2] Warren W. Wiersbe, *On Being a Servant of God,* Baker Books, Grand Rapids, 1993, p.30

[3]John Maxwell, *The 21 Indispensable Qualities of a Leader,* Thomas Nelson Publishers, Nashville, 1999, p.121

[4]Carter G. Woodson, *The Miseducation of the Negro,* Haskin's Publications, Philadelphia,1933, p. XIII

[5] David A. MacLennon *Entrusted With the Gospel,* The Westminster Press, 1951. P. 31-32

[6] Gary L. McIntosh and Samuel D. Rima, *Overcoming the Dark Side of Leadership,* Baker Books, Grand Rapids, 1997, p. 36

[7] Ibid., p. 44

[8] D.A. Carson, *The Cross and Christian Ministry: Leadership Lessons from 1 Corinthians,* Baker Books, Grand Rapids, 1993, p. 95

[9] Reinhold Niebuhr, *The Irony of American History,* The University of Chicago Press, 1952, p. 52

[10] John Maxwell, *The 21 Irrefutable Laws of Leadership,* Thomas Nelson Publishers, Nashville, 1998, p. 138

[11] Eugene H. Peterson, *Under the Unpredictable Plant,* Wm. B. Eerdmans Publishing, Grand Rapids, 1992, p. 27

[12] Alan E. Nelson, *Leading Your Ministry,* Abingdon Press, Nashville, 1996, p. 21-22

[13] David Marcum and Steven Smith, *Egonomics,* Simon & Schuster, New York, 2007, p. 24

[14] William H. Willimon, *Pastor: The Theology and Practice of Ordained Ministry,* Abingdon Press, Nashville, p. 49

[15] George Barna, *The Power of Vision,* Regal Books, Ventura, CA. P.28-29

[16] Karl Barth, *The Word of God and the Word of Man,* Peter Smith, Gloucester, MA, 1978, p. 119

[17] Ibid., p. 124-125

[18] *The Complete Works of Wesley*, Vol. 8, p. 38-39, "An Earnest Appeal to Men of Reason and Religion"
[19] Samuel D. Proctor, *The Certain Sound of the Trumpet*, Judson Press, Valley Forge, 1994
[20] Charles Wesley, *A Charge To Keep I Have,* 1707-1788

BIOGRAPHIES

(alphabetical order)

DR. CLAUDE R. ALEXANDER, JR. has served as the Senior Pastor of University Park Baptist Church in Charlotte, North Carolina since 1990. Born in Waterloo, Iowa and reared in Jackson, MS, Dr. Alexander received a Bachelor of Arts Degree with honors in Philosophy from Morehouse College, a Master of Divinity Degree from Pittsburgh Theological Seminary, and a Doctor of Ministry Degree from Gordon-Conwell Theological Seminary.

Dr. Alexander has been appointed Vice-President of the Hampton University Ministers' Conference and inducted into the Martin Luther King, Jr. Board of Preachers of Morehouse College.

During Dr. Alexander's tenure at University Park Baptist Church or "The Park", the church has grown dramatically both in numbers and in ministries. "The Park" now has three locations in the Charlotte area, with a membership that has grown from less than 500 to more than 8,000. Under Dr. Alexander's direction, more than 80 ministries and services are now available which reflect the diversity of age groups and the needs and interests of the congregation and community.

Dr. Alexander's dynamic messages are broadcast nationally on The Word Network, The Inspiration Network and XM Radio. Having purchased 54 acres of land, on April 15, 2001 University Park Baptist Church moved into its new $13 million sanctuary and Family Life and Wellness Center. The church purchased 46 acres in the South Charlotte area and dedicated The Park South sanctuary on August 22, 2004. Future plans include senior citizens bungalows and the development of a residential community.

REV. DELMAN L. COATES, Ph. D. graduated magna cum laude from Morehouse College in Atlanta, GA with a Bachelor of Arts degree in Religion in May 1995, and received the Master of Divinity degree from Harvard Divinity School in Cambridge, MA in May 1998. He has also earned a Master of Philosophy degree in Religion in 2002 and a Ph. D. in 2006 from Columbia University.

While at Columbia, he served as the Youth Pastor at the Metropolitan Baptist Church in Newark, New Jersey, an urban congregation of 5,000, from 1999-2004. Dr. Coates also worked in the Community Development Grants unit of JP Morgan Chase & Co. in New York providing grants to faith-based institutions and non-profit organizations engaged in the development of affordable housing, childcare centers, and other community and economic development projects.

Dr. Coates has served as the Senior Pastor of the Mt. Ennon Baptist Church in Clinton, MD since 2004. In just over four years, the congregation grew in excess of 4,000 members. In September 2007, Dr. Coates initiated a campaign entitled *"The Enough Is Enough Campaign for Corporate Responsibility in Entertainment"* to protest the corporate sponsorship of images and messages that degrade women, glorify criminal activity, and propagate negative stereotypes of black and Latino men as pimps, gangsters and thugs. It has received national coverage on CNN, ABC News 7 (Washington, DC), NPR, the New York Times, Essence Magazine, The Michael Baisden Show, and many other major media outlets.

In the summer of 2008, he was honored by the African American Pulpit, the nation's premier journal for African American preaching, as one of the "20 To Watch."

BISHOP WILLIAM P. DeVEAUX, upon graduation from high school, entered Howard University and was elected Junior and Senior Class President and Basileus of Omega Psi Phi Fraternity. While at Howard, he answered the call to ordained ministry. Following in his father's footsteps he later served in the United States Army as a chaplain. In the midst of enemy fire, he brought comfort and solace to troops in combat during the Viet Nam Conflict.

In addition to a bachelor's degree from Howard University, he attained a Bachelor of Sacred Theology from Boston University as well as an M.A. and Ph.D. from Vanderbilt University. He has served on the faculties of Meharry Medical College, Princeton Theological Seminary and Howard University School of Divinity.

In the field of theological education, Dr. DeVeaux is recognized for his achievements as the Executive Director of the Fund for Theological Education Inc. During his tenure, scholarships to Black, Hispanic and North American students were granted to support their theological education.

On July 2, 1996 the Reverend William P. DeVeaux was consecrated as the 113th Bishop of the African Methodist Episcopal Church in Louisville, Kentucky and was assigned to Southern Africa where he lived and served for four years. He also served as the presiding bishop of the 16th Episcopal District of the A.M.E. Church which includes the following conferences: Guyana/Suriname, Windward Islands, Virgin Islands, Dominican Republic, Haiti, Jamaica, and London/Holland. He is currently the bishop assigned to the Sixth Episcopal District, the state of Georgia.

REV. DR. FLOYD H. FLAKE a former U.S. Congressman is the senior pastor of the more than 20,000 members Greater Allen A. M. E. Cathedral of New York in Jamaica, Queens, and President of Wilberforce University in Ohio. During his 31-year pastorate, Allen has become one of the nation's foremost Christian churches and development corporations. The church and its subsidiary corporations operate with an annual budget of over $34 million. The church also owns expansive commercial and residential developments, a 750-student private school founded by Flake and his wife Elaine, and various commercial and social service enterprises, which has placed Allen AME among the nation's most productive religious and urban development institutions. Allen Church's net assets are valued at over $100 million.

Flake served 11 years in the U.S. Congress, and was a member of the Banking and Finance and Small Business Committees. During his tenure, he established a reputation for bipartisan, innovative legislative initiatives to revitalize urban commercial and residential communities. Most notably, the Community Development Financial Institutions Act of 1993 contained provisions Flake authored which provided incentives for financial institutions to make market-oriented investments in destabilized urban and rural economies.

Dr. Flake earned a Doctorate of Ministry degree from United Theological Seminary in Dayton, OH and a Bachelor of Arts degree from Wilberforce University.

He has authored the best-selling book, "The Way of the Bootstrapper: Nine Action Steps for Achieving Your Dreams", and co-authored with his wife the book, "Practical Virtues: Everyday Values and Devotions for African American Families", published by Harper Collins. His latest book, "The African American Church Management Handbook", published by Judson Press was released in December 2005.

DR. TERESA HAIRSTON is the founder and publisher of Gospel Today Magazine (the world's #1 Christian Lifestyle Magazine); creator of the Gospel Today TV Show (a newsmagazine show which airs weekly on the Word TV network via DirecTV); host of a weekly "Gospel Today" radio update on "The Light" Radio Network; and, founder of The Gospel Heritage Foundation, a non-profit organization that hosts an annual "Praise & Worship Conference"—which attracts thousands of pastors, youth, musicians and praise dancers.

But Teresa Hairston's story is more amazing than her achievements!

Back in 1989, as a divorced mother of three small children, all she was able to scrape together to invest in her "dream" of becoming a publisher was $300. That's it. *She had $300, three young children, no husband and a dream.* Today, Gospel Today Magazine is a reality, and is the most respected Urban Christian lifestyle publication in existence. Steve Harvey, Bishop T. D. Jakes, Denzel Washington and more have graced its covers. GT is a fixture among progressive ministries and Christians who want inspiring reading material.

In step with her mission to inspire, educate, inform and inspire, Hairston has maintained her strong connection with her Gospel musical roots. In 2005, she launched Gospel Today Entertainment, an independent label that has released two national CD projects. In 2008, Hairston earned her Doctor of Ministry Degree and now travels the globe preaching the Gospel. She is currently single and lives in Atlanta. Her motto is: "When God gives you a vision, He'll make the provision!"

BISHOP DONALD HILLIARD, JR., D.MIN. earned a Bachelor of Arts degree from Eastern College (now Eastern University) in St. David's, Pennsylvania, a Master of Divinity degree from Princeton Theological Seminary in Princeton, NJ and a Doctor of Ministry degree from the United Theological Seminary in Dayton, Ohio, as a Samuel DeWitt Proctor Fellow. A sought after preacher, lecturer and intellectual, Dr. Hilliard's contributions include serving as the Pastor/Scholar-in Residence and Mentor for the Doctor of Ministry in Renewal Program at Palmer Theological Seminary in Wynnewood, PA, membership on the Oxford University Round Table Advisory Board and chapel speaker at Princeton University, Howard University and Wheaton College. Dr. Hilliard has also served on the Advisory Council for the Yale University Center for Faith and Culture National Working Group.

In 1983, the young and fiery Hilliard stepped to the challenge of shepherding the Second Baptist Church of Perth Amboy, New Jersey. Under his transformational leadership, the church has experienced tremendous growth and the surrounding community has been revived both spiritually and economically. Cathedral International is now one church in three locations: Perth Amboy, Asbury Park and Plainfield, New Jersey.

At the hand of Bishop John H. Bryant, Pastor Donald Hilliard, Jr. was consecrated to the Office of Bishop in 1995. The Covenant Ecumenical Fellowship and Cathedral Assemblies (CEFCA) was born and has grown to include pastors and churches throughout the east coast and as far as Dominican Republic, South Africa and Liberia.

REV. REGINALD T. JACKSON graduated from Delaware State University with a Bachelor Degree in History and from Interdenominational Theological Center, in Atlanta, Georgia with a Masters Degree. In 1981 he was assigned to the pastorate of St. Matthew AME Church, Orange, New Jersey. During his ministry more than 2,000 persons have responded to the invitation to accept Christ and become a part of St. Matthew Church. Under his leadership, St. Matthew has adopted the theme, "The Servant Church of the Oranges" and instituted over twenty ministries that serve church and community and minister to the spiritual, emotional, physical and financial needs of people, including St. Matthew NIDA (Neighborhood Improvement Development Association).

In addition to his pastoral responsibilities, Rev. Jackson was named Executive Director of the Black Ministers Council of NJ in 1996, representing more than 600 African American churches. In this position he has been a prophetic voice for social justice, engaging almost every major issue facing the state, including parity funding for low income schools. His leadership on this issue resulted in the State Supreme Court ordering the state to spend hundreds of millions of dollars in poor school districts, increasing charity care funding for those who are uninsured, and forging legislation to end predatory lending targeting minorities. He is best known however, for his leadership in the fight against racial profiling and reform which led the NJ legislature to pass and the governor sign legislation making NJ the first state in the nation to have a law making racial profiling a crime.

Rev. Jackson has received numerous awards and serves on several Boards within the state including Chairman of the Board of Trustees of Essex County College. He is also a Life Member of the NAACP and Phi Beta Sigma Fraternity.

BISHOP T.D. JAKES is a quintessential leader known for his service to the church and the global community.

Bishop Jakes has global reach through missions around the world, record-breaking events, and weekly, with his diverse congregation at The Potter's House, where he shares his message of hope, inspiration and God's love with over 30 thousand members in Dallas, Texas. The Dallas-Fort Worth community is also home to Clay Academy, the college preparatory school for leaders of the next generation; the Metroplex Economic Development Corporation, a resource for aspiring entrepreneurs; and Capella Park, a charming single-family housing development.

Having written over 30 books, Bishop Jakes is a New York Times best-selling author several times over! One of his most recent runaway successes, *REPOSITION YOURSELF: Living Life Without Limits*, has over a half-million copies in print in less than a year's time! His message is also communicated in print and broadcast media through interviews and features in Time, Forbes, and Essence magazines, the Washington Post, USA TODAY, CNN, Fox News and more. His life-enriching wisdom is highly sought after, from the pulpit to TV screens across the country—as seen on his many appearances on the Dr. Phil show.

His worldwide outreach is strengthened by his weekly television broadcast, The Potter's Touch, which reaches millions of households globally. From the small screen to the silver screen, Bishop Jakes has added the title of filmmaker to his list of pursuits, transmuting his message of empowerment and encouragement into *WOMAN THOU ART LOOSED: THE MOVIE*—his first motion picture. This moving story of a woman plagued by the ills of domestic abuse highlights Bishop Jakes' emphasis on social issues. His latest film, *NOT EASILY BROKEN*, is the tale of what happens when calamity meets an already-troubled marriage. The movie—the first of a multi-picture deal with SONY—is directed by Bill Duke and stars Morris Chestnut, Taraji P. Henson, and Jenifer Lewis and hit theaters in early 2009.

From Dallas to Washington DC to Nairobi, prison inmates, Hurricane Katrina evacuees and Kenyan natives alike have been touched by the message of faith and God's love through the ministry of this servant and pioneer.

DR. SIR WALTER L. MACK, JR. was formally educated at Elon College in Elon, NC (Bachelor of Arts), Duke University in Durham, NC (Master of Divinity) and United Theological Seminary in Dayton, OH (Doctor of Ministry), He completed a continuing education program at Harvard University which focused on economic development and community revitalization where he was both a pupil and invited guest preacher. He was also a guest lecturer and round table participant at Oxford University in Oxford, England that focused on the role of religion in education and the government. Dr. Mack currently serves six students as their academic advisor and theological mentor through the doctoral program at United Theological Seminary, which focuses on developing leadership for effective programming ministry in the Post-Modern Era.

Released by Harrison House Publishers in October of 2005, Dr. Mack's book Passion for Your Kingdom Purpose is transforming the lives of believers and framing the Kingdom of God for the unchurched. Dr. Mack has also appeared on Trinity Broadcast Network (TBN) on numerous occasions proclaiming the gospel of Jesus Christ in various forms.

Pastor of Union Baptist Church in Winston Salem, NC, Dr. Mack's leadership has fostered the church's expansion from 300 to over 3800 members, requiring three services to meet the needs of attendance. Through a Drug Dealer's Conference he created, hundreds of drug dealers were galvanized in his church to enhance their knowledge of God, self and society. As a result of the phenomenal nationwide media response, a he established a prototype for communities throughout the country.

Dr. Mack was cited as one the top 20 preachers under 40 by the *African American Pulpit Journal*, and is the recipient of numerous awards including the NAACP Community Service Award, Phi Beta Sigma Fraternity – Community Excellence Award," and Fox 8 News "Content of Their Character" Award.

PASTOR ANTHONY G. MACLIN earned his Bachelor of Business Administration and Master of Divinity degrees, from Howard University. He received an Honorary Doctor of Divinity degree from the Richmond Virginia Seminary in Richmond, VA.

He became Pastor of The Sanctuary at Kingdom Square (formerly Glendale Baptist Church) in July 1986. He led The Sanctuary from a membership of 192 active members to its current membership of more than 5,000. He developed and currently leads nearly 75 active ministries.

Pastor Maclin birthed the Multicultural Worship Center (MWC) in 2000. In January 2005, MWC was officially planted as a separate congregation. He has directed the purchase, lease, and renovation of more than $20,000,000 in properties for church use.

In 2004 Pastor Maclin led the church in purchasing the Hampton Mall Complex, now called Kingdom Square. Kingdom Square has grown to become a thriving business community that is home to several nationally connected businesses and eating establishments.

He continues in his groundbreaking, precedent setting efforts by embarking on a major redevelopment of Kingdom Square into a complex where the community can live, work, play and worship. Housing, shopping, retail businesses and a major worship facility are part of the planned development.

Pastor Maclin is a member of the Executive Board of the Kingdom Association of Covenant Pastors, and serves as the First Assistant to Bishop Walter S. Thomas, Sr., Presiding Prelate. He is also Vice President of the Collective Banking Group of Prince George's County and Vicinity and is a member of the Lott Carey Baptist Foreign Mission Convention. He also led the Churches United for Hurricane Relief effort assisting residents along the Gulf Coast who had been devastated by the aftermath of Hurricane Katrina.

PAUL P. MARTIN, ESQ., an attorney with over 18 years of trial experience, served as an Assistant District Attorney in Bronx County, New York from 1989-1995. As a trial assistant in both the Narcotics Bureau and the Trial Division he prosecuted a variety of cases and was responsible for all phases of criminal litigation from the authorization of an arrest to the Grand Jury presentation to the Trial.

After serving as an Assistant District Attorney, Martin accepted a position at Macloon & Friedman, P.C., a medical malpractice defense firm. Both working as an Assistant District Attorney and as an Associate prepared him as he ventured on his own, opening his own office in 1996 in midtown Manhattan. As a sole practitioner Martin represented clients in all five New York City Boroughs, as well as Westchester and Long Island. He has tried numerous cases to verdict and won acquittals on numerous high profile cases. He litigates civil matters, such as medical malpractice cases, false arrest and imprisonment cases, contract and police misconduct cases. In 2005, he joined with Gregory Preston and Jesse Wilkins to form the general practice law firm of Preston, Wilkins & Martin PLLC. Martin is a frequent commentator on numerous television shows which discuss legal issues.

He also represents a number of Not–For-Profits and serves as general counsel for numerous churches and not-for-profits in the New York City Metropolitan area.

Mr. Martin is a graduate of Wilberforce University, Wilberforce, Ohio (B.A.) and St. John's University School of Law, Queens, New York (J.D.). He is a member of the New York State Bar, and is admitted to the US District Court of the Southern and Eastern District.

BISHOP RICHARD FRANKLIN NORRIS leads the First Episcopal District of the African Methodist Episcopal Church, which covers the Northeast section of the country and the Isle of Bermuda.

He received his B.A. Degree from Rutgers University, New Jersey. Having received the call to ministry at age 15, he later attended the New Brunswick Theological Seminary and the New York Theological Seminary, where he earned his Doctor of Ministry Degree.

Bishop Norris has since received honorary doctorates from Lee Theological Seminary and Monrovia College. His fellowships have included the Ford Foundation Urban Training Center (Chicago), the Lilly Foundation, the New York City Mission Society and the New York Theological Seminary.

Bishop Norris has pastored throughout the First Episcopal District of the A.M.E. Church, including Pennsylvania, Bermuda, New Jersey and New York. From 1986 through 1993 he pastored the mother church of African Methodism, Mother Bethel in Philadelphia.

In June 2000, at the Forty-Sixth Quadrennial General Conference, Bishop Norris was elected and consecrated the 116th Bishop of the African Methodist Episcopal Church. He was sent to serve the 14th Episcopal District in West Africa, which includes Nigeria, Togo, Benin, Liberia, Sierra Leone and Cote D'Ivoire. There, Bishop Norris was an able and effective leader. He rebuilt churches, schools and universities that had been destroyed in the ongoing unrest in the area. He has traveled to and from Africa frequently for the good of his pastors and the people, even when his life would have been in jeopardy.

In June 2004, at the Forty-Seventh Quadrennial General Conference of the African Methodist Episcopal Church, he was selected to serve the First Episcopal District as Presiding Prelate. During his tenure, the District has prospered in spirit and substance.

BISHOP ALFRED A. OWENS, JR. graduated from Miner's D.C. Teachers College with a Bachelor's degree in English. He later satisfied the course requirements for a Master of Arts degree in English from Howard University, and received his Master of Divinity and Doctor of Ministry degrees from Howard University School of Divinity.

In 1966, Bishop Owens founded Christ Is The Answer Chapel, which merged in 1976 with the Mt. Calvary Holy Church forming what is now known as Greater Mt. Calvary Holy Church. Bishop Owens has been blessed to see the membership grow from 7 members in 1966 to an adult membership of over 8,000 persons today. Because of his faithfulness and diligence in ministry, Bishop Owens was consecrated a Bishop in the Mt. Calvary Holy Church of America, Inc. In 1988, and was appointed as the Vice Bishop in 2001. In 2008, Bishop Owens was elevated to the position of Presiding Prelate and Senior Bishop of the Mt. Calvary Holy Church of America, Inc. In addition to serving as the Dean of the Joint College of African American Pentecostal Bishops since the year 2000, Bishop Owens, on August 20, 2009, was also elevated to the esteemed position of the Archbishop of the Joint College. Bishop Owens continues to serve as Adjunct Professor at Howard University School of Divinity, where he teaches classes in the field of Homiletics and Church Leadership and Administration.

Bishop Owens' preaching ministry has caused him to travel extensively across the United States and to such foreign territories as Africa, Canada, England, Italy, Germany, Switzerland, and the West Indies. He is the instrument the Lord used for the Mt. Calvary Holy Church to be located in California, Florida, Illinois, Texas, London, England; Trinidad, Jamaica, Ghana, and India. In addition to his extensive travel, Bishop Owens is also the author of "Sermons for a Victorious Life," and his latest release: "Help Thou My Unbelief".

Bishop Owens shares the pastorate of Greater Mt. Calvary Holy Church with his wife, Co-Pastor Susie Carol Thomas Owens, to whom he has been married since 1972. He attributes much of his success to his wife and his sainted mother, Susie Elizabeth Crowder Owens.

CO-PASTOR SUSIE C. OWENS is a graduate of Bethel Bible Institute, where she earned an Associate of Arts degree in New Testament Studies in 1970. In 1972, she graduated from Brooks College with a Bachelor of Arts degree in Early Childhood Education. In 1999, she received a Master of Arts degree from Howard University School of Divinity, and she is currently pursuing a doctoral degree in African American Leadership from Fuller Theological Seminary in Pasadena, CA.

Evangelist Owens serves alongside her husband in ministry as the Co-Pastor of Greater Mt. Calvary Holy Church. She serves as Vice President and an Instructor of the Calvary Bible Institute, an accredited Bible School under Greater Mt. Calvary Holy Church. She also serves as a member of the Evangelistic and Trustee Boards of Greater Mt. Calvary Holy Church and Executive Director of the Women's Alliance.

Evang. Owens has been in ministry for over forty years and has traveled extensively throughout the US and abroad. Her unique presentation of the gospel has enabled her to minister to many denominations and organizations as a much sought after preacher, teacher, leader, and counselor. She has ministered on national platforms to tens of thousands, serving at various retreats, conferences, seminars and services.

Evang. Owens has received numerous awards and citations; most noteworthy among them, the distinct honor of Mother of the Year for the District of Columbia, an honor bestowed upon her by the American Mothers Association for her outstanding work in the field of parenting.

She is the author of two books: Unless Two Agree and Memorable Moments. She is the proud mother of two children, Alfred Thomas and Kristel Moneek and grandmother of five: Nathan, Darian, Nicholas, William, and Kaiden.

BISHOP DENNIS V. PROCTOR presides over the Western Episcopal District of the African Methodist Episcopal Church. A graduate of the Syracuse, New York public school system, he received his Bachelor of Arts (Summa Cum laude) from Livingstone College, Master of Arts in Pastoral Care and Counseling, from Ashland Theological Seminary, {a C.P.E. Diploma from Western Reserve Psychiatric Habilitation Center}, a Juris Doctor from The Ohio State University college of Law, and a Doctor of Ministry from the United Theological Seminary where he was named a Samuel D. Proctor/Otis Moss Fellow. He was inducted in Martin Luther King, Jr. Board of Preachers at Morehouse College, Atlanta Georgia and was honored to receive the Doctor of Divinity degree from Hood Theological Seminary and Livingstone College, his Alma Mater. Bishop Proctor has been a featured lecturer at the prestigious Hampton University Minister's Conference. In addition, one of his sermons is publish in the book o *"Outstanding Black Sermons Volume 4"* Judson Press.

Bishop Proctor has held three pastorates, St. James A.M.E. Zion Church in Massillon, Ohio where he led the congregation in the building of a new church and purchased a parsonage; the St. Luke A.M.E. Zion Church of Wilmington, North Carolina, where he led the congregation in remodeling the church and purchased a new parsonage. He currently pastors the historic Pennsylvania A.M.E. Zion Church in Baltimore, Maryland. He was elected bishop on July 18, 2008 at the 48th Session of the General Conference as the 97th bishop in succession of the A.M.E. Zion Church.

Bishop Proctor is the Founding President of the Congress of National Black Churches (Baltimore Affiliate). He serves on the Connectional budget Board. He Co-authored, *"Christians Under Construction"* with Dr. Staccato Powell. He is the Chair of the Finance Committee of the Philadelphia-Baltimore Annual Conference (Mid-Atlantic II Episcopal District)

REV. DR. RAQUEL A. ST. CLAIR is the first woman to serve as Executive Minister to the 6000 members of the historic St. James African Methodist Episcopal Church in Newark, NJ where Rev. William D. Watley is the Senior Pastor. Her primary task is to execute the God-given vision of the Senior Pastor by overseeing all ministries, supervising the ministerial staff, equipping and resourcing lay and clergy for ministry, and participating in the preaching and worship leadership of the church. In 2006, St. James became "One Church in 2 Locations," opening a second worship site in suburban Essex County. Rev. St. Clair is the ministry leader for that site and is responsible for preaching, site development, and discipling the membership. Rev. St. Clair is also the founder of the Women's Ministry, which currently includes two weekly women's Bible Studies and special events.

Dr. St. Clair received her Ph.D. in New Testament Studies at Princeton Theological Seminary. She was the recipient of the Presidential Doctoral Fellowship, the highest award given to incoming Ph.D. candidates, the New Testament Fellowship and the Expository Preaching Prize. In 2000, Rev. St. Clair had the distinction of being one of nine African American Ph.D. students in the nation to receive a Dissertation Fellowship from the Fund for Theological Education. Rev. St. Clair has served as a Teaching Fellow in both introductory and advanced level graduate courses and as a Teaching Assistant for New Testament Greek. She is also proficient in the Biblical languages of Hebrew and Aramaic.

Dr. St. Clair is a published author. Her first publication, *The African Presence in the Bible: Gospel Sermons Rooted in History,* was co-authored with her pastor, Dr. William D. Watley. Dr. St. Clair's article, "Womanist Biblical Interpretation" is included in *True to Our Native Land,* the first New Testament commentary written exclusively by African American with earned Ph.D.'s. Dr. St. Clair's first solo publication, *Call and Consequences: A Womanist Reading of Suffering and Discipleship in Mark's Gospel*, was released in Fall 2008 from Fortress Press. She has forthcoming articles in *More Power in the Pulpit, New Interpreters Bible Handbook on Preaching,* and *A Handbook of Feminist Biblical Theology*

Dr. St. Clair holds a Bachelor of Arts in Religious Studies from Yale University and a Master of Divinity degree from Princeton Theological Seminary.

REV. WILLIAM D. WATLEY, Ph. D. has served as Senior Pastor of the historic St. James African Methodist Episcopal Church in Newark, NJ for over 25 years. Under his leadership the membership has more than tripled and the annual church income has increased by 700%.

He established the St. James Social Services Corporation which oversees a feeding program and food pantry that dispenses over 89,000 meals annually, a clothes closet that distributes over 20,000 articles per year, an Intergenerational After School Care Program and Safe Haven Summer Peace Camp for children, as well as various emergency service, mentoring, literacy and employment training programs for adults. In addition, Rev. Watley is the chairperson of the Board of Directors for the 220 unit St. James Towers.

Most recently, Dr. Watley has launched a contemporary, multicultural Sunday worship service which is held in the suburban Essex County area and a Dot.com ministry that makes the weekly worship services, sermons, bible studies, and prayer ministry easily accessible to the masses via the Internet where viewers from over 45 countries regularly log on.

Dr. Watley has preached on the continents of Africa, Asia, Australia, Europe, and South America in addition to the island nations of Cuba, Barbados, Bahamas, Bermuda, and Trinidad.

A mentor and educator, Dr. Watley served as President and Distinguished Professor of Religion of Paul Quinn College in Waco, Texas. He has served as a visiting professor at the New Brunswick Theological Seminary, New York Theological Seminary, and Princeton Theological Seminary as well as a guest lecturer at Harvard University, Andrew Rankin Memorial Chapel at Howard University, and Payne and Turner Theological Seminaries.

A prolific author, Dr. Watley has written nineteen books and has authored several booklets and articles. He is the founder and C.E.O. of New Seasons Press, the publishing division of William Watley Ministries.

He has served on the Board of Directors for Beth Israel and Horizon/Mercy Hospitals, the United Negro College Fund and the Fund for Theological Education. In addition, he has been a member of the Advisory Boards for First Union Bank, the African American Pulpit, and the Interpreter's Bible Commentaries.

Dr. Watley received his Bachelor of Arts in Theology from St. Louis University and a Master of Divinity from the Interdenominational Theological Center. He received a Master of Philosophy and his Doctor of Philosophy-Ethics from Columbia University. In addition, he completed post-doctoral work at the Ecumenical Institute in Celigny, Switzerland and Harvard's Institute for Educational Management.

REV. LANCE D. WATSON, D. MIN. is a three time Summa Cum Laude graduate of Wayne State University in Detroit, Michigan from which he holds the Bachelor of Science in Psychology, the Bachelor of Arts in Philosophy and the Master of Arts in Guidance and Counseling.

He is a Magna Cum Laude graduate of the Samuel DeWitt Proctor School of Theology at Virginia Union University from which he holds a Master of Divinity and a Summa Cum Laude Graduate of the Presbyterian School of Christian Education at Union Theological Seminary in Richmond, Virginia. He completed his doctoral studies at United Theological Seminary earning the Doctorate of Ministry degree.

He serves as Senior Pastor of the Saint Paul's Baptist Church of Richmond, Virginia and *chief visionary* for its corporate affiliates, *Destiny Child Development Center, Destiny Christian Academy, Destiny Center for the Performing Arts, Charisma Books and Gifts, Saint Paul's Federal Credit Union, Saint Paul's Community Foundation, NIA, Inc. of Greater Richmond and Positive Power Media Group.*

He is host of the telecast *"Positive Power"* seen nationally on TV ONE Network. Saint Paul's has been noted by the Virginia General Baptist Association as one of the fastest growing churches in Virginia and as one of the fastest growing churches in the nation by Outreach Magazine.

This young, progressive and forward-looking congregation for *"People On the Grow"* serves as the spiritual home for more than 12,000 persons and supports mission and ministry causes around the globe.

Dr. Watson is on Facebook and Twitter, and is the author of several books, including the soon to be released, *That Was Then, This is NOW* available through all major bookstores and www.lancewatson.org.